Rhiannon Lucy Cosslett and Holly Baxter co-founded *The Vagenda* blog in February 2012. It was a viral sensation and instant hit and received over 7 million views in its first year. It has attracted widespread media coverage and has received praise from Caitlin Moran, Lauren Laverne, Chris Addison, Jenny Eclair, and India Knight. Rhiannon and Holly are journalists in their twenties. They live in London.

HOLLY BAXTER AND
RHIANNON LUCY COSSLETT

The Vagenda

VINTAGE BOOKS
London

Published by Vintage 2015

2 4 6 8 10 9 7 5 3 1

First published in Great Britain in 2014 by Square Peg

Vintage
Random House, 20 Vauxhall Bridge Road,
London SW1V 2SA

A Penguin Random House Company

Penguin
Random House
UK

www.vintage-books.co.uk

www.penguinrandomhouse.com

A CIP catalogue record for this book
is available from the British Library

ISBN 9781784700430

The Random House Group Limited supports the Forest Stewardship
Council® (FSC®),the leading international forest-certification
organisation. Our books carrying the FSC label are printed on
FSC®-certified paper. FSC is the only forest-certification scheme
supported by the leading environmental organisations, including
Greenpeace. Our paper procurement policy can be found at
www.randomhouse.co.uk/environment

Printed and bound in Great Britain by CPI Group (UK) Ltd, Croydon, CR0 4YY

To our mums, for their unwavering emotional support;

and to our dads, for their technical support.

We could not ask for better or more hilarious parents.

Contents

Introduction

What's a girl to do?

(or, How we realised between cocktails that there was something very wrong in Magazineland)

Back in February 2012, a pair of impoverished graduates launched a blog dedicated to humorously lambasting women's magazines. We called it 'The Vagenda', a term we stole from a broadsheet article about women in the workplace with a hidden agenda. Of all the stupid portmanteau terms we had come across while reading magazines – manthropology, shoemageddon, hiberdating – 'vagenda' was the most ridiculous. And we found not only that the amalgamation of 'vagina' and 'agenda' was pleasing to the ear, but that the word perfectly encapsulated the aims of the blog: to expose the silly, manipulative and sometimes damaging ulterior motives of women's magazines.

We were experts only insofar as we had consumed an awful lot of glossy trash over the years – glossy trash that had been telling us how to look, think and behave since we first left the local newsagent's clutching a copy of *Mizz* in our sweaty little sherbet-covered fingers. Women buy thousands upon thousands of magazines each year, and, despite the advent of the internet and, for some publications, tanking circulation figures, they remain extremely popular. It's said that women look at between 400 and 600 adverts a day, and with the ratio of advertorial to editorial in magazines rapidly increasing, that number is likely to rise. Magazines' editorial content and the adverts that target you with age-specific products alongside it (lip gloss for tweens, padded bras for teenagers, plastic surgery for twentysomethings, overpriced 'shabby-chic' sideboards and Le Creuset kitchen paraphernalia for the middle-aged cohort) have been an unavoidable part of the female consciousness for most women raised in the Western world since the 1930s.

Even publications that used to celebrate women's liberation in the seventies and eighties have been increasingly watered down and replaced with easily recycled, oversexed content pandering to an advertising team who've got your money on their mind. Nowadays, it can feel as if their index fingers are pointing accusingly at you from behind the page, primed to deliver you a hefty shot of insecurity to complement your morning Botox.

As tweenagers, we graduated from the romance comics, spooky stories and 'I kissed a boy during my first period, am I pregnant?' problem pages in *Shout*, *Mizz*, *Sugar* or *Jackie*, dependent on your age, to those with a more mature demographic such as *Just Seventeen* (later rebranded as *J-17*). For our own generation, *J-17* (which everyone knows you read when you were 13 and hid from your scandalised mother, lest she find the bit about 69ing) was the go-to magazine for sex advice, trading as it did primarily in information and revelations about boys in the same way that *Jackie* traded in romance and engagement stories in the 1970s. But these sorts of stories have a sell-by date, and by the time you're a teenager, you're being steered headlong into *Cosmopolitan*, *Company* and *Grazia*. An addiction that lasts a lifetime is born. We haven't got past our twenties yet, but we're looking forward to the terrifying content of 'mature' magazines such as *Red* and *Easy Living* ('Do his sperm hate your vagina?' 'Will your consumption of guacamole affect your fertility?' 'Is off-white a suitably calming colour for the nursery of a baby with "unconventional sleeping patterns"') Alongside all this, the celebrity magazine grew to gargantuan proportions throughout the noughties. Where once *Hello!* and *OK!* stood slightly shamefacedly in the corner of the news racks, *heat*, *Closer* and a variety of other younger sisters now jostle for room, emanating a combination of disjointed newzac and bilious body snark like the cidered-up drunk on your corner. 'Is it a baby or a burrito? Our experts decide!' scream headlines next to a magnified image of Celebrity X's stomach. 'Celebrity Y breaks down over unbearable pressure from paparazzi!' proclaims the next headline, with a blurry picture of said celeb's hand across a lens as ironic illustration. On the face of it, you wouldn't think that that sort of banal content would reel in a substantial audience – yet we fall for it again and again.

If Page Three is the sexist builder hollering at you in the street, then *Grazia* and *Cosmo* are the frenemies who smile to your face and bitch behind your back. It worried us that women such as us, reared on a diet beginning with problem-page questions about tampons in *Bliss* magazine and graduating on to *Company*, weren't being offered any of the necessary critical tools to deal with increasingly sinister content. There comes a certain point (probably around the time that you've picked up your tenth issue of *Cosmopolitan*) when your brain is encased in such a large volume of fluffy bullshit that you switch off and start thinking, 'My elbows are fat. You're right, *Cosmo*, they are really bloody fat,' as you stare at the latest photoshopped model. Open up one of these rags and you'll be confronted with a tirade of mixed messages: an article about women having a lower sex drive than men, followed by a problem page in which a man complains that his girlfriend is always gagging for it, for example. In the case of the latter, the agony aunt's response to the gentleman in question is naturally that his missus is definitely, definitely a nymphomaniac and needs therapy as a matter of urgency. Such contradictory material is enough to drive a woman to drink. One minute you're being told to love your body and embrace it as the imperfect vessel that it is, and the next you're manically rubbing coffee granules into your arse cellulite instead of drinking them in your morning latte (which, by the way, makes you fat).

You'll also face a constant deluge of articles which supposedly question what it is, and isn't, OK to do (Can I sleep around? Can I eat carbs? Can I shave my pubes and still believe in feminism/world peace/string theory?) Rather than reassure you that you can do all these things and that you should stop worrying about them, the editorial staff continue to busy themselves setting up fictitious taboos ('Proposing – his job or yours?') which just serve to make you even more worried about your already hellishly hectic life. Many of you will be familiar with the 'Hey, it's OK' section of *Glamour* magazine, which features 'jokey' reassurances related to modes of behaviour deemed typical of all females. Yet rather than saying, 'Hey, it's OK that you don't want a baby,' or, 'Hey, it's OK that you don't have the time or inclination to shave your legs between October and April, if at all,' or even (God forbid) 'Hey, it's OK to eat carbs,' they rely instead on crass, deliberately uncontroversial generalisation. So it's 'Hey, it's OK to dish the dirt on your sex life to all of your friends but convince yourself he'd never do the same to his,' or 'Hey, it's OK to browse the babywear section even if you don't have a baby' (both real-life examples from April 2013). What's a girl to do?

It was high time, we felt, that we took it on. The Vagenda aimed to shine a critical light on women's media, moving from piss-takes of the most ridiculous sex tips in *Cosmopolitan*, to why the female celebrity is always painted in the same way by tabloids, to the ongoing media obsession with female diet and beauty. As our readership grew, we began to address much broader issues affecting women's lives, from maternity leave to the under-representation of women editors in the media and the depressing prevalence of ultra-violent porn. Our starting point was the magazine world, but as we dug deeper we saw that the dysfunctional habits of *Glamour* and *Grazia* were reflected and repeated in film and TV, on billboards and in advertising, throughout newspapers and across mainstream websites. That is why this book predominantly criticises women's magazines, but also makes mention of the surrounding media that influence them, and vice versa.

Almost as soon as we launched, hordes of women, from the age of 13 right up to 85, were getting in touch and wanting to add their voices. The Vagenda has now covered everything from the weave to the vajazzle, miscarriage to motherhood, the position of women in the workplace to the position of the fortnight. We've done this with the help and contributions of women (and men) from all over the world. They got in touch to point and laugh and rant and rave at the ridiculous media stereotypes that surrounded them, whether they were university freshers, new mothers, or engineers at the start of their career, and the response was humbling. It made us realise that we weren't the only ones who felt like crap when we read women's magazines or watched MTV.

A study by Bradley University in Illinois in 2012 found that just three minutes spent looking at a fashion magazine led to 70% of women feeling 'guilty, depressed, and shameful'. Similarly, the University of Missouri–Columbia conducted a survey involving 81 women and found that, after three minutes of looking at images of fashion models, all of them felt worse about themselves, regardless of size, weight, age or height. When *Seventeen* magazine was first published in 1944, the average model was around 5 ft 7 in. and weighed 130 lb (9 stone 3). These days, the average model is 5 ft 11 in. and weighs 115 lb (8 stone 2). It's a pretty drastic change. Since the mid-twentieth century, the bikini-body ideal has done a complete 180, with women then being implored to 'gain 10 to 25 lb the easy way' in the same way that they are now being told to lose it. Looking at an advertisement from that period really hammers things home. 'How do you look in a bathing suit?' it demands, illustrating its message with two female figures. The very slender woman looks demonstrably unhappy, while the smiling Monroe-esque 'ideal' woman of the age is well pleased with herself. Yet, looking at such images now, it's the former type which would be lauded as the ultimate ideal, while the latter would be consigned to the plus-size section. In other words, the goalposts are always shifting, and women are continually expected to live up to some form of arbitrarily decided 'ideal body'.

There's no doubt that all this obsessive body monitoring is having a negative impact on our self-esteem, but it's not just our physical appearance that is under scrutiny. This book looks at how the media attempt to dictate everything from your bikini wax to your body language, your diet to your 'sex moves', your pants to your personality, and we hope that you come to see it as something of a survival guide. Because it's high time we all called bullshit.

1

Women's Magazines

Where did it all go wrong?

WHAT TO READ: A GOOD WIFE'S GUIDE

In the beginning, there was the home-making magazine. Back then, 'woman' was synonymous with 'wife', so you moved quickly from children's stories to magazines that taught you how to cook a loaf from scratch without annoying your husband too much. This fairly accurately reflected how life was for women in the 1700s, when these manuals started to emerge: childhood, then the next fifty or so years as willing domestic servant and mother. Often, these magazines weren't actually targeted solely at women – they were 'family editions', with a section for children and sometimes even helpful hints for the hubby. Because books weren't as easily available as they are now and the internet was a mere twinkle in someone's great-grandfather's eye, these publications also used to print chapters of popular fiction for the family (in 1897, *Cosmopolitan* serialised *War of the Worlds*. Seriously).

The first British women's magazine was launched in 1693. It was called The *Ladies' Mercury*, and, like its male counterparts, it operated out of a coffee house. Unlike its male counterparts, however, it preoccupied itself with relationship problems, promising to answer readers' queries about 'Love, etc'. It only lasted for four issues, but it was the first time that 'women' as a special-interest category existed in the journalism world. The altogether more successful *Lady's Magazine*, which first appeared in 1770, was targeted at the upper echelons of society and reflected their presumed interests: royalty, and sentimental stories. No home-making tips here – leave that to the staff – but lots of titillation on offer, in the form of 'romantic fiction' which invariably involved the (chastely expressed) deflowering of a virgin. These two types of magazine and their content were beginning to merge by the mid-nineteenth century, with the creation of a much larger middle class. Samuel Beeton's *Englishwoman's Domestic Magazine*, for example, featured fiction but also domestic advice on such varied subjects as 'How to treat dysentery' and the best way to stew liver. Not long afterwards, the bodice-rippers like those found in the *Lady's Magazine* were cosying up next to gardening advice, and in the mid-nineteenth century the fashion plates joined them. The *Lady's Magazine* even featured a 'Cupid's Post Bag' page that dispensed romantic advice, which for a brief period featured erotic missives about the sexual thrill of a tightly laced corset. The *Englishwoman's Journal*, meanwhile, campaigned for women to be allowed to train in various professions, though only in the absence of a male provider, and was decidedly undomestic in this respect.

In the 1890s women entered the world of journalism in record numbers, and not just as magazine contributors (often unpaid novices and ladies of leisure) but also to work for the women's pages in newspapers. According to Anne O'Hagan, one of the 'Hen Coop' assigned to a small room in the offices of Hearst's New-York-based *Evening Journal*, these sections were 'sacred to currant jam and current gossip'. She noted, sarcastically: 'No woman is ever mentioned on a "woman's page" who is not, if not transcendently beautiful, at least gifted with "a charm of manner all her own". No actress is there whose home life is not of a sort to gladden every mother's heart. No woman lawyer or doctor is anything but "deliciously feminine.""

Femininity was exactly what editors were looking for when they hired women journalists to provide the 'woman's angle' on news stories. Female reporters who wrote human-interest stories – the emotive, 'soft'

side of the masculine 'hard' news – were dubbed 'sob sisters', and feature writers were expected to occupy themselves primarily with the four Fs: family, food, fashion and furnishings.

By the turn of the century, the number of magazines targeted at women had doubled: some survivors of that era include *Harper's Bazaar*, *The Lady* (from 1885), and *Woman's Weekly*, which was launched in 1911 to meet the demand of newly office-employed women. Its content combined 'real-life romance' stories (the first ever edition featured a man recounting how he 'fell in love over a bath chair') with cookery tips and knitting patterns, demonstrating the merge of the upper-class women's publication and the working woman's 'family manual' into a new kind of magazine altogether. *Woman's Weekly*, for instance, was in 1915 combining advice on how to get rid of 'salt cellars' (an old-fashioned term for bingo wings) with tips on how to become a 'lady detective'.

There were more risqué efforts, too, such as *Freewoman*, a feminist weekly founded in the same year as *Woman's Weekly* which, as well as the usual topics of housework and motherhood, also covered the movement for women's suffrage. WH Smith refused to stock it on the grounds that it was 'disgusting' and 'immoral'. In contrast, working-class women had fiction magazines which serialised romantic melodramas involving steamy transgressions of class boundaries.

After the First World War, editors started to realise there was money to be made from a new kind of independent woman. Bizarrely enough, some of the magazines published in the 1920s (the era of the new breed of chain-smoking, Charleston-dancing, sexually liberated flapper girls) seem progressive even by today's standards. A copy of *Modern Woman* from 1925 includes an article called 'Life is sweet, sister' that reads like a manifesto for female liberation. 'I doubt whether any other period of women's history could show a time when it's so wonderful to be alive,' it begins, before continuing with, 'What sweeter money is there than money you earn yourself?' and, 'There's nothing like a good job and your own regular income to keep your mind happy.' It also contains early prototypes of the same beauty advertisements that you'd see in today's magazines, but nevertheless puts forward a vision of womanhood that's altogether much more multifaceted, featuring fiction and theatre reviews alongside cookery and interior decoration.

In the late 1930s, publications such as *Woman* encouraged women to look outside the home and into their communities. They showed flickers of feminism, discussing double standards on smoking (something considered by men to be 'uncouth' in a woman) and asking why it was that women had to wear skirts. *Woman* magazine even asked for flexible working hours for mothers. For a brief period in the interwar years, it looked as though women were gaining serious ground.

However, after the war many women who had achieved financial independence were ousted from the jobs they'd had during wartime and sent back into the kitchen to make way for the returning soldiers. While *Modern Woman* was still taking a forward-thinking stance (in February 1946 it ran an article celebrating 'our 24', the number of women in parliament at the time, which said, 'All 24 have something to offer – what woman hasn't?'), other magazines were well on their way to becoming the home-making bibles we associate with the 1950s.

The magazines of the 1950s provided an aspirational 'dream world' for those who had experienced rationing and poverty. Like the Victorian 'angel in the house', the 1950s housewife perfected her art with the use of a manual which dispensed helpful domestic tips. What differed was the sheer range of new commercial goods available to the housewife, who became a target for advertisers. Suddenly, fridges, washing machines and electric ovens had become an affordable option, and they freed up a huge amount of time previously wasted in domestic drudgery. (No wonder *Mad Men*'s resident housewife Betty Draper mounted hers.) These darlings of the domestic world dominated the pages of magazines to the extent that their adverts started to affect editorial content for the first time. In 1956 the first advertising 'arrangement' took place when a nylon manufacturer booked $12,000 worth of space in the US edition of *Woman*, and the editor agreed not to publish anything about natural fibres in the issue.

According to Katharine Whitehorn, the function of women's magazines was to 'teach women how to be perfect', with adverts sending the message that 'they would be perfect only if they used the product'. Full-colour page spreads started to appear in *Woman* in 1956, a precursor of today's glossies. In the same period, magazine readership skyrocketed, and competition was so fierce that an article in *The Economist* referred to the market as 'the petticoat battleground'.

Magazines like *Good Housekeeping* enjoyed storming success as the go-to rags for fifties housewives in need of domestic tips: '101 decorating ideas', 'Clothes to make a new baby', and 'How do you measure up against the stars?' ran alongside recipes (Spam suppers, 'Bacon Cookery Special'), adverts for new 'life-changing' home appliances; and girdles (tagline: 'Because you insist on freedom'), and tapeworm diets ('Eat! Eat! Eat! & always stay slim!'). And, of course, endless flower arranging torture, as illustrated by a ten-page 'Summer Flower Arranging Special' from May 1955. 'The good wife's guide' which ran in *Housekeeping Monthly* in the same year instructed its readers: 'Remember: his topics of conversation are more important than yours', 'You have no right to question him', and 'A good wife always knows her place'. All of these catered specifically to an audience of housebound females.

It should go without saying that the more time you spend bored at home, the more stuff you're likely to buy, making advertising in these magazines extremely lucrative for the average business. Tailoring content to a solely female readership was turning out to be such a good idea that more women – lots of them – had to be hired full-time by the publications to keep relevant content churning. But aspiring journalists weren't the only ones to embrace the increase in employment opportunities: more and more women were entering the workplace, and that meant they'd be spending much less time bored off their tits buying consumer items such as household goods, and much more time being bold and busy in the office. Gradually, women's magazines, with their staid domesticity, started to look hopelessly out of step. They didn't speak to the 'new woman', who was often unmarried and in employment. A new selling tactic would have to be used as a way of getting them to spend their money at the same rate as housewives. As Naomi Wolf explains, there was a 'transfer of guilt' as anxieties about household dirt transformed into anxieties about physical appearance. Baking tips weren't going to cut it in the age of independence; the beauty industry needed to step in. As Wolf puts it, we'll buy more things if we are kept in the 'self-hating, ever-failing, hungry, and sexually insecure state of being aspiring "beauties"'. In fact, the more supposedly liberated women became, the more they were confronted with articles such as 'Want a new nose? Complete information' (*Cosmo*, October 1963) and 'Legs a man can't forget – they can be yours' (*Cosmo*, April 1963).

In the 1960s, women's liberation and 'free love' changed Magazineland. *She* was the first magazine that made no attempt to target a specific group of 'housewives' or 'career gals' but instead aimed to appeal to women across the board. It had been launched in 1955 but came into its own in the sixties, by publishing a mixture of social commentary, politics, and tongue-in-cheek articles such as 'Weight-lifting for bust-lifting', 'Your old banger: how to make it last', and 'Womb music: once heard, never forgotten'. The similarly refreshing *Nova* launched in 1965 and, like *She*, its intended readership was wide: a 'new magazine for a new kind of woman', whether or not she was married, employed, university-educated or a mother. A typical cover of the time was *Nova*'s 'Yes, we're living in sin. No, we're not getting married. Why? It's out of date.' Instead of targeting people by social class or income, the new women's publication targeted according to attitude. And that attitude was becoming increasingly liberal.

'NO ONE LIKES A POOR GIRL' – The *Cosmo* Girl is born

As women became increasingly distanced from the home, rates of magazine consumption, which had been so high in the 1950s, started to fall dramatically, and someone needed to turn this around. *Cosmopolitan* was remodelled in 1965, and turned from a 'family read' to the gal's handbag companion that we might recognise today. Helen

Gurley Brown, the new editor, who had just written a wildly successful pulling manual called *Sex and the Single Girl*, would stay with *Cosmo* for thirty-two years. With her perfectly manicured hand at the helm, and a new focus on gaining the readership of the independent, 'fun, fearless female', features like 'Favourite toys for little Timmy' morphed into juicier versions such as 'Meet Timmy, your favourite toy boy'. Magazines like *Good Housekeeping* were rapidly becoming the exception rather than the rule. The beauty industry tightened its stranglehold, with the number of diet articles rising by 70% from 1968 to 1972, and there was an increasing focus on sex. *Cosmo* articles from the time include 'World's greatest lover – what it was like to be wooed by him' (July 1965), 'The 600 calorie diet to make you skinny without hysterics' (November 1974), and 'Morals, ethics and that *Cosmo* Girl: how far out can (and should) she go?' (February 1975).

Brown believed in 'sex without shame', and the *Cosmo* Girl was absolutely synonymous with the liberated woman of the sixties. She didn't wait for a husband to turn up on a white horse, fill her up with babies and stick her in the kitchen with a fondue set. She had boyfriends and 'lived in sin', had one-night stands and enjoyed them, and even dipped her toe into the pool of married men, all the while looking perfectly turned out and permanently euphoric (think *Mad Men*'s Joan Holloway). *Cosmo* also ran advice on how to set up home alone ('The perfect apartment for that Cosmopolitan Girl' – October 1970), on managing your money, and on how to know your cystitis from your polycystic ovaries. Its message was revolutionary in its time, positioning men as complementary to a woman's life rather than central to it (and it still is, compared with the airbrushed pages of today's *Cosmo*). But it claimed to provide a more palatable, less threatening, 'sexy feminist' alternative to what Brown termed the 'dour, angry feminism' of the time.

Because while Brown had been revolutionising *Cosmopolitan*, something else had been going on in the magazine racks of everyone's local corner shop. Overtly feminist magazines enjoyed their salad days in the seventies and eighties. One of the best examples of these was *Spare Rib*, which was launched in 1972 by a collective including Rosie Boycott and Marsha Rowe. It was an important self-described 'women's liberation magazine'. Though it featured many of the most pertinent debates of the time, the humour was thin on the ground; presumably aware of this, its own editorial team once ran a feature called 'Why is this magazine so depressing?'

WH Smith, ever the pusher of boundaries, refused to stock *Spare Rib* because of its explicit content and its edgy rejection of gender norms ('A woman doesn't have to be a virgin, wife or mother'), giving the feminist publication a certain underground appeal. When Rhiannon's granddad went into a bookshop and asked for a copy for his daughter, a confused store clerk imagined a very different kind of young woman and redirected him to the cookery section.

Spare Rib ceased publication in 1993, just as consumerism reached fever pitch and political commentary in women's magazines all but disappeared for ever. *Ms.* magazine, the monthly liberal feminist magazine launched by American feminist Gloria Steinem in the same year, continues to this day, though it is now quarterly.

Many other women's mags took *Spare Rib*'s lead, interspersing their make-up tips with articles about career progression and equal pay. Along with the women's sections of newspapers, magazines such as *Woman* and *Woman's Own* were playing a crucial part in the feminist revolution. They took many of the themes covered by the feminist press – 'battered wives', the unfair division of domestic labour, sexual harassment, and equal pay – and tailored them to a mainstream audience. Suddenly the war was being fought from kitchens and laundry rooms up and down the country. What looked like a harmless, fluffy women's magazine being read directly under a husband's nose was actually encouraging his wife to demand equality in every sphere.

By the 1970s, women were picking up *Cosmo* and its little sister *Company* in their droves. Both magazines paid homage to feminism in the form of a sassy, assertive individualism while still retaining their sexy consumerist focus, with articles such as 'How to be a millionairess' (*Company*) and 'Lose weight in bed – the lovemaker's diet (*Cosmo*). The teen market that *Company* tapped into had been established by *Honey* in 1960, and since then had seen a boom in readership. Popular teen magazine *Jackie* saw its sales rise from an initial 350,000 readers at its launch in 1964 to 605,000 in 1976. It struggled to compete with the racier *Just Seventeen*, which was launched in 1983 and, despite its demise in 2004, probably remains the most influential teen magazine ever created.

But by the end of the eighties, the 'campaigning magazine' had been all but swallowed up by the much raunchier glossies, as well as the more high-end fashion magazines such as *Vogue, Marie Claire* (launched in the UK in 1988 with an average circulation of 195,000) and *Elle* (1985). As for *Cosmo*, by the eighties and nineties, any pretence of feminism had been fully overshadowed by raunch, with features such as 'Why liberated couples drive each other crazy' (September 1983) and 'When too much sex is not enough' (August 1992).

Helen Gurley Brown had set a precedent for the magazines that were to succeed – and the direction was confusing and often self-contradictory. She told women to take the shame out of sex, and to plan their careers around themselves rather than around their future husbands, but under her editorship, *Cosmo* tips for single women revolved around how to get a man, and bedroom tips focused on how to please him, even in the articles featuring in the so-called 'feminist' *Cosmo* of the 1970s and '80s: 'What I want in a wife', 'Things to say in bed', 'What your legs say about you', and 'Twenty ways to make him come on strong'. While apparently every girl has it in her to 'Smock around the clock' (yes, really), not everyone, according to *Cosmo*, is 'thin enough for a thong'. *Cosmo*'s 'please your man' to please your advertisers message intensified throughout the nineties and noughties, until the magazine ended up where it is today: a publication hell-bent on perfecting your body for the sex he wants. The *Cosmo* Girl didn't have to be an angry feminist with armpit hair, but suddenly what she *did* have to be was a shaven, shiny babe right down to her Sloggis, spending her Saturday night in complicated lingerie becoming proficient at a striptease, or coordinating her look with the boyfriend she wants to attract. (A common feature has men lining up and judging a female celebrity's dress style, so you can find out in advance of your trip down to H&M whether Keith from Coventry prefers high-waisted jeans or hotpants.)

But what had pushed boundaries in the sixties became a tedious reiteration of the status quo a few decades later. *Cosmo* began pumping out the same boring conveyor-belt content every month, often borrowed from previous issues of years before, or from other magazines: one 2013 feature asking whether you're having a 'normal' amount of sex had already run in a 1987 edition of *Bella* ('Making love – how often is normal?'). Gurley Brown herself was a woman of contradictions who celebrated the 'fake look' with almost admirable tenacity, both through public advocacy and private choice – she even wrote an article about how to remain beautiful during sex while wearing a hairpiece. She may not be solely responsible for what happened to the women's magazines we now consume, but her own contradictory attitudes towards women go a good way to explaining the inconsistencies that her longtime publication came to suffer from.

There is some irony in the fact that *Cosmo* turned the magazine market around. Before it, unmarried women had been largely ignored by other publications, which were considered to be the domain of men. *Cosmo*'s highly sexual content paved the way for a variety of imitators, most notably the now-defunct *more!*, a magazine that catered to self-identifed teenage 'ladettes'. Magazines such as *Minx* prided themselves on their sexual frankness and targeted 'young, assertive, rather scary young women' who 'don't buy women's magazines'. But their raunchy content led to battles with advertisers, who weren't really fans of the groundbreaking work *Minx* was doing on subjects like female ejaculation (according to an ex-employee, an article on this was sent back with strict instructions to 'go away and de-quim it'), and this blighted the publication. It eventually folded in 2000, due to falling circulation. The journalist Polly Vernon, who wrote for *Minx*, felt it was different to the 'silly, vacant, extravagant and often cruel' (*Guardian*, 3 July 2000) magazines out there. She now works for *Grazia*.

Throughout the late nineties and early noughties, plastic surgery advertorial became increasingly common, even for magazines preaching 'body confidence'. In this newly aggressive landscape, magazines seemed to want to provoke insecurities in their readers by encouraging them to buy into a certain body ideal, then selling that insecurity on to advertisers for financial gain in the most insidious way. They sought an upwardly mobile, young, aspirational readership for this very purpose: it was a readership that was easy to sell to advertisers. *Glamour* magazine, which was launched by Condé Nast in the UK in 2001 as a pioneer of the 'handbag-sized' format and continues to be the bestselling women's monthly, produced a brochure for advertisers which seeks to describe this highly sought after readership: 'With an average age of 27, these readers are upmarket, high spending and aspirational or upwardly mobile, and with lots of disposable income.' It continues: 'They buy a fashion item every eight days and a beauty product every nine days. They take holidays twice a year and need a glamorous car to project their personality and get them around their busy lives.' In short:

Glamour is

For successful, independent modern women who know how
to have fun, how to dress, and how to spend

They do: shopping, friends, bars, travel

They don't: window shop, stay at home, have a problem
spending

They buy: clothes, shoes, make-up and jewellery. Their
vices? A new handbag every month for each new issue of
Glamour

They are: ABC12 women aged 18–34.

'*Glamour*, The Philosophy and Profile', cited by Rosalind Gill
in *Gender and the Media. (2007)*

For us, the *Glamour* profile is ironic considering we bought the magazine when we were at our most skint and living off 15p instant noodles, but it makes fascinating reading. Furthermore, its emphasis on female beauty has remained steadfastly the same, as demonstrated by the fact that in May 1958 the US edition was running articles such as 'What to wear with what to be pretty', and in February 2012 it opted for the slightly screechier but nonetheless identical 'We're all going to be soooooo pretty!' Still, we suppose that's better reading than their damning tragic spinster exposé of January 1972, entitled 'What it's like to be 27 and unmarried'.

Cosmo appeals to a similar demographic to *Glamour*, though, according to Jan Adcock, *Cosmo*'s publishing director until 2007, 'It's not an age thing, it's an attitude thing . . . it's glamorous and sexy, and it's about success – some people are scared of that, at whatever age.' It's hard to reconcile this independence with the ideal *Cosmo* Girl you can catch a glimpse of on the Hearst digital website, a woman who 'follows celebrities and emulates their style', but then that's the fundamental contradiction. The 1990s saw forthright, sassy, feminist-lite content that lauded independence, juxtaposed with rather anti-feminist advertising. Naomi Wolf pointed out that women's magazines have split personalities, but the conflict between serious, pro-women content and advertising that she wrote of in 1990 has now largely become irrelevant: advertisers have truly won the battle.

It started to seem as though the only way these women's magazines could survive in this cold, capitalist world was to make sure that their readership felt just insecure enough to keep buying issue after issue. In 2012 there was a bit of a stir about whether we'd all gone wrong. As *Cosmo*'s fortieth birthday approached and blogs that mocked its content became popular, the powers-that-be in Cosmopolitan Towers launched The F Word campaign to 'bring feminism back'. Celebrities came out in tight-fitting T-shirts proclaiming, 'We use the F word, do you?' while doing duckface and/or bedroom eyes to the camera. Despite the fact that feminism has nothing to do with what you're wearing on your genitals, a debate they held at the Women of the World Festival in 2012 was entitled 'Can you be a feminist and vajazzle?' Hard-hitting stuff, we're sure you'll agree.

CELEB-BASHING AND YOU

But woman cannot dine on vajazzles alone. A new kind of magazine had burst on to the scene in the nineties to threaten the behemoth that was *Cosmo*: the celeb magazine. By the noughties it dominated the news-stands – so much so that it's hard to believe this phenomenon actually crash-landed on the British landscape relatively late. While France had had *Paris Match* since 1949 and Spain ¡*Hola!* since 1944,

Hello! only reached British shores in 1988, with *OK!* following in 1993. Before being hounded by the paparazzi became a full-time occupation, the stories that appeared in the celeb-watching rags such as *Hello!* were often directly endorsed by the respective celebrity's PRs. 'C-List Celeb shows off her hand-sewn leather pouffe by the pool, available under her own label from John Lewis,' an article might read, accompanied by a grinning portrait of said C-Lister and her three beautiful children. Sure, the glowing profiles of the celebrities in these pages might now and then raise a little cynicism, but you basically knew what you were getting when you slipped a copy of *OK!* into your shopping trolley on a guilty Saturday stock-up. Solid gold trash, with the celeb seal of approval and the willing, cosy collusion of some PR execs and their friends in journalism.

By the late nineties, society's celebrity obsession was in full swing. Weeklies *Closer, Now, Reveal, New* and *heat* all followed, with some boasting enormous circulation figures (as of 2004, *heat* was read by half a million people every week). New-kid-on-the-block *Grazia* (launched in 2005) became as beloved of the British public as its 'generic women's mag' counterparts like *Cosmo, Company* and *Elle.*

But as celeb mags became a bigger deal, public figures started biting back at the idea of having their children photographed building their first sandcastle and started going to court to try to prevent the media from publishing their most private and often shameful stories. And lo! the age of the super-injunction was upon us. It turns out that having enough money can secure the protection of the court as the papers are about to reveal your sleazy extramarital affair, just in the nick of time. The rise of the super-injunction showed just how irrational celebrity magazines and tabloids had become as they got a taste of real popularity. Back in the early noughties, when everyone was still somewhat blasé about a cheeky up-skirt shot if you ran away quickly enough, one paparazzo was found at the christening of Madonna's son, having hidden in the cathedral organ for over 24 hours and pooing in a bin bag. He almost got away with a film of just under half an hour, before security guards found him sneaking out. This was the year when *Celebrity Big Brother* aired for the first time. The lens of the pap was becoming a ubiquitous symbol of fame and its consequences. By 2012 – just over a decade later – our own royal family was suing some of the most determined celebrity photographers for invading the privacy of a family holiday between Prince William and his then-new bride Kate Middleton by snapping topless photos of her.

Women suffered the most at the hands of these dogged photographers. The paps knew very well that a snap of K-Middy's breasts would sell like hot cakes – and despite the great pro-royal loyalty of the British press who promised not to buy and publish those particular photos, the pesky celeb mag counterparts in other countries weren't quite so protective. Of course, this wasn't the first time a scantily clad lass had been shamed by the press, but it was a boundary-pushing moment. Alongside the Leveson Inquiry – which had exposed phone hacking and other dodgy journalistic practices that showed the depths to which some hacks would sink to get their story – it told consumers what they were really buying into when they flicked through a full-colour 'source reveals all' article on this month's top model. And in many ways, once some official hand-wringing was over, the magazines themselves stopped pretending that they had any real integrity, and continued going hell-for-leather to procure the best snap of Former Child Star X's neon thong as she slipped out of the nearest limousine.

As the decade progressed, the tabloids starting getting in on the act and coverage of female celebrities increasingly became focused on their bodies and their flaws. The *Daily Mail* and the Femail section of its website – which by 2010 had become the most popular news website in the *entire world,* a title it certainly hasn't relinquished at the time of writing – regularly used its infamous 'sidebar of shame' to present a tasty variety of body-shaming tactics every time a famous woman left the house. (Once they wrote five articles in a single day on Lady Gaga's perceived weight gain; perceived, that is, by one of their own reporters.) If a nipple slipped, a muffin top wobbled, or a pair of particularly chiselled cheekbones got caught at a dramatic angle, according to the 'sidebar of shame' the woman in question was a slut, a fatty or an anorexic.

Sweat patches on T-shirts, too-obvious tit tape and hairs out of place were gleefully pointed out in such classy ways as via *heat*'s 'circle of shame' or 'hoop of horror', which highlighted the offending body part with the undisguised mocking sneer of a school bully on coke. The ratio of males to females in the 'circle of shame' feature is undeniably skewed.

These celeb-dominated magazines also focused on personal relationships – again, with a glaring gender divide, usually casting their female leads as 'devastated', 'gobsmacked', 'out of control', or another variant of the unhinged emotional woman, while their 'aloof' male counterparts hovered in the background. They run bikini-heavy cover stories with headlines such as 'Kim's BIG FAT GREEK HOLIDAY' (*heat*, 7 May 2013), and constantly collate celebrities' dress sizes with their romantic destinies ('LOVESTRUCK BODIES: Kelly comfort eats as Danny fails to commit – SIZE 12' – *Closer*, 29 June 2012). Men sometimes suffer, but women are afforded a special kind of scrutiny. If a celebrity managed to make it along a street full of ruthless flashing Nikons without flashing anything herself, then the expression would have to say it all. The headlines in magazines such as *heat*, *Closer* and *Grazia* increasingly speculated on (almost always) female celebrities' inner thoughts, according to the pose they'd caught them in, and based upon crude stereotypes of the female population. Thus Jennifer Aniston becomes a 'tragic spinster', whether she is dating someone or not. Indeed, *Grazia*'s apparent lack of respect for the truth coupled with its futile attempt to keep up with internet celebrity news was clear for all to see when it ran a cover announcing 'Jen: It's OVER' on the same day that Aniston announced her engagement. Because simple sells, maybe even more than sex, and who cares if it's bullshit at the end of the day? It isn't really changing anything important, right?

The procurement and marketing of these photos has become one truly unflattering reflection of the modern age. Celeb mags make money out of targeting, labelling and shaming their victims with fervour – indeed, some of their 'victims', via their publicists, even encourage it. The magazines then use that shame to sell you lippy and lipo. Before you know it, you have your own mental 'circle of shame' every time you look in the mirror. It's no surprise, then, that in the modern day visiting the newsagent's can feel like teetering on the edge of a mental Mordor. There's a spewing, spitting volcano waiting to swallow you up.

SO WHY THE HELL DO WE BUY THEM?

Whenever confronted with the simple question of why it is we buy magazines, it's helpful to use the analogy of an uncomfortable pair of knickers. Many, many women go about their days wearing extremely uncomfortable – and sometimes even borderline painful – pants, and yet it's not as though we've ever stopped wearing them. We suspect that many women have a similar relationship with their magazines; sometimes they hurt, but we're convinced nonetheless that we need them. And indeed, for a long time we did need them. From where else were you supposed to glean information about what other women were doing and thinking? Not the main newspapers, which were apparently purely for men, and not television, which didn't exist. For many women, magazines offered a rare glimpse into the world of the feminine, and for that reason they gained a disproportionate level of importance. It's not as though anyone else took women's interests seriously.

As it began to be acknowledged that women amount to no less than 50% of society, we developed a much more love–hate relationship with magazines. In Naomi Wolf's 1990 book *The Beauty Myth*, one young woman articulates this perfectly. 'I buy them as a form of self-abuse,' she says. She reads them, she tells Wolf, and thinks:

'Yes! Wow! I can be better starting from right this minute! Look at her! Look at *her*!' But the feeling is short-lived: 'right afterward, I feel like throwing out all my clothes and everything in my refrigerator and telling my boyfriend never to call me again and blowtorching my whole life.' Tell us about it.

Those working in the magazine industry will always cite the laws of supply and demand as a defence to keep peddling their vagendas. Healthy circulations are taken as an indication that readers actually enjoy 'learning' about what the shape of his foreskin reveals about his inner feelings for you, but what those journalists are unwilling to admit is that there is still little alternative available in the women's market, at least not in printed form. Although almost everything on offer is a bit of a disappointment, when you want something to kick back with in the bath, you go with it. When every mag is spinning the same old spiel, it doesn't really matter which glossy ends up sodden with Radox on your bathroom floor.

Supply-and-demand arguments also ignore just how ingrained our participation in the cycle of insecurity and consumption can be, as the rest of this book will go on to explain. We read magazines to feel bad about ourselves – in other words, they confirm what we have been taught to buy into throughout our lives: the idea that, as women, we are in many ways lacking. And then we buy the things they tell us to buy to make ourselves feel better. Until, inevitably, we start to feel bad about ourselves once more, and again look to the magazines for a remedy. It's a horrible spiral of shame: we know – we've been trapped in it for years. But by the time you finish this book, you may never want to buy another magazine again.

2.
Body Politics

YOU'RE NOBODY, IF NO BODY LOVES YOU

When was the last time you tried something on in a shop under fluorescent lighting and emerged wanting to hang yourself from the nearest rack of skintight jeggings? Although it may alarm passing children, let's face it, they have to find out about mortality one way or another. Meanwhile, your dreams of pulling off a leather minidress were just crushed by the iron fist of reality as you caught sight of your reflection in one of those disturbing three-way mirrors that allowed you to see your profile in all its chinless glory. Suicide is seemingly the only viable option.

It's a sad fact that, although most women have never uttered the immortal words 'Does my bum look big in this?' – mainly because it's such a terrible cliché – pretty much every woman (even, we suspect, the Victoria's Secret Angels) has at one point said or thought, 'I hate my body'. Words like 'I'm so ugly' or 'I'm so fat' come tumbling out of women's mouths with alarming frequency, confirming everything that we've been led by the media and its cycle of insecurity-mongering to believe about ourselves: as though we are born vain, insecure and self-obsessed as a sex, rather than moulded that way. After years of our

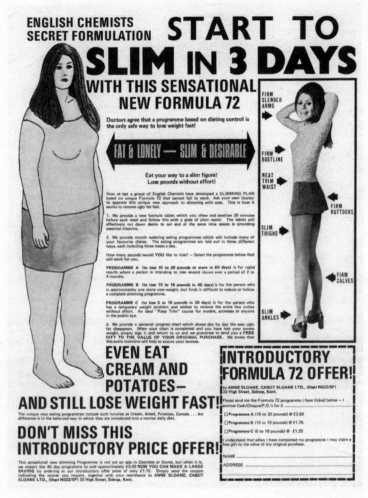

bodies and their individual parts (camel toe, cankles, sideboob, bingo wings, et al.) being viewed as legitimate topics, is it any wonder that some of us engage in body-shaming 'fat chat' with our friends and loved ones?

Blokes apparently don't worry about such trivial things: if and when they develop the frown lines and porcine bellies of middle age, it merely lends them a jowly distinction that commands the respect of man and beast alike: just look at the Cabinet! Of course, in reality, there is an escalating pressure on men to conform to certain body types as well, but the most piercing scrutiny has always been fixed firmly on the gals: our (hopefully large) breasts, our (hopefully tiny) waists, our (hopefully fulsome but rock-hard) bums, and everything in between. Magazines take an instructive role, claiming to be able to teach you everything you need to know about being a woman, before presenting you with a parade of bodily problems which need 'fixing', and then laying on advertisements for miraculous products which can supposedly do just that. Indeed, Mitchell and Webb's excellent parody advert captured just how many things advertisers can find wrong with your body: 'Women: you're leaking, ageing, hairy, overweight and everything hurts, and your children's clothes are filthy. For God's sake sort yourselves out' (the men's slogan was 'Men: shave and get drunk, because you're already brilliant'). Such advertising is so heavily oriented towards women's innumerable 'problem areas', and so pervasive, that you're a fully paid up lady consumer before you know it: a lady customer who knows that the only way to remedy her flaws is to spend, spend, spend – and the only way to know what to buy is to read yet more magazines.

Meanwhile, despite the fact that the size of the average woman in the UK oscillates between a 14 and a 16, we're force-fed the notion that there's nothing better than being skinny. Magazines such as *Closer* ruthlessly document the yo-yo dieting of D-List celebrities and always ensure that there's a 'bloated' bikini body on the cover. Other magazines hammer home the fact that your body is a work in progress, and reassure you that you can guarantee yourself a 'flab-free holiday' by following 832 simple steps. A Danish television show called *Blachman*, after its creator Thomas Blachman ('the Danish version of Simon Cowell', according to the *Telegraph*) even made body-bashing its central premise in 2013: a naked woman would stand before a panel of (male, fully clothed) judges while they delivered merciless feedback on her body, cellulite and all. A May 2013 article in *Time* magazine stated that 'Blachman purportedly created the show to get "men discussing the aesthetics of a female body without allowing the conversation to become pornographic or politically correct."' Oh, and did we mention the fact that the woman under review isn't allowed to speak?

Despite what Thomas Blachman may think, male scrutiny of the female body in the media is not lacking: it is, instead, very much in hyperdrive. How has this state of affairs become so normalised? Perhaps you buy into the idea that a trickle-down from porn has led to the shiny, plastic, hair- and cellulite-free bodies we're confronted with on every billboard; or perhaps you think that the ageism of Hollywood and the fashion industry has more to answer for – but either way, as they say at Alcoholics Anonymous, the first step is admitting we have a problem. Unfortunately for women, certain men have always regarded our bodies and our ladyparts as common property, to be prodded and ogled and lusted after like sexy livestock at an agricultural auction, and as women have come closer to achieving equality with men, the pressure we are under to embody unrealistic physical ideals increases exponentially.

In today's visual media, the objectified female body is so prevalent that many of us don't even notice it any more; we just accept our decorative status as fact. Most lasses we know wouldn't blink an eye at the average grinding, frotting, rutting sweaty sex-fest of a modern pop or hip hop video, or think twice about Jay Z's assertion that he collects 'Money, Cash, Hoes' (despite the fact that money and cash are *the same thing*). A fleeting glance at a stack of US-based *Seventeen* magazines proves that women are 'trained' to accept objectification from an early age: one 2013 cover had 'Find your BEST LOOK INSIDE' ('make-up artist tricks & more') juxtaposed with 'THE HEALTHY DIET' ('look and feel better in just 2 weeks') and 'How to be a great date (and get

asked out again!)', deliberately collating beauty, dieting and social acceptance. Another issue of *Seventeen* ran 'SPRING BEAUTY SECRETS'
('sexy eye make-up, hot new lipsticks') above 'DOES HE LOVE YOU?
Find out now'. It sounds like the stereotype of a middle-aged housewife's
paranoid mind from a Dear Deidre strip, but it's the cover of a magazine
beloved by America's young teens.

So how did we get here, to the self-hatred in the changing rooms and
the public figures vilified for not doing their hair right, and the 'sexy eye
make-up' tips that will make somebody love you? It seems we stood by
fairly sedately as the standards of beauty in media outlets, helped by a
great big dollop of photoshop, became increasingly difficult and then
impossible to emulate. It happened gradually; we took it all in our stride.
And then one day we looked up at the doe-eyed, gazelle-legged movie
star on the latest billboard whose digital manipulation had gone so far
that she was almost indistinguishable from the cartoon beside her, and
realised that no human in the world – including the woman who posed
for the picture – actually looked like that, yet the magazines are telling
us we need to spend our lives vainly pursuing that ideal. And so we all
continue to nod along, pinching the fat on our thighs resignedly as we
refuse another cheesecake; or we keep silent.

MARKETING INSECURITY

Reading a contemporary women's magazine is often like waiting for
an insecurity bomb to go off. One minute you're looking at a nice
harmless little feature about a group of women who set up their own
coconut yoghurt factory, and then – BAM! – you and your enormous,
gelatinous arse are running for cover as giant capitalised letters implore
you to 'Take your butt to bootcamp'. Then just as you've recovered and
have turned over to find out about a new kind of dance meditation that

everyone in showbiz insists you *have* to try, the second bomb detonates with an almighty CRASH because they've said your thighs should be no wider than eighteen inches in circumference and yours are twenty-freaking-five. Before you know it, you're lying face down in a puddle of your own tears and wondering how many pounds you'd lose if you amputated your legs from the knees downwards. *Woman's Own* once ran a front cover with a radiant, smiling Dawn French, dressed up for a press event, splashed across it. The accompanying text was: 'Dawn – FAT AND OUT OF CONTROL? PLUS: Fern and Denise – their skinniest bodies ever!' If that's not enough to make you cry at the counter, what is?

Meanwhile, the UK government has had to resort to sending out leaflets to parents to advise them on how to talk to their children about body image, because young children cannot differentiate between bodies that are photoshopped and ones that aren't – and most adults can't either. By the time a girl is 13, magazines are telling her 'love your body, but try this diet', in preparation for a complete and utter indoctrination by *Cosmo* and *Glamour,* who'll print saccharine articles on body confidence and the importance of self-esteem, and then whack them next to a cosmetic surgery advertorial. Confused? You're not the only one.

Picture the scene: you're 13 or 14, maybe even younger, and all hell is breaking loose in your body. Somehow, pubes have started sprouting overnight, your nipples are in agony, and you're bleeding from that hole in the middle that you weren't even totally ready to believe existed yet. Copiously. In fact, your vagina is basically Stalingrad. Every time you look in the mirror, the war seems to have broken out on a different front. You're developing lumps and bumps in places where previously there were none and you're grouchy and irritable, and massively hormonal. Your mum doesn't understand you and, on seeing your first bout of virgin acne, feels it appropriate to announce to the dinner table that you're just 'going through puberty' but 'still look pretty underneath, despite the obvious'. And if that wasn't bad enough, a strange foreign animal species called 'boy' that smells vaguely of Lynx, knobcheese and Hubba Bubba is starting to show an interest in you through the tried-and-tested methods of insult and torment (usually by asking you why you haven't got any tits and then pinging your bra strap while his other hand readjusts his knackers). If you could, you'd sleep 18 hours a day and never talk to anyone again. No one speaks to you the way that Courtney Love/Alanis Morissette/Avril Lavigne/Lady GaGa/Taylor Swift does (delete according to age and taste). It's no wonder so many of us end up backcombing our hair, throwing on an oversized crucifix necklace and becoming goths for a couple of years: being a teenage girl is shit.

In the midst of that adolescent whirlwind, just as your strange new body is being transformed into that of a woman – whichever sort of woman your genetics have already dictated that you'll be – you're told that you should either be aspiring to have the skinny, bony frame of a child, or be transforming yourself into a pneumatic pornstar with tits the size of melons and a bald vagina not unlike the one you had before your pubes hit. That we live in a society where young teenage girls who are not even fully developed yet are begging their mums for a boob job makes us want to down our seventh gin and grow a penis (which could, in all fairness, make for a spectacular night on the town).

It's not as though baby girls emerge from the womb already hating their podgy thighs, yet a study by University of Central Florida professor Stacey Tantleff-Dunn and Sharon Hayes published in the *British Journal of Psychology* in 2009 showed that half of 3- to 5-year-old girls worry about being fat, and that by age nine, half of them have already been on a diet. We can just see them in the back garden now – 'No mud pie for me, ta, a moment on the lips means a lifetime on the hips!' – and it's not a pretty picture. The same piece of research found that girls between the ages of 11 and 17 cite 'looking good' as their number one aim in life;

once this mindset is developed, advertisers quickly jump in to define exactly what 'good' is, before the girls have time to think for themselves.

We live in a world now where we are able to vote and work and even sometimes run whole countries, so hasn't feminism achieved its goals? Where's the beef? Well, our main point of contention is that, while we're technically *allowed* to do all these things, we're still supposed to have a cracking cleavage while we're doing them. (A man, meanwhile, can be a political tour de force while simultaneously looking as rough as a badger's sphincter. But we're mentioning no names.) If you have the audacity to be a woman and walk around cultivating a prominent career for yourself, it's pretty much taken as read that your appearance will be used by the media to discredit you. Take the website HillaryUgly.com, which was set up to mock Hillary Clinton for being 'one ugly old Hag' with 'ideas . . . even scarier than her looks' – or the cover of the *New York Post* which ran an unflattering picture of her angrily discussing Benghazi politics with the headline: 'No wonder Bill's afraid'. Or perhaps the numerous women's magazines that ran 'Margaret Thatcher style' features in the wake of the former Prime Minister's death, yet neglected to mention any of her policies. Or the comments made by the leader of the Liberal and Democratic Party in Russia, who stated that US diplomat Condoleezza Rice was an ugly woman whose political stance on Russia is negative because 'this is the only way for her to attract men's attention'.

The fact of the matter is that ever since women became a target group for those shadowy suits known as advertising executives, the media have been creating a lack of body confidence and then using the resultant anxiety as a marketing tactic. One advert for Palmolive from the 1950s shows a drawing of a woman sitting in front of a mirror and carries the strapline, 'Most men ask, "Is she pretty?" not, "Is she clever?"' (Just in case you were unsure as to where your life priorities should lie.) Indeed, the 1950s were prime time for advertisers hell-bent on insecurity-mongering and their campaigns created neurosis wherever they went. They interrogated the magazine readers of the time, shaming them for every natural bodily process going, asking product-oriented questions that included: 'Does your husband look younger than you do?', 'Why couldn't Grace get partners? Because her nervousness and worry brought on NERVOUS B.O.' and 'YOU, 5,000,000 women who want to get married: how's your breath today?' No wonder poor Grace was so sweaty.

Meanwhile, over twenty years later when the feminist revolution was supposed to be well under way, Black & Decker, which at that time made exercise machines, gave us a pretty hefty taste of 'same shit, different decade' with a bitchy ad that read: 'Are you twice the woman your husband married?' Nice. The thing is, that when you look at these adverts they can seem charmingly quaint and retro. 'Ha ha!' you chuckle, 'How silly and ignorant those advertisers were back then. Thank God we've all moved on.' But look a little closer, beyond vintage imagery's current trendy status, and you'll realise that advertisers' tactics have barely changed. In the last few years, magazines have run adverts for diet pills and plastic surgery that used the taglines 'I hated every kilo on my body' (diet pills advertised in *Reveal* magazine, April 2012) or 'I just had my breasts done, but the biggest smile you'll see is on my face' (Transform Medical Group's adverts for plastic surgery, plastered across the London Underground and *Cosmopolitan* magazine throughout 2012).

We're not saying we're against cosmetic surgery as a choice per se, but it becomes less of a choice and more of an imperative when every picture of a woman that you see is trying to convert you to surgery with the persistence of an airbrushed Jehovah's Witness. What does send us on a trip to Outrage Mountain, however, is the notion that it's the *only* option. Magazines tend to opt for some simpering twaddle to disguise this, such as the unforgettable line in *Glamour* magazine: 'Let's get one thing straight: at *Glamour*, we don't want you to have plastic surgery. We love you (and ourselves, thanks) just the way you are', before undoing it all by going on to say 'all the experts we spoke to confirmed that, in the right patient, at the right time, aesthetic procedures can have powerful positive outcomes', and advertising five different Harley Street clinics in the back pages. Much like your ex-boyfriend, *Glamour* doesn't really love you at all. It only wants you for your body, and you deserve better.

The revelation that advertisers and magazines create our insecurities as a selling tactic is nothing new, but their cynicism does seem to have jumped up a notch. In late 2013, media news outlet *Adweek* reported on research which revealed when female consumers are at their most insecure. This turned out to be Mondays, a 'good time' to market 'quick beauty rescues', apparently. And magazines not only try to capitalise on your existing insecurities but also create new ones ('back fat', anyone?) until you become dependent upon them for cures for all your horrible flaws. Without them, you're on your own: a fat, unattractive loser who has no idea what probiotic frozen yoghurt is and thinks 'free radicals' either means a nineties band or a Cold War era film about communists on the loose. 'We'll be your friend,' they bleat from the supermarket racks. 'We'll show you how to pass in this crazy world, how to wear the right clothes, discuss the right topics, and eat the right foods.' Much better to pick up the latest copy and join the body-trashing ranks. As keen consumers of women's magazines ourselves, we both noticed that the more we bought them, the worse we felt about our bodies.

Magazines' obsession with women's bodies at the expense of their minds is obvious. We once counted 45 'body terms' used in a single issue of *Cosmo* (words such as 'bum', 'thigh', 'curves', 'figure'), compared with 9 'mind terms' ('mind', 'brain', 'think', 'thoughts') – and that wasn't an unusual edition, by any means. Their obsession becomes your obsession, and once they've created it within you, they live to feed it.

A GAL'S GUIDE TO BODY-BASHING

So how can you go about spotting this confidence-damaging content in magazines, especially when it can be so subtle that your brain doesn't even notice it's soaking it all up like a sponge until it's punishing you in front of the full-length mirror later? The first step is understanding their tactics. A prime example of their cunning bitchiness is the way magazines and newspapers will call a woman 'curvy'. 'Celebrity X celebrates her new curves!' the headline will say, giving the impression that the article is about body acceptance and female empowerment, when in fact the main text alludes to 'yo-yo dieting' and 'struggles with weight gain'. While 'curvy' may initially have been used as a way to describe larger women without being downright rude, it has now become a catch-all term for anyone with a little bit of flesh on her bones. The *Mail Online* has even taken to referring to pregnancy as 'getting curvy'. Another classic is the phrase 'womanly shape' or 'real woman', as though having a 'non-womanly shape' makes you some kind of fake mannequin woman masquerading as human. Size 8 Daisy Lowe famously referred to herself as 'curvy' in a *Grazia* interview in early 2013 ('Being skinny doesn't suit me'), having previously done so in the *Daily Telegraph* back in 2010. It was surprising to hear a successful, slender model talk about going to shoots 'where the clothes didn't fit and you feel horrendous about yourself', but her admission that she loves being 'curvy' seemed to provoke a kind of curvy warfare, with the *Telegraph* choosing to pick up the story with a piece entitled 'Daisy Lowe is not "curvy", says fellow model Zara Martin'. People tied themselves up in knots to decide whether 'curvy' meant 'curvy' or not. Was Daisy fat-shaming herself? Are size 8 girls allowed to call themselves 'curvy' if it's actually a euphemism for plus-size? You may well think that you give zero fucks, but it turns out that enough people care to make a mini media storm.

What's even more perplexing about the use of terms such as 'curvy' is the fact that by the early noughties, body fascism had become so universal that any woman going about her business who *didn't* look like a malnourished size zero was immediately lavished with praise for her 'body confidence'. As Kim Kardashian has regularly demonstrated to us, simply being a female with an arse has become a noteworthy occupation (if you're taking a 'belfie' of it, even better); the same with Christina Hendricks and an ample chest. Being a celebrity with a 'womanly figure' means having shit-tons of journalists praise you for the 'bravery' and 'individuality' you exhibit simply by owning a pair of tits. It seems that, if you're not busy lamenting your cup size and your unwilling membership of the Itty Bitty Titty Committee, then your hourglass figure is being flaunted as proof that you're courageous. It's a D-cup, darling, not a battle with leukaemia.

Advertisers realised that it was high time to cash in on all this 'body acceptance', and launched the Dove Campaign for Real Beauty (perhaps that's a bit of a cynical take on it, but hear us out). The campaign focused on celebrity photographer Rankin's portraits of 'real women' (not all those skinny bitches who apparently don't count) with insecurities that, it was implied, had been developed by the beauty industry. One demonstrably slim young woman who featured appeared with the tagline 'Thinks she's fat'. Another poster showed underwear-clad women of all sizes cavorting together in wondrous merriment like a basket of puppies on adoption day. 'Dove has liberated us from the shackles of media expectations!' they seemed to cry, as they let their love handles jiggle wild and free. Despite the fact that one of these campaigns was for a cream that supposedly smooths out cellulite (because we all know *that* is simple enough to shift), at least the portrayal of diverse body types spearheaded by Dove could be seen as one step in a positive direction. Unfortunately, however, nothing seems to have changed very much since then, and certain corners of the media continue pitting various female body types against one another and labelling them either 'real' or fictitious.

A particularly insidious form of body-shaming subjects women to the scrutiny of 'trained celebrity nutritionists'. Nice, normal women are photographed in their bras and pants before being called fat and ugly in a variety of backhanded ways by a team of pseudo-scientific 'experts' with a printed-out qualification from the College of Body Contouring Remedies. 'You need more wheatgrass in your diet,' they'll say, clutching their empty clipboards. And they're not the only ones who seem to know what's best for women's bodies while covertly feeding them expensive poison.

Then there are the leading questions. Women are often asked, 'What's your least favourite part of your body?' or, 'What's your ideal celebrity body?' as part of PR-led surveys for nefarious companies, which then end up recycled and regurgitated and placed in amongst the genuine news: '65% of British women detest their noses!' the headline will say, when in fact it's nearly always just 65% of the women who happened to be passing a certain spot on that particular Saturday afternoon, a spot which, coincidentally, is just around the corner from the rhinoplasty clinic that they were heading to. Next, there is the kind of feature where a couple are interviewed about each other and the guy gets 'Does your girlfriend prefer her bum or her boobs?' while the girl is asked 'Does your boyfriend prefer the James Bond franchise or Tarkovsky?'

It's not just the shape of your body that you should be paranoid about, however, it's also the way it smells. In 2013 'intimate wash' company Femfresh had to pull its 'Woohoo for my FrooFroo' campaign after a massive social media backlash (which, let's say, we were not uninvolved with) during which the company's Facebook page was swamped with 'VAGINA' comments and a hefty serving of future suggestions for Femfresh flavours, including 'houmous' and 'mojito'. People were angered that they were being told their vaginas were somehow naturally dirty, when in fact they are far more inclined towards self-cleaning than testicles and penises (and yet wiener cleaner is not available on the market). The rule of thumb that 'if the guys aren't doing it, it's probably sexist' applies here.

It's as though the media want us in a constant battle with the processes of our bodies, as though they want us to remove all traces of anything natural, such as body hair or crow's feet or freckles, to become a doll-like version of femininity. These bodies exist in a world where when you get your period blue liquid comes out, cystitis is non-existent and no one ever, ever gets the kind of yeast infection where you're constantly crossing your eyes as well as your legs and cutting every conversation short to resume your quest for a toilet cubicle in which to scratch yourself to oblivion.

In the eyes of these magazines, these advertisers, these executives, a woman is only the sum of her squeaky-clean parts (and sometimes, owing to the over-zealous use of Photoshop, they aren't even her own parts). As a result, she becomes piecemeal, fragmented: a collection of boobs and thighs and bum and waist and calves, as though these body parts are somehow separable from her. Women such as Germaine Greer and Susie Orbach have been saying this for years, of course, but nothing has really changed. In fact, it's getting worse. The overwhelming message is that a woman's individual body parts mean more than she does. Take *Cosmo*'s '50 great things to do with your boobs' (because, y'know, you have the time), an article which implies that your breasts are such fascinating appendages that you've been searching for years for a way to maximise their usefulness. Unfortunately, the magazine's 'boob fun' suggestions were nowhere near as fun as those of our readers, mainly because *Cosmo*'s, funnily enough, all seemed to revolve around men ('Put temporary tattoos of his name around your nipples, and give him a peek when you bend forward in an undone button-up'). Not nearly as enjoyable as one reader's suggestion, which was to 'get an arty friend to paint them with a leaf design then hide topless in a hedge'. (After all, if you're going to spend a significant part of your life worrying about your body parts, you might as well use them to conduct interesting experiments now and then.) The point is, they're *our* breasts, and we don't need an instruction manual full of helpful suggestions and rainy day activities to help us enjoy them (especially when we can just take them to a gig), just as we don't need to call our vaginas 'minkies' in order to talk about them, because we're not six-year-olds). And, while this may all seem fairly trivial, it doesn't take a procession of justifiably disgruntled pro-choicers holding up placards to politicians saying 'Keep your rosaries off my ovaries!' to remind you that women's bodies are still considered everyone else's business – and no more so than when it comes to the humble *vagine*.

MINGE MADNESS

Whether it's another majority-male debate on abortion in the White House or the House of Commons, a pharmacist telling you that you should have kept your legs closed when you've gone in for the morning-after pill, or another tedious Vagisil advert, everyone's got something to say about your vagina and what you do with it. Getting all its hair torn off is commonplace; labiaplasty is now de rigueur, and we've paid hundreds of pounds in VAT – or 'tampon taxes', if you will – here in the UK, because the stuff needed for your monthly visit from Aunt Rose apparently counts as 'luxury goods' in the eyes of the government (they were, however, kind enough to lower the VAT rate from a whopping 17.5% to 5% in 2001. Yippee.) Go ahead and luxuriate in the feeling of shedding your womb lining, girls – you deserve it.

But the interest in what's inside your knickers doesn't end there: anti-abortion campaigners will openly debate whether the rights of an adult woman not to be penetrated against her will by a vaginal ultrasound are less important than the rights of the month-old foetus living in her womb, and certain politicians seem fetishistically obsessed with our vaginas, telling us what should be going down up there. It's surprising any of us even bother to continue taking off our knickers of a Friday night (don't say we're not troopers). Indeed, the man calling for vaginal ultrasounds, US Republican Ryan McDougle, considered himself an expert on the inner workings of women's bodies until his Facebook page was inundated with vaginal updates ('During my last period, I had to use the Super tampons because I had some chunky blood issues. Do you know anything about that?'). Others of the McDougle ilk have been overwhelmed by hand-knitted uteruses (uteri?) sent anonymously through the post: craftivism at its best. As a wise American woman once said during one of these protests, 'If I wanted the government in my vagina, I'd fuck a senator.'

So what is it exactly that makes everyone so loose-lipped about labia, and where will this obsession with our vaginas end? For a while it seemed that the appearance of your vag, safely encased as it was in a pair of pants (most of the time, at least) was beyond reproach, even if the rest of your body was dissected by media moguls. What (and who) you did with it sexually was, and still is, another matter, but if you fancied cultivating a massive 1970s bush then that was your prerogative. But it was not to last, and partly since the skyrocketing growth of the adult entertainment industry in the 1980s and '90s, we're now at the point where even our vaginas are supposed to represent porno pussy perfection and, as a result, a variety of products and treatments have sprung up. (Vajacial, anyone? It's like a facial, but for your vagina. Cos that's, like, totally your other face.)

In 2011 and 2012, a number of advertising campaigns in Thailand and India appeared which hinted strongly that women would be more desirable to men if they bought vaginal whitening products (seriously) because shades of brown just make for a vulgar vulva, sweetie. Meanwhile, a 'genital cosmetic colorant' (vag dye, basically) called My New Pink Button was being marketed in the English-speaking world as a way to get back the 'youthful' colour of your flaps and 'increase sexual confidence'. As one reviewer drily noted, 'I would never buy this product. Instead I like to get a sick thrill from skulking around in the shadows, tricking men into my beige vagina.' We don't know about you, but the colour of our clits never really factored in to our sexual confidence. We were too busy worrying about whether the 'happy pancake' really was a sex position (it is, apparently) and whether the condom had wiggled to the end of the guy's knob or not, rather than whether or not we had fifty shades of grey labia. But if we don't come back at the onslaught of these 'developments' with a massive 'I DON'T CARE', while wielding a big vagina-shaped tennis racket to bat this load of balls out of the court, then they'll keep trying to convince us that we do.

Just to top off the mountain of 'WTF' vajayjay-changing products out there, the particularly brazen company Ultratech also suggested that they had made a 'vaginal tightening cream' in 2012 to reinstate that oh-so-fetishised state of female virginity. If that's not enough to turn your stomach, maybe the fact that it was called '18 Again' will – or try

YouTubing the commercial, featuring an actress singing that 'it feels like the first time all over again' (because *that's* a sexual experience every woman out there is just gagging to repeat). Meanwhile, plastic surgeons the world over offer the 'beautification' of vaginas and 'reattachment' of hymens, despite the fact that, in our personal experience, losing your hymen is about as pleasurable as having someone rap your knuckles with a frozen veggie sausage. It is now routine for surgeons in the US to perform labiaplasty operations, because it's such a lucrative business, and feminist and medical groups have argued in the last few years that such procedures, which can lead to recurrent bleeding, infection and permanent scarring, should count as genital mutilation. In 2011, there was even a 'Muff March', organised by campaign group UK Feminista and performance art group The Muffia, down Harley Street, London's plastic surgery haven, in protest. At the dawn of the 'designer vagina' craze in the early twenty-first century, the NHS reported that double the number of labiaplasty operations had been performed in one year (2006) than had been performed during the previous four. In 2013, WhatClinic reported a 109% increase in enquires regarding the operation, while The *Cosmetic Surgery Guide* reported that 24% of their female readers would be interested in hearing more about vaginal rejuvenation. Clearly, this one is a continuing trend.

Like most new products for women, this veritable smorgasbord of idiocy came with the promise that it was the latest 'solution' for females. Funnily enough, we didn't know we had half of these problems in the first place, but when we're surrounded by these messages daily, we start to believe that our bodies have flaws that *do* need fixing. And nowhere has a campaign to 'solve' women's bodies been more successful than in the case of hair removal.

FIGHTING THE FUZZ

You might be forgiven for forgetting that a natural part of puberty for women involves growing thicker, darker hairs on their legs, ladyparts and underarms. After all, magazines are full of pictures of smooth, shiny, hairless women and any female celebrity who has decided to do something more important than get the razor out is immediately lassoed with a magazine circle of shame or declared part of a 'Celebrity armpit hair face-off' (*Metro*, July 2012), like Julia Roberts and, more recently, Pixie Lott. Poor old Pixie was even subjected to the headline 'Pixie Lott explains why she was flashing armpit hair on the red carpet', followed by the tagline 'Popstar doesn't seem embarrassed by her red carpet fail' in *Reveal*, despite the fact that she'd merely accidentally shown some stubble while posing with her hand on her hip as opposed to, say, parading through the premiere with hirsute arms in the air and a women's rights placard over her naked breasts (although *that* would have been amazing). Dare to suggest that any fuzz might be allowed to stay in place – barring, perhaps, a small triangle perched above the labia charmingly known in beauty salons as 'the landing strip', useful in a world of increasing ambiguity to signify that you actually have sat your Year Nine SATs – and there will be an outcry.

Thanks to pre-teen exposure to magazines, learning the word 'pubes' comes hand-in-trembling-hand with 'Veet' and 'tweezers' and 'G-string wax': just consider the fact that Uni.K.Wax salons in the US held a promotion offering 50% off waxing for the under-15s back in the summer of 2012. The world of women's grooming is mad keen to point out that if you're going to have sex, you're going to have to make sure you look the part, and that includes pubic grooming. Much affectionate fun has been made of the teenage boy's first shave, bound as it is to leave a few blood-soaked tabs of toilet paper in its wake, but little has been made of the shamefaced tiptoe of the teenage girl into her parents' bedroom to seek out Daddy's razor blade and apply it to her newly furry areas. Sure, aftershave stings (we imagine) – but try ingrown hairs along your knicker line, cuts near your sexy parts, and the itch of regrowth in a place God never intended to itch when healthy and functional. The jumpy 17-year-old who eventually deflowers you will most likely forget to glance down anyways but be prepared in case he does, lest you break his spirit with your untamed lady-garden and consign him to a lifetime of hysterical celibacy.

The anti-pube brigade dictates that women should look basically prepubescent all the time; ideally even when they're knocking on for the menopause. We're not saying that how you choose to tame your minge isn't your choice (believe us, we couldn't care less what you do with your pubes), but the suggestion that landscaping the front garden is now absolutely necessary for a normal sex life is so prevalent that it's become an obligation. If you've ever seen porn, you'll know that the acceptable pubic hairline is rapidly receding. This all ties in with the shiny, vacant, sterilised version of sex that the media and its delinquent cousin pornography sell you.

We've both fallen prey to the brigade ourselves in the past. Having bought some budget own-brand waxing strips as part of a two-for-one deal using her pocket money, the intrepid 15-year-old Rhiannon waited until her mother was out and then locked herself in the bathroom. She applied the wax strip to the left half of her nether regions, but as soon as she actually grasped the reality of what she was about to do, she suddenly lost every ounce of plucky resolve and became too frightened to tear it off. An hour later, after several tentative attempts, she finally ripped it off like a plaster, screaming blue murder. She was stuck with the resultant half hairy/half baldy fanny for weeks. And there's not much better waiting for you in a salon, where Holly fainted during a particularly brutal 'G-string wax' at the embarrassing age of 21. It's another situation where the ladies are under pressure to do something that the boys aren't (sexism alert), and yet, in our experience, men never seem to respond well to suggestions that, if they want a smoothy-smooth snatch to play with then they should respond in kind by removing all their bollock hair. If it hurts more than your last heavy period and you need a hot water bottle and a good cry afterwards, then it's not *just* a beauty routine, whatever the sadist with the electrolysis machine tells you.

For women to show any hair from the neck downwards has always, to an extent, been frowned upon, especially pubic hair, which, as a sign of rampant sexuality, has long been regarded as immodest. Indeed, nude depictions of women in painting often neglected to feature pubes (though it should be noted that upper-class Victorian lovers gave one another their pubes as souvenirs). However, there wasn't really any attempt to control what the masses did with their body hair until the early twentieth century, when sleeveless dresses came into fashion and unshaven underarms suddenly seemed obscene. This was closely followed by legs, then, with the advent of the two-piece bathing suit, V-zones, back in the time when the phrase 'bikini line' hadn't even tunnelled its way out of the glossy pink woodwork, never mind the concept of a vajazzle.

It was US magazine *Harper's Bazaar*, targeted at the 'better sort' of women, that published the first advertisement warning against fanny fuzz in May 1915. Back then, ads were still getting into the swing of subtle manipulation, so they just went out there with a pretty straight-forward message. 'Summer dress and modern dancing combine to make necessary the removal of objectionable hair', read the snappy tagline – despite the fact that body hair had never been 'objectionable' before. The late-Edwardian 'fash pack' pushed the idea that a 'woman of fashion' would never be seen compromising her new sleeveless outfit by daring to bare hair, and slowly this message trickled down to most

I LOVE MY HUSBAND
FAR TOO MUCH
TO RISK GETTING
DRY, LIFELESS "MIDDLE-AGE" SKIN!

women in North America, the UK and, yes, despite the hairy stereotypes, France (where a 'landing strip' is referred to as a *ticket metro*) – though surely French feminist group La Barbe, committed fans of novelty hair – which the BBC delightfully described as 'fighting inequality with sarcastic humour and fake beards' – are sure to be vociferous in the defence of their bearded clams.

But why is fanny fuzz such an issue at all? When we published an article on the Vagenda website written by our friend Emer O'Toole describing how she had turned her back on the razor, the response was overwhelming, and while lots of readers praised our contributor's straight-up attitude to her hairy bits, just as many reacted against her decision to boycott the whole shebang. The controversy surrounding one young woman's thoughts about her armpits, legs and fanny was such that she made national headlines, showed off her pits on *This Morning,* and was even asked to do a topless shoot by that classy tabloid the *Sunday Sport* (she said no, FYI). If we needed proof that women's bodies were still subject to dizzying levels of social judgement, then this was it. Body hair is, after all, just a natural part of being an adult: dye it, braid it, pull it out, sew charming Yuletide scarves with it. But if you really, truly find it revolting to the point of disturbance, we invite you to go ahead and watch a 'back, sack and crack' waxing session (if you can ever find a willing live male to undergo it in front of you). The resulting mess looks like a passionate night in with honey gone wrong, and when a slightly furry fanny turns your stomach more than that, you must be truly chaetophobic.

Many would argue that their decision to wax or not to wax is their choice, and on the most basic level it is. But there doesn't seem to be much out there in the way of pube positivity – the anti-muff brigade is certainly winning. Bikinis are embroiled in a bitter dispute with the postage stamp to see who can take up the least space in the world at any one time, and for many years the Brazilian wax was the rule rather than the exception. Once upon a time, the 'muffstache' was something it was considered poor taste to mention in polite company, but now you're expected to be porno-perfect in preparation for that close-up money shot at all times. In this day and age, most beauty therapists seem to privately consider you a bit of a hippie if your waxing regimen hasn't included getting on all fours and allowing them to get acquainted with the minutiae of your bumhole. With that much societal pressure, coupled with the fact that we hardly know anyone who will freely admit to not shaving, the decision to remove the hair isn't so much a decision as an imperative. Perhaps it's time to say a muff is a muff (sorry) to the notion that pubic hair is somehow repulsive or disgusting, and to the myth that only after a close shave, a bit of colonic irrigation, and a sesh of bleaching your arsehole (preferably not in that order) will your privates be just about decent enough to get intimate with.

3
Beautiful Lies

(or, Hey, is that a vagina on your face?)

THE PRICE OF BEING PRETTY

It's impossible to walk past a display of women's magazines without being hit in the face at full force with the semen facial of their beautiful lies: the covers alone will tell you most of what you need to know. 'Get Bigger Eyes! Redder Lips! The Perfect Skin Tone! Whiter Teeth!' they whisper in shrill, insidious Voldemort style, as you march through WH Smith en route to a discount Chocolate Orange. '612 Beauty Myths That Turned Out to Be True!' cries the latest edition of the first glossy you fully focus your eyes on – and that's it, you have to know. Undeniably intrigued, you pull it cautiously off the rack, hoping that one of the resurrected myths isn't the Victorian belief in puppy urine's anti-ageing qualities. Flick through the pages to the feature in question, and it might as well be, for all the sense it makes, recommending as it does everything from seaweed hair wraps to eyelash perms to vajacials, oxygen facials (because going outside just isn't enough), and placenta-based hand cream. Welcome to the everyday world of beauty journalism, where everyone has something to sell and, as you're about to see, is willing to try everything from bribery to manipulation to emotional blackmail in order to get you to buy into it. Whether it's getting you to sign up to some 'amazing' new procedure you never thought you needed, like waxing your eyebrows off before having them tattooed back on again, or making you obsess over your nonexistent moustache, the beauty section's on to it. This is a place where the sheer quantity of products being marketed as 'everyday solutions' or 'necessities' outweighs the number of hot dinners you could ever be expected to consume, ten times over. Tread carefully, because the carpet is made of 100% hand-woven self-loathing (and it's been dyed to match the drapes).

No wonder we keep complaining about the culture of 'having it all' – it seems a pretty tall order to ask the average woman to actually *live* her life in between 'priming up that beach bod' and 'fighting the winter flab', moisturising and exfoliating and polishing and trimming and powdering until there's nothing left but a small, generic lump of regulation girl-flubber. Every few weeks, a new 'must-have' product comes on the market to remind you that last week's perfection wasn't quite perfect enough. Surprise – it costs an even higher percentage of your pay cheque than the last one did, and the pressure to have it at hand will reach fever pitch within weeks. Soon, you'll be the only one lacking a tube of the gunk in your purse; by next year, you'll feel naked without it.

The cosy relationship between beauty PRs and the journalists writing 'content' for the beauty sections of magazines is well known throughout the industry: the free spa breaks and the free backhanders of Crème de la Mer and 'real diamond' nail polishes hundreds of pounds out of any reader's price range, and the unspoken threat that if you don't lavish glowing recommendations on their providers that cushy lifestyle might be taken away. This essentially means that at the consumer end, all we hear about is the 'must-have' pair of fake nails which make you feel 'simply gorgeous'. The writer is hardly going to mention that they make her feel a bit like Cruella De Vil and she can't open the boot of her car (and if her boyfriend wants his prostate massaged then he can just forget it), not when next week's promise of a free bikini wax is dangling in front of her. She's embroiled in a world where beauty therapists on commission are reminding her that waxing away her pubes is 'clean' and 'normal', but she hasn't got any money left because she's underpaid and over-criticised. She just spent her last pay cheque on a 'treatment' made of whale spunk. Do you really trust what she has to say about moisturiser?

Beauty editors face an ever-increasing mountain of beauty products to coo over, 'test' and add to the wish list, and the range is staggering. When you've complemented your full face of slap with a caffeine roll-on under the eyes, added in a can of hairspray, invested in the latest perfume, slathered your thighs with anti-cellulite complex, painted on some cuticle treatment and cleaned the overnight whitening gel off your teeth, all before you've run a comb through your hair, it seems downright bizarre that you're still only just keeping up with what you 'must, must, *must*' do as a bare minimum for respect as a human being. The magazine article that advises on how to get the 'natural look' (clue: go out without any make-up) and yet recommends over thirty different products is well known. *Vogue* Australia even ran a feature in October 2013 called 'Experts on how to do the new natural make-up', where catwalk directors and make-up experts collaborated on seven detailed steps ('From the skin, to the cheeks, eyes and lips') on how to look like you're not wearing any make-up at all. How much more can you physically layer on to your skin or into your pores before you start vomming retinol A-complex over your cornflakes and excreting anti-ageing serum? We're not entirely sure – and we're not going to test it – but we've definitely wasted a large enough proportion of our brains on contemplating whether 'extract of bull testicle' will make our eyelashes more voluminous or not. Maybe it's time to reclaim the tiny lump of duck-egg grey matter in our 'silly' female brains – you know, the organ that's currently dedicating itself to articles with titles such as '100% hotness' (*Glamour*) or 'Get pretty now' (*Teen Vogue*) – once and for all. Despite what the industry may tell you, it's still the most important thing about you.

WHERE BEAUTY BEGINS

Whether it's a study on the age-defying properties of semen or an advert promising you a peachy posterior, the message that we need to, that we *must*, be beautiful is all around us. Can it just be coincidence that, as women have been increasingly liberated and emancipated, these beauty ideals have become all the more tyrannical? While once there was one kind of mascara to fit all, there are now umpteen promising you different, sometimes physically impossible, results (can you imagine if your lashes really did go on 'for ever', like physics-defying, man-catching tentacles?). The adverts, the products, the stores are everywhere, and it's not until you sit down and *really* think about it that you start wondering why beauty is consistently used as a stick with which to beat women, but almost never men.

As little girls, we were told to scrub our dirty faces. So far, so normal (a snot-and-jam face mask is never attractive, or hygienic), but that simple existence didn't last long before we were being told fairy tales about gorgeous princesses who were effortlessly beautiful and in constant flight from older stepmothers, who were evil, ugly and vain. At around the age of six you're given (or your friend is given) a disem-bodied blonde woman's head made of plastic, which you're supposed to 'style' using hair bobbles and 'kiddy make-up'. (Where the hell did this decapitated monster come from?) A quick scan of the Argos catalogue reveals a multitude of resolutely pink and purple products for toddlers and above, ranging from nail transfers (made by Crayola, of all people!) to a Minnie Mouse vanity set, to dummy hairdryers and straighteners. We're encouraged to play hairdressers in the same way that boys are encouraged to play pirates, despite the fact that having strands of your hair wrenched through a swimming cap with holes in it while your stylist wanks on about her holiday in Tenerife is nowhere near as fun as hunting for lost treasure.

Meanwhile, parents have told us of their daughters' first trainers coming with a 'play' sparkly lip gloss attached. In November 2013, the free gift in bright pink girlie mag *Animal Friends* (aimed at girls aged 3–10) was a 'Sparkle Set' of 'funky bracelets', 'cool tattoos' and 'lush lipshine', despite the fact that the magazine's content revolves around a love of animals (as the name suggests), and the Christmas issue of *Angel Princess* ran with thirty-six free gifts including 'lipshine' and plastic jewellery. That little girls under ten years old are already being sent the message that beauty and grooming should be high on their priority list, that they should be sitting in front of a plastic illuminated mini dressing table when they could be running around scraping their knees and climbing trees without worrying about the impact on their hair, makes us want to set fire to the 'princess' section of Toys 'Я' Us, stat.

From an early age, girls are taught that they're supposed to follow a very specific beauty blueprint. This was highlighted expertly in 2013 by deviantART user Oceanstarlet, who created a Disney Girls Tutorial breaking down the various components of a Disney princess, and comparing it to the average female form in real life. According to her guide, the Disney princess invariably has an enlarged, childlike head sitting on an extremely slender neck, ginormous eyes with permanently dilated pupils, impossibly small feet, but no muscles or hips. With *Brave* in 2012, Disney created a princess who didn't fit this stereotype for the very first time – a feisty Scottish tomboy called Merida, who refused marriage and excelled in archery, complete with uncontrollable ginger hair. Despite the fact that Merida had been hailed as a progressive step by a company famed for its saccharine depictions of femininity, Disney sadly redrew her for her initiation into the Magic Kingdom's Princess Hall of Fame. She was given make-up and a cleavage while they were at it. Criticism was vocal, but perhaps we shouldn't have been so surprised; after all, these were the people who had stretched out Minnie Mouse to a super-skinny frame at Barneys in New York for a cartoon catwalk sequence because, as Barneys creative director Dennis Freedman put it, 'The standard Minnie Mouse would not look so good in a Lanvin dress.'

By the time we were teenagers in the 1990s, we'd read enough articles in *Mizz* magazine called things like 'Make-up to make you happy' to know that we should be covering ourselves in roll-on neon body glitter and bindis if we ever wanted to get down to 'Brimful of Asha' with that 'luscious lad'. At around this time, Rhiannon devoted an inordinate amount of energy to bleaching out her freckles using 'fade out' cream. 'You'll end up like Michael Jackson,' her mum warned, to no avail. Both of us also begged our mums to iron our hair, and by our twenties we were fully paid up beauty consumers, spending much of our hard-earned lady cash (and let's remember, that's still significantly less than man cash) on identical products differing only in their jazzy packaging and pseudo-sciencey claims that promised the world.

This is cradle-to-grave marketing. Despite the fact that women over 50 tend to disappear from our television screens the minute they stop conforming to our fresh-beauty paradigm, they're expected to do everything in their power to return to their former youthful appearance, despite the fact that this is, well, BIOLOGICALLY IMPOSSIBLE. (Admittedly, this is not something that seems to trouble publications for this age bracket. *Red* ran a piece called

'Can you anti-age your eggs?' Short answer: no.) When they're not creating new insecurities for a whole generation of older women (yes, your 'post-pregnancy tummy' or your 'flabby upper arms' are now supposed to be your 'main weakness', and you may as well follow *Red* magazine's genuine hashtag #WhatToEat if you don't want to let that 'newly slowed metabolism' get the better of you), magazines such as *Easy Living* and *Good Housekeeping* tirelessly flog anti-ageing creams and moisturisers, dropping in impressive-sounding phrases such as 'penetrating micro-particles' and 'multi-level moisture'. 'I've seen evidence in the mirror that anti-ageing creams can make a huge difference,' bleats a feature in *Easy Living*'s beauty section, 'particularly as I haven't gone down the road of having Botox, fillers or lasers (yet!) From your 30s upwards, it's genuinely worth the effort to set up a proper routine, and you need to stick to it every day for at least 4–6 weeks to get results.' Just long enough to need to buy the biggest bottle of the freebie product they gave you in exchange for editorial, then? Gotcha. But since when did 'a proper routine' morph from learning the choreography in the music video for Beyoncé's 'Single Ladies' into a toe-curlingly mundane application of various lotions, night after night, in front of your bathroom mirror? That beauty has become akin to a full-time job seems to us like nothing more than a conspiracy to make women's lives chronically boring.

As anyone who's tried to wash their Afro using own-brand shower gel will tell you, certain lotions and potions do actually work better than others. But as Dr Ben Goldacre points out in his myth-busting *Bad Science*, most moisturisers are essentially the same when it comes to, erm, adding moisture to your skin. These companies stun you with sciencebabble about the 'pro-retinol complex' or 'biopeptide' in the creams, which, despite sounding only a little more convincing than Danone's 'bifidus digestivum', will apparently deliver unto you the gift of eternal youth and hotness. The thing is, although these ingredients always claim to have miracle properties, they are most often present in over-the-counter face creams in such minuscule quantities that the only thing they'll do is sweet sod-all to your skin. All that will happen is that you'll end up thirty quid poorer and looking exactly the same as you would had you smeared a three-quid tub of Vaseline on to your chops. As a case in point, a couple of years ago there was a rush on Aldi's £3.49 anti-ageing serum after a BBC *Horizon* programme found it outperformed all of its bankruptcy-provoking rivals.

One of the many things that is so disturbing about the beauty industry is how the faces smiling out from cosmetic surgery adverts all send the same message: changing your appearance can change your life. Beauty, more than anything else – including personal or psychological wellbeing – has become the goal towards which women are told to aspire, and what's alarming is that we rarely question it; it's just taken as a given.

THE PURSUIT OF PERFECTION: BEAUTY IS PAIN

Why are we willing to put ourselves through increasingly painful and bizarre procedures in an apparent quest for perfection? If you're anything like us, you probably check your reflection at least several times over the course of a day, and you may have even perfected the 'subtle shop-window check', where a thorough inspection of your flyaway fringe is disguised as a nonchalant perusal of the mannequins. On average, the self-checking window gaze is much more prevalent amongst women (Holly once checked herself out in the back of a serving spoon during a roast dinner), but it's not because there is a special female gene that makes you care more about your appearance. We care more about our appearance because we've been *told* throughout our lives that that's where our priorities should lie.

You've probably heard the phrase 'beauty is pain' at one point or another. Although often said flippantly, it reveals a fundamental truth about the things women put themselves through in the pursuit of physical perfection. And it's nothing new – just look at the corsets and lethal lead make-up of yesteryear and pity poor old Elizabeth I, who spent most of her time in a corset made of whale bones. However, with the number of women undergoing cosmetic surgery currently increasing year by year, the masochistic aspects of the beauty industry and its followers are definitely in competitive hyperdrive. 'I went through hell to look this good,' the magazine articles scream. The 'hell' that is described will often involve unregulated procedures, surgical mutilation, enormous health risks (sunbeds, extreme dieting, faulty implants, etc. etc.), and months and months of self-imposed misery. While the end result may be appealing, the means for getting there are extreme. Is going to such lengths really all that worthy of admiration? When we hear that Celebrity X works out for five hours a day before going to bed encased in a cling-film mud wrap, it makes us wonder where she finds the time – and how we're ever supposed to emulate that, unless we're replacing sleep with butt crunches.

Being beautiful doesn't just involve pain, the media remind us: it also takes time and money. Think about all the time you've spent worrying because of the beauty police – it probably amounts to at least the length of a language course. You could be fluent in Italian, living *la dolce vita* in Rome, stuffing your face with pizza and partying with men called Antonio who comb their pubes over the waistband of their diamanté-studded trousers, had it not been for all those hours you spent fretting about your blackheads.

Not to mention the dollah it deprives you of, which in Britain amounts to an average of £18,000 on face products alone in a lifetime, according to one 2013 survey by Superdrug (whose head of cosmetics was quoted in the *Daily Mail* as saying that 'we're sure most women would agree it's money well spent'). In 2011, TV shopping channel QVC's more comprehensive research found that when you combine all the products for face, hair and body maintenance, the average British woman will end up forking out £133,000 in her lifetime. That's quite a few luxury holidays spent on a white-sand beach with a toned waiter serving you cocktails; or, you know, a deposit on a house. When you consider that women are still paid on average 14.9% less than men, it really hits home how being a woman can put you at an economic disadvantage. There have been times when both of us have been on the dole, and yet have felt it necessary to spend our paltry Jobseeker's Allowance on new foundation rather than food – and not because we're especially vain, but because as women we're made to feel that we need to look a certain way in order to be considered acceptable. It's perverse that we should crave a smooth, dewy complexion over a filling, nutritious meal, and will happily live off teabags on toast if it means that we are able to achieve it (plus we might lose a few pounds in the process). But this is the way we live now.

When we see a baby girl looking at herself in the mirror and smiling, we already know that this is probably the happiest that she is ever going to feel about the way she looks. From then on it's all downhill, so she'd better get used to the implication that, unless she loses 10 lb, she'll die fat and alone in a pool of her own chocolate-flavoured SlimFast. Although she will grow up in a supposedly modern society where she's told that she can achieve anything – be a doctor, or a politician, or an academic, just like a man – there remains a double standard at work. Women are still repeatedly told that physical attraction is the most they should aspire to – or, that if they do intend to pursue an important career path, they should attend to their looks or be prepared to be judged for them first. This can have an effect on both self-esteem and a person's own level of ambition: what's the use in being Prime Minister if all people notice is your hair? Just look at the way female politicians are treated by the media. When MP Clare Short complained about Page Three being sexist, *The Sun* branded her 'fat' and 'jealous', while Angela Merkel was allegedly called an 'unfuckable lard-arse' by fellow politician Berlusconi, the thought of whose company is enough to put anyone off sex forever. And if you thought it was bad for politicians, it's even worse for feminists. The efforts of the Suffragettes were once referred to as 'plain talk for plain women'. To an extent, that stereotype persists.

IMPERFECTION CORRECTIONS

The cover pages of publications like *Marie Claire* and *InStyle* can easily give the impression that being 'beautiful' is a full-time job. The sheer number of tasks on the to-do list alone makes you wonder if there are just enough hours in the day to take '292 tips and tricks' and '50 beauty secrets' on board. These rags have done away with the idea that beauty is in the eye of the beholder, and joined in with some completely different – and highly marketable – mantra. You can count on the latest lacquered publication to serve up pages of products you need to 'tame' your hair, 'correct' your flaws, and 'identify' the ways in which 'he' thinks you're lacking so that you can 'GET SEXY NOW!' (that's an order). When they get sick of peddling the same old foundation reviews, a new product comes along that we're suddenly ugly without, from 'beauty balm' to 'miraculous' bust-firming gel (FYI, no cream can make your tits bigger – we've tried), and yet we didn't even know we needed it until somebody told us.

Now, don't get us wrong. We've all invested in a bottle of blue hair mascara or five (well, it was cool very briefly in the nineties. In the north), and we've all frightened flatmates and/or lovers with a 'home-made' face mask straight out of the pages of *Glamour* (you gotta love that drowning feeling of getting pulverised banana up your nose). We've all briefly fallen for the idea that 'body brushing' will get rid of your cellulite and 'drain out impurities' that were stuck to your hips, just waiting for a bristling motion across your epidermis to make a break for freedom. But when you have a breakdown on a Sunday evening because you've tripped over your steaming bowl of organic aloe vera wax while trying to pull on your 'instant tan' leggings during a 'bust-enhancing' yoga ritual and accidentally waxed your perfectly threaded left eyebrow off, you know there's got to be something wrong.

The reasoning behind the idea that you need this stuff is, of course, that you're unacceptably imperfect and you need to look better, lest you offend the pot-bellied builder who locks eyes with you over his egg sandwich as you order yourself a hangover breakfast in the local caff. 'Your mascara might have lengthened those lashes, love, but it's clear you've neglected to give them a curl!' he might leer, as an unexpectedly runny yolk oozes down his overalls and you cover your peepers in shame. Sounds, well, fucking stupid, doesn't it? But someone out there *has* to persuade you that you need a good fixing, lest you realise the total unlikelihood of eyelash critiques in the real world you inhabit – so they need some good hard stats to back them up. And that's when the measuring tape comes out.

PERFECT PROPORTIONS

More often than not, there's a great big dollop of pseudo-science backing up a publication's assertions about your bum-to-cheekbone ratio being seriously out of kilter. 'The perfect female face' is something that crops up again and again in the media, mostly from the tabloids (usually in the 'women's section' – talk about having a target audience for anxiety-mongering), but also in magazines. Whether it's 'Using the golden ratio to discover the perfect human face' (*Elle*, April 2008), 'Perfect face dimensions measured' (BBC News, December 2009), or 'Beauty summed up: to tell if a woman's attractive, it's all in the figures' (*Mail Online*, August 2010), once you start noticing these articles you see them everywhere. And all of them are, of course, illustrated solely with pictures of women.

Say it with us: THERE IS NO SUCH THING AS THE PERFECT FACE. This doesn't stop scientists with far too much time on their hands dedicating a quite frankly insane number of hours to measuring the distance between our eyes (they obviously don't have a bathroom ceiling to de-mould), often in ways that smack disturbingly of eugenics, and are just as racist (the 'perfect female face' is always, always white). Once the results of the study are in, journalists either skim-read and recycle them, or just slap a press release thick with marketing speak up on their websites. Every month or so, these truly Nobel-worthy scientists will emerge from their musty hidey-holes, blinking like badgers in the sunlight, and announce that, after years of research, they have finally hit upon the elusive and complex formula that denotes female beauty. Of course, they often conveniently work for someone who makes face plumper or eye cream or skin lasering technology.

And it's not just our faces but our bodies, too. You'll probably have seen them, these 'perfect female' composites. They pop up with terrifying regularity everywhere from *Men's Health* to the *New York Post* ('Here's the perfect woman!') to women's titles such as *Grazia*. All these publications naturally tout different qualities (*Men's Health* said small feet and narrow hips, the *Telegraph* stipulated 'women with hourglass figures and perfect waists') and they almost always illustrate the piece with a 'fantasy' woman cobbled together using photographs of various female celebrities. There are even composites dating from the early twentieth century, such as one from 1930 that gave exact measurements, so that you could aspire to Greta Garbo's 33 in. chest and silent-film actress

Aileen Pringle's 18 in. thighs. Yet female composites have been around even longer than that – they've been doing the rounds since Ancient Greece, when artist Zeuxius made a picture of Helen of Troy using five different models in order to create a pinnacle of ideal buffness, much like a pervy Photoshop retoucher on the staff of a pre-biblical version of *Nuts* magazine. Plato spoke of 'ideal proportions', while Da Vinci tried for years to paint such a woman, which is how, they think, he ended up with the *Mona Lisa* (although nearly as many people think she is Da Vinci dressed up as a woman, so go figure). These ideal female types can still be seen today in the pages of newspapers and magazines, with features that scientists deem a mathematically perfect distance from one another. We're constantly told that in order to attract a male we need to have small eyes, or big eyes, or a babyish mouth, or rosy cheeks, for what are nearly always given as evolutionary reasons. A May 2012 article in *Grazia* entitled 'Is this the sexiest ever face?' perfectly sums up this kind of thinking. It essentially tries to use science to get you to buy more make-up and pluck your eyebrows by telling you that 'there's nothing feminine about a strong brow, which in scientific terms is a mark of testosterone', while your eyes should be 'small, and positioned halfway down your face, like a baby's'. We anticipate the all-new eye-repositioner with bated breath.

While no one who writes these articles is outright *saying* that the women who don't resemble the 'perfect female face' should be sent to an Ugly Home and prevented from mating, there's a *suggestion* that those who do not conform are less likely to be chosen by a male because they do not possess the range of features that men are supposedly pre-programmed to go after (and yes, the implication that men are mindless sex robots incapable of overriding their penises to make their own decisions is pretty patronising in itself). The suggestion is that the more symmetrical a woman's face, the more likely she is to attract a mate on the basis that she is 'healthy' and free from hidden genetic defects. Plus, your face is more likely to be symmetrical when it is not sagging, so symmetry also equals youth, which equals fertility, which equals BONER CENTRAL. And yet the fantasy woman pictured doesn't exist, because her face has been created using a thousand others. These symmetrical masks, with their emotionless look of the automaton, are essentially the faces of biological determinism. It's the same school of thought as that pronouncing the omnipresent ideal waist-to-hip ratio, which is that, if you are lucky enough to possess it, it's enough to make you bang tidy in the eyes of the opposite sex. No room for environmental and social factors here, folks: according to these guys, attraction is all down to biology. We like to call this 'sexist bullshit', but more sympathetic people tend to call it 'evolutionary psychology'. Strangely, you never see a diagram of 'the perfect man'.

Even scientific studies which don't necessarily result in a 'sexist bullshit' outcome will end up with one once they reach the pages of a newspaper. Journalists will also cherry-pick the studies that suit their own agenda. Thus if they are working on an article about 'differences between the sexes', when a 'women are shit at parking' study comes their way, they might ignore any studies that say otherwise in order to meet their deadline and give their editor the headline he or she wants. This works similarly in book publishing, where the determination to 'get in on the zeitgeist, quick' results in book titles such as Allan and Barbara Pease's *Why Men Don't Listen and Women Can't Read Maps*. Cultural ideas about gender, including the aforementioned myth that women's role as decorative, beautiful objects has some kind of evolutionary function or fits into an undisputed Darwinian truth, therefore end up going unchallenged.

This theory that men are typically drawn to certain evolved traits was something even Darwin found a bit sketchy, believing as he did that there were few universal ideals of beauty because there is so much variety in appearance and preferences across human groups. In other words, we live in a diverse world, a world in which there exist many different, equally diverse kinds of beauty, and yet, so often, we only ever see one type. Not only is she almost always young, slim and white, but, apparently, 'objectively' beautiful, more likely to be selected by men to procreate because hey, it's only natural.

SURVIVAL OF THE FITTEST

Next time someone tells you that your lady-brain is wired a certain way because of what cavepeople were up to thousands of years ago, you should call their bluff. Scientists actually know very little about the lives of our ancestors and why we are the way we are. And even if they did know how cavepeople behaved, we are intelligently evolved enough to choose not to emulate much of it (hence we no longer shit on the floor). Even the supposedly definitive December 2013 study by the University of Pennsylvania that found male brains had far fewer connections between the left and right hemispheres than female brains essentially told us very little about the real world. According to the BBC report on the research, experts argued, on seeing the results – which had already been hailed as world-changing by hundreds of publications – that 'it is a huge leap to extrapolate from anatomical differences to try to explain behavioural variation between the sexes' ('Men and women's brains are "wired differently"', BBC News, 3 December 2013). Of course, this didn't stop a deluge of headlines suggesting that the key to gender had finally been found.

Needless to say, an offshoot of this is that scientists are also *obsessed* with trying to find a biological payoff for the existence of the female orgasm (with absolutely no success), and with the apparently different characteristics that men and women desire in a mate. (Wait until your stomach is feeling quite settled and then google the term 'uterine upsuck'.) The old cliché that men are attracted to youth and physical attractiveness while women crave wealth and status appears again and again in the media, and, sadly, is perpetuated by women almost as much as men. Take the *Marie Claire* article (yes, they're repeat offenders) in which a woman recounts an affair with her boss, who is then fired. 'Stripped of his former title, his influence, and his company credit card, he suddenly seemed emasculated,' the journalist wrote, before unceremoniously dumping him. Nice. This completely unsound hypothesis is endlessly promoted in a world that has always been run by and for men, and in which women have had very little power of their own (and thus needed rich men in order to gain it). No one is born a gold-digger, but, as usual, nature garners more media attention than nurture. It's just so much more convenient to believe that we're all pre-programmed to choose our sexual partners according to the same set of assets or values, rather than because of power imbalances in the culture – or even because of criteria which vary from person to person, such as, just for example, liking Simon and Garfunkel (or not), delivering excellent head, and knowing how to make a grade-A falafel wrap.

If you're in the market for a man and your baby eyes or perfect cleavage have yet to evolve, not to worry. Magazines inform us that there is some hope, in the form of 'experts' who can teach you the best ways to attract a man, one of which is to make yourself look as though you're having sex all the time. The least you can do to please society is to pull off the tousle-haired look of the recently post-coital. As a *Grazia* article informed us, a 'pink cheek mimics the natural flushing which occurs during sexual arousal'. Never mind if the wheelbarrow position is the last thing on your mind when you're standing in line at McDonald's for a caramel McFlurry, you need to look like you're about to grip the skinny shoulders of the bespectacled teenager behind the counter and furiously shag the acne right off his adolescent face beside the deep fat fryer. According to these 'experts', the list of how you can look like sex is pretty much endless, so beware if you've stuck on some red lipstick only because you thought it looked edgy with your outfit. Red lipstick is, according to newspapers, magazines and journals alike, *the* prime way to look instantly shagtastic. Why? Because decorating your upper lips signals to the outside world that you've got a vagina ON YOUR FACE. Of *course*!

One study, 'Does red lipstick really attract men? An evaluation in a bar', managed to waste valuable space in the *International Journal of Psychology* in June 2012. And according to research published in *Medical Daily* and *Live Science*, waitresses who wear red lipstick get more tips, due to its association with 'heightened sexual arousal'. Then again, as Rosie Cowling, editor of ohdearism.com, pointed out on the Vagenda blog at the time, 'it's surprising that those clever science boffs couldn't work out that there's nothing that makes an overworked, underpaid waitress any less moist than being forced to smile coyly as a sweaty overweight businessman who smells like a Lynx factory pulls you on to his lap by your skirt (happened)'.

The idea that you should look as if you're ready to take the commuter next to you, right here, right now, underlies a few of the more unusual pieces of advice we've come across in women's magazines – and some have even taken it that little bit further. One 'top tip' that's trotted out surprisingly regularly (it's definitely popped up in the hallowed pages of *Cosmo* a few times in our collective reading experience) is that if you're looking for a man to bed, your 'natural secretions' can take the place of your usual perfume. Yes, *Cosmopolitan* has seriously advised you to rub vagina juice on your neck (because, like, hormones), and it wasn't an April fool. The pheromones in your daily discharge will 'drive him wild', according to a resident sexpert we can't remember due to subsequent traumatic blackouts. He totes won't know how to resist you when it smells like you've got a fanny on your face, so why not go all out and get a bottle-full to smear all over your Sunday best? Or you could take the easy route and buy Vulva Original, an honest-to-God real-life perfume that could, maybe, help you 'catch that man'. Your new musk might attribute a whole new meaning to the term 'flapper dress', but hey, it's tough being single.

Despite what scientists-for-hire might tell you, there's only so much that having a face that smells like a day-old pair of underwear can do when it comes to your pulling technique. Unless you go for a serious overhaul, you're always going to look the way you were genetically programmed to. We're talking DNA, but not in the 'perfect composite' way. It's your mother and father you can blame for being an hourglass or a brick, a cello or a goblet (all genuine, bona fide 'body types' posited by beauty gurus Trinny and Susannah in their *Body Shape Bible* back in the dark ages of 2007). Holly once brought herself and her mother to tears as a young teenager, by accusing said mother of passing on an unjustly oversized arse through the evils of defective DNA. Needless to say, her mum hadn't even entertained the idea that her bum was big until that moment. You can spend all the time you want yelling at your paternal grandmother for the boobs that just won't stop sagging, or the great-great grandad that hailed from Scotland for the skin that just won't tan, and you still won't get anywhere fast. When you realise that the anger you feel can't be immediately translated into results through yelling at the root cause, it turns into action to deal with the effects: you need that spray tan *now*, and you need it before anyone else realises that your cheekbones are misaligned and your natural shape is an 'apple' (as if we hadn't realised that 'apple' is just a bitchy way of saying 'round'). 'The essentials' might mean food and shelter to your male counterparts, but you know very well that to survive as the female of the species it's vital to make sure the bags under your eyes don't detract from the credibility of your keynote speech. After all, the magazine in your handbag whines like incessant noise: the two are inextricably linked.

Whether or not you've hit the 'genetic jackpot' looks-wise, however, really depends on what era you're living in as much as it does where you live. Just look at the chubby nude beauties hanging in art galleries: mere decades ago, *they* were the ideal. The Jazz Age saw women bandaging down their breasts to achieve a masculine look, while in the 1950s it was the Pin-Up girls, with their tiny waists but buxom breasts, that ruled the roost. So, while to you and us it may seem as though the current beauty ideals of extreme thinness or porno plastic bodies have been in place for ever, they're actually relatively new (which is curious, considering how they're supposedly 'pre-programmed' into the male brain, isn't it?). As for this idea that women should aspire to be beautiful because, well, they're more likely to get laid that way and therefore ensure the continuation of the human race: it doesn't even really make sense. Aside from the fact that you could use the 'it's just natural' logic to justify a plethora of unacceptable behaviour including rape and murder (and, sadly, some do), the insistence that the female of the species is always decorative is little more than an excuse to silence an entire sex. In the animal kingdom, it's often the males of the species that tend to pretty themselves up in order to attract a mate – hence the lion's mane and the peacock's vibrant feathers, a lads' competition in action. In other words, if we really were to base our assessments of human behaviour on the shitty premise of what the animals were up to, then it would just as likely be the men, as the ladies, who'd be forced to compete in a visual hierarchy of hotness. Not that it matters, because, goddammit, there's no objectively unified definition of hotness in the first place.

So why exactly do we wear make-up? OK, so it may give you confidence and make you feel good – we're not saying that beauty routines can never be pleasurable – but we've seen enough features on 'brave' celebs without make-up to start to feel that going out unaltered is positively radical. As long as we're told that beauty is a static quality that exists objectively, rather than a concept which differs from person to person, and decade to decade – as well as the only thing that women are really good for – then most of the female population are likely to be suffering from feelings of inadequacy and low self-esteem. We're told that beauty just 'is', men are hard-wired to want that and only that specific quality, and women are hard-wired to please men. (Pipe down, lesbians and assorted others who dare to deviate from the sexual norm.) From this evolutionary perspective, women are *meant* to aspire to beauty, while men are only meant to respond to it – and that, quite frankly, is a scientifically shaky falsehood.

PLASTIC FANTASTIC

Despite knowing this at some level, increasing numbers of us are inflicting painful and expensive procedures on our bodies in pursuit of the ideal form. The only-slightly-creepy toy beloved of so many young children, Barbie, has literally impossible proportions: various studies that have attempted to recreate her in the real world (scientists with tape measures again) have claimed variously that she would topple over from the weight of her humongous breasts on an otherwise unusually petite form, or that her torso would be unable to hold her internal organs. Truly, there's nothing like a visible small intestine to make you appreciate a hulking pair of tits. In 'What would a real-life Barbie look like?', *BBC Magazine* estimated that a 5 ft 6 in. Barbie would have a 20 in. waist, 27 in. bust and 29 in. hips: not entirely impossible, but certainly unusual. And Barbie wasn't a one-woman pioneer; chances are that the dolls you played with in your youth enjoyed very little facial or body diversity, much like the photoshopped images we see in magazines today.

One thing that being a regular reader of women's magazines teaches you is that the jump from modelling your looks on impossible types to nodding along with the 'special reports' in your woman's weekly on plastic surgery and where to get your Botox done is not as great as you might think. Magazines are always cautious when it comes to encouraging plastic surgery. 'Not that we're telling you to fix your face, girl,' they trill. 'We're just saying: plastic surgery could be the best thing you ever did. Or not. Whatever. Here's a number for a local surgeon, and further details in our advertising section in the back. No pressure.' A prime example of this kind of searing hypocrisy can be found in an April 2011 *Glamour* article entitled 'Plastic fantastic?' that details surgical procedures and emphasises their 'positive outcomes' but then tells you that it's fine if you like the way you are as well. Perhaps because the back pages feature no less than five advertisements for plastic surgery practices, we see the writer treading a somewhat disingenuous line between condemnation and endorsement.

If they don't get you with the subtle hints, though, they'll start to ask you questions. And with every so-called question, the writers of the magazines we know and love (read: have complicated, abusive relationships with) give you less and less choice over your own definition of beauty. Instead of 'Do you want curly hair?' followed by a recommendation of products or techniques, it's become 'Do you want gorgeous eyes?' or 'Do you want beautiful lips?' or 'Do you want flawless skin?' Rather than whether you want curly hair today, these are questions that posit only one reasonable answer. You're hardly going to sit back and mentally reply, 'No, actually, I'd rather be a puffy, bloodshot, frizzy-haired harridan with a visible skin disease' – so you more or less have to engage with their so-called suggestions. No more do you make choices about the look you might want to create, you just have to agree to 'be flawless' or 'be gorgeous' or – probably the most sly of all – 'be even more beautiful'. If it feels like a backhanded compliment, there's a reason, and part of the reason is that the advice and features pages are rubbing shoulders with advertising executives whose slogans say things like 'your skin, only better'. We might all have started to accept this sort of advertising as if it's really just kindly advice, but if you imagine walking out of your sixth form on results day, happily clutching your A Levels in an excited hand before your best mate with six A*s describes her achievements as 'your grades, only better', you can see where we're coming from.

All of this brings us back to the products that we never knew we needed. The media can't go on convincing you to sign up to pore minimiser for ever.

BUYING INTO BEAUTY

Beauty is an industry, indeed one of the fastest-growing industries in the world, pervading every page of every magazine you read, from celeb news to fashion to reviews to the holiday section ('have a cellulite-free summer!'). It was one of only a handful of sectors to grow during the most recent recession in the UK and US – referred to as 'booming' by the *New York Times* and 'recession-proof' by UK-based *Businesses for Sale* – and the people who work in it invest thousands in knowing what your life is like. In 2012, when other businesses were still routinely going into administration following the most recent financial disaster, Cosmetic Executive Women UK found that the UK beauty industry was 'in better shape than it has ever been', with a workforce of almost a million and a value of over £15 billion.

Of course, none of this could change the fact that most young people were out of work and scraping pennies from behind the sofa; so, having clocked this disparity between their own bubble and the rest of the world, the savvy PRs behind Debenham's Beauty Hall decided to create yet more insecurity in their target market by selling a story to the *Daily Mail* ('The REAL REASON you aren't getting that job') about exactly why their target demographic remained jobless (chipped nails, split ends, the wrong colour lipstick) and how to ensure that you no longer commit these heinous errors (home manicure, professional haircut, new products). An actual quote from someone in the beauty department stated that 'your beauty regime holds the key to that dream job', as though you could suddenly be made Secretary-General of the United Nations provided you sorted out your wiry man-brows and that persistent kink in the back of your hair. The *Daily Mail* advised that split ends – which your interviewer will of course be ogling while attempting to throw you off by asking a completely unnecessary question about your expertise in oncological medicine – imply you're 'lazy'; overdone make-up says you're 'power crazy'; and a lack of slap says you're an emotional wreck who doesn't even bother with the mascara wand any more because it will be 'inevitably cried off within hours'. This may be one of the most sinister marketing ploys to have come out of the economic downturn.

Magazines tend to make you doubt that little inner voice which says, 'My lipstick is less important than my A Levels' or, 'A pear shape *can* damn well rock a pair of wet-look leggings' or even, 'I know what I really want.' That last one is key: magazines have a tendency to make you feel like a useless oik, a pig in knickers who's in desperate need of their help, and that they're the only people who can transform you from a frumpy fatty into a fabulous filly. You might think the Groupon deal you got for a weekend of zorbing followed by Monkey World sounds ace, but your weekly mag reckons you'd be much more suited to a spa vacation – and you're supposed to go along with it. You might think that a 'girlie spa week' where you steam out your 'impurities' over a bucket of lavender oil is totally eclipsed by the much more preferable idea of a 'girlie Spar week', with its two-for-a-fiver deal on sparkling rosé, bargain bin DVD of *Beaches*, and three tubs of full-fat houmous only a few minutes past their sell-by date, followed by the dusting off of an old Blink 182 album with a few friends who'd never tell. You might think that you don't need a lymphatic drainage machine in your bathroom, or that microderm-abrasion sounds more like something you'd rather avoid like the plague than expose yourself to willingly on a seasonal basis, but people's wages now depend on convincing you that an arse-draining massage and one less layer of skin is just what you *really* wanted when you reached for that Snickers bar and the remote control. Women's magazines pride themselves on convincing their readership that they don't really know what they want any more. And, like really creepy shepherds, they lead their flock down to the colonic irrigation clinic faster than you can say 'Why doesn't this gown have a rear?'

TOXIC TREATMENTS

The media have spent a long time convincing women that they have to be beautiful and that most of them are not. So long, in fact, that every-thing's become a bit weird out there – especially the substances they tout as solutions to your hideousness. And since you might have lost sight of how the culture of beauty has become downright bizarre, after the deluge of marketing and editorial material that backs it up, we've put together our favourite examples of beauty industry idiocy from the last decade for your expert perusal.

Venomous lip balm and face cream

Holly tried on some lip balm purporting to be made of snake venom one evening and choked on her JD and Coke in front of a very attractive man, so we had to do some digging. Turns out that most lip products purporting to be 'venomous' in some way actually just contain irritants like cloves, cinnamon and peppermint oil to cause a low-level reaction in your lips. It's the slightly more advanced version of pinching your cheeks to make them red, but more along the lines of all-out bitch slap. Meanwhile, face masks to 'tighten' your skin are being developed with the use of bee venom.

Caffeine-infused tights

Yep, these ones are real – and they exist in legging form as well. The best-known suppliers of coffee derivatives in hosiery are SkinKiss, a company who reckon they've seen 'unprecedented demand' for tights with 'cellulite busting' microcapsules inside that are activated by the heat of your body. So while you're busting a move on the dance floor at the student club, or hawking a pram down the street, there's an espresso on your thighs giving the fat cells a cheeky little workout.

Fun with your colon

Perhaps you remember Gillian McKeith, the controversial nutritionist who did a brief stint in the *I'm a Celebrity . . . Get me Out of Here!* jungle and, over a particularly illustrious career, earned herself the title of 'the awful poo lady' (a moniker that every woman surely envied). Essentially, this was all because of her belief that you need to get up close and personal with someone's excrement to really know what they're like inside, and she got a lot of stick for it. But the truth is, the beauty media have been excited about poo for way too long (let's never forget that 'Poo: the last taboo' was a genuine feature in the aristocratic pages of none other than British *Vogue*. As Rhiannon's mother pointed out at the time, if they were really in the market for taboo-busting, they would have called it 'shit'). 'Colonic irrigation' has taken the spotlight for a number of years now, having become a staple option in many a respectable spa, and literally every national publication has had something to say on the matter. Even The *Guardian* sent a journalist off to a Thai resort where you could clean out your bum and bond with new friends while you were at it, proving that while holidaying with your mates from school in Magaluf might well *feel* like enduring tens of enemas and hundreds of laxatives, someone out there has already packaged up that precious feeling and turned it into a separate commodity. Just in case you're wondering, it costs upwards of a grand.

Fish pedicures

Garra rufa fish eat dead skin (usually off other fish), and they had their heyday between 2010 and 2011. Fish salons popped up everywhere and people paid £20 an hour to have their calluses nibbled off by aquatic creatures. But it seems the days of the fish pedicure are numbered. Due to the risk of infection, getting your mani-pedi done by a *Garra rufa* is on the way out.

Nose straighteners and eye wideners

The nose shaper is big in Japan. It's a plastic contraption that clips your innocent nostrils into place with the aim of producing something altogether slimmer and perkier. Some digging has proven that there's a variety of brands to choose from, but our personal favourite is a 'bestselling nose clip' called Nose Up. The science behind it sounds a little over-optimistic – like believing a push-up bra might one day induce a spontaneous boob job – but the clips remain wildly popular amongst their target demographic.

Similarly, there are plastic contraptions out there that claim to 'widen eyes' to make South-East Asian women look more Caucasian – and these aren't only sold in the salon. They've made an appearance in the little girls' toy sections of children's stores in the last few years.

The semen facial

Finally, we'd just like to take a moment to debunk the popular myth (CONSPIRACY) that semen is the ultimate beauty tool. In an interesting turn that has seriously made us wonder whether women's mags are being secretly controlled by mac-wearing, greasy-haired perverts, semen has made a cumback. Facial, fertility aid, toothbrush substitute, a healthy and low-cal mid-afternoon snack: all of this and more has been promised of the lowly sperm by media moguls. Let's clarify right now that it's way less nutritious than a superfood salad, will never do for your face what a flannel and some warm water will, and hasn't yet been upheld by the NHS as a cure for depression (although we have it on good authority that if a man is diabetic then it *can* taste like watermelon). Magazine hacks: letting a man spaff in your face is not the key to eternal youth. It's nothing more than penis propaganda. Swallow *that*.

BECOMING UNREAL

The funny thing is, the media and the advertisers behind these products and reviews know themselves that there's a problem with their tactics, but, given who they are and what they're aiming for (profit), it's nigh on impossible for them to address the issue seriously. Whether you're telling ladies euphemistically that they need to 'enhance' their 'true selves', like Dove, or taking the other tack, it's all lotions and potions. Tellingly, Dove's parent company Unilever was criticised for hypocrisy after it emerged that they also own the skin-lightening brand Fair & Lovely. In case you're not familiar with Fair & Lovely, they market lightening products to darker-skinned women in several countries across the world. But if you're whiter than an anaemic ghost then you won't get away with ditching your optimistic can of St Tropez yet. Because there's a perfect shade to aim for out there, and you haven't quite achieved it yet.

In fact, skin colour has been marketed to us as if we don't all have a natural skin tone, and it could be seen as the apotheosis of everything that's wrong with the beauty-pushers. 'Look healthy with a spray tan!' commands the shopfront of every salon, as if most redheads are luminously white because they share a stubbornly unhealthy lifestyle. Meanwhile, a 'winter glow' of 'soft fairness' is sold in countries such as India, for girls who have turned the wrong colour during the warmer months because of a petulant and unnatural habit of walking around in the sunshine. All the big brands are in on it – Vaseline's Healthy White is just one example of a skin-lightening product that has been marketed in Asia of late. 'Boost your complexion' is a common phrase used to convince light-skinned women that they should be darker and dark-skinned women that they should be lighter, which is a bit like someone marketing you stilettos to 'boost your tallness', a quality that you've been hiding for too long by secretly refusing to let your legs grow longer.

In today's society, one of the worst things you can say to a woman is that she is ugly (and the other is that she is fat). But a world in which only 5% of teenage girls say that they wouldn't change a thing about their appearance (Girlguiding UK research, 2012) and the percentage of young girls reporting unhappiness with how they look increases year on year (*Girls' Attitudes Survey*, 2013) is not a world that we're keen to live in. It's a world in which standards of beauty are becoming increasingly homogenised and Westernised. It is a world where nobody is perfect, where toddlers think they're fat, where black women are bleaching their skin with whitening creams and white women are risking cancer for the perfect tan, and women of all races are mutilating their facial features in the futile pursuit of perfection, and, by extension, happiness. Charities such as Media Smart, which helps children understand the distorting techniques used by the media and teaches them to differentiate between photoshopped and non-photoshopped images, are leading the way in helping children to dissect what they see around them, but it's an uphill struggle which needs an enormous cavalry force. After all, the advertisers get 'em young, so it's important we do too. The internet is awash with articles and videos showing the 'before and afters' of image production, such as Tim Piper's *Evolution* for Dove in 2006, and it would be even better to see something like that being turned into a national campaign by a group of people who have no incentive to sell a product. How else can we work towards a world in which the next generation escapes the fate of its predecessors?

While we'd rather see something from Dove more along the lines of Debenham's announcement that they'll ditch airbrushing altogether, drawing attention to the beauty process which begins with a make-up brush and ends on a computer is a step in the right direction. Meanwhile, those who still insist on airbrushing invariably end up in tit-for-tat bitchfests: take the case of a Christian Dior mascara ad featuring Natalie Portman in 2012, which was reported to the UK's Advertising Standards Agency by rival company L'Oréal because Portman's eyelashes were airbrushed. The ASA agreed that Dior's airbrushing meant that it 'misleadingly exaggerated the likely effects of the product' – but then again, L'Oréal's own mascara ad using Penelope Cruz had been banned in 2007 for the very same reason. Businesses reporting each other for commercial advantage is all very well – but stricter standards should be set to avoid the widespread use of digital manipulation in beauty product adverts in the first place.

The internet, with its ubiquity and scope, has proved to be a powerful force in the campaign for beauty diversity: it gives a platform and a voice to the kinds of people, and lives, that remain practically invisible in the mainstream print media, and demands that we question why they aren't represented elsewhere. It's our belief that one of the most important things we can do is constantly challenge that status quo with the power of the consumer: wielding the power of social media when things don't look right; calling out the sheer volume of plastic surgery pushers in a country where medical procedures are supposedly banned from advertising; demanding that photoshopped images come with warning labels, specifying what is real and what is not; and, when publications and other outlets cross the line, voting with our feet. Because when you really dig beneath the smooth, beautiful surface, the media's underlying motive is revealed as the opposite of what they want you to be. That is: horribly, hideously ugly.

4
Sex in Magazineland

POPPING YOUR MEDIA CHERRY

The Modern Experience of Sex begins with the Sexual Awakening, which is a polite term for your first uncomfortable dream about that guy in school whom you were happy just plain hating before, but who your body now desperately wants you to hate-fuck instead. Yes, you're 15 years old and you now want sex with everyone, including yourself. You're not exactly sure what sex is, you've only recently found out that there is actually a third hole down there, and you feel about as attractive to the opposite sex as the slimy lovechild of Margaret Thatcher and an algal bloom (with even greasier hair and skin). But suddenly you're getting some weird horny feelings to complement your new physique – and by the way, kid, good luck out there.

No doubt many of you will recall taking a sneaky peek at the sexy bits of your mum's issue of *She* or *Red* when she wasn't looking, but it's often the teenage magazines that provide young women with their introduction to all things sexual. Pre internet porn and Snapchat, teenage magazines assigned themselves an educative role, perhaps in the knowledge that sex education was (and often still is) so shoddy – ask any woman you know and we guarantee she'll know at least one person

who thought they were bleeding to death when actually they had just started their period. The magazines of our adolescence such as *Just Seventeen* (*J-17*), *Bliss*, *Mizz*, *Shout* and *Sugar* were filled with advice on sexual problems, along with more information about vaginal discharge than you could shake a douche at. *J-17* in particular pushed this frank approach to the limit, and received many an outraged parental letter as a result.

Magazines such as *Bliss* now try to counteract the demands to 'BE A SEX GODDESS. NOW!' (a real headline) that are ubiquitous in the magazines targeted at a slightly older audience by such campaigns as 'Be Sexy, Be Sussed' ('Sexy girls have the confidence to say "No"'), and the well-qualified agony aunts and uncles (usually sexual health clinic workers and youth consultants) generally respond to questions about the birds and the bees with refreshing honesty. But even *Bliss* is guilty of running backward editorial such as their 2014 online quiz 'How do lads see you?' (For the sake of research, Holly did this quiz herself and got 'Lads see: Mate not Date. You're easy-going, confident and can talk to anyone . . . Problem is, lads are so busy having a laugh with you, they forget to see you as possible girlf material. Don't stop being your sociable self, but maybe it's time to let lads see the flirty side too.')

The emphasis isn't all on sex and flirtation in the land of the girls' mag: with pre-teen magazines especially, for every problem page explaining that you can't get pregnant from a blowie, there's a collection of 'embarrassing moments', a spooky story, or a picture of a kitten to cover your physics book with. But much practical advice was gleaned from these semi-glossed pages in our childhood.

Once their readership outgrew 'how to kiss with tongues', successful girls' magazines of the 1990s followed a similar format to their slightly more adult counterparts and moved on to 'how to do that corkscrew thing with your tongue that your boyfriend saw in porn last week'. As the nineties progressed, magazines became more and more risqué, to the point where even the establishment was shocked. In 1996 Conservative MP Peter Luff proposed a bill that would require publishing companies to put age suitability warnings on the cover of magazines aimed at young women. Needless to say, it failed.

Grateful as we were for the information they dispensed, these magazines were never devoid of agendas. *Sugar* magazine, for instance, collated 'boy tips' with celebrity news, promoted an annual modelling competition (Rhiannon actually went to university with the winner of 'Britain's sexiest sixth-former', as voted for by *Sugar* readers), and had enough 'real-life stories' to make you feel the right mix of *schadenfreude* and personal inadequacy. A common feature in *Sugar* was to discuss how to do 'flirty fashion', a look which usually involved a crop top and some glittery lip gloss. The emphasis on boys was clear, as demonstrated by topics such as 'The big boy-mate question: to snog or not to snog?', 'How to be irresistible', 'Vanessa [Hudgens]: How I got Zac [Efron] . . . and kept him!', 'Pretending to have sex made me popular', and, perhaps most depressingly, 'Frenemies: why you should be friends with the girls you hate'. These early messages, which breed suspicion of other women alongside the dodgy subtext that changing yourself, or putting out, is how you get people, and especially men, to like you, weren't even improved by the occasional red herring of a real-life story ('I came home to find Mum ironing a chicken' is a personal favourite of ours).

While touting 'confidence', *Sugar* pointed out the flaws in female celebrities through a number of those beloved backhanded compliments which would later morph into outright ruthlessness in the pages of *Glamour* and *Grazia*. Chock-a-block with make-up ads, and constantly correlating physical beauty with romantic and sexual success, it introduced its readers to the mentality that would make them susceptible to the grown-up mags' plastic surgery push in their twenties. From *Sugar*'s free lip balm making your smackers 'soft and kissable', to the cover of *Closer* telling you that some reality star's lipo means that 'sex is amazing', magazines wrestle you into a stranglehold from your first vague notion that sex exists, and keep hold of you until you admit through choking tears that yes, getting implants in your bum might make your partner enjoy doggy style that little bit more and that a Hollywood wax might be worth it, even if you have to spend half an hour with your ankles on the shoulders of some professional sadist who has the sick humour to carry the innocuous-sounding title of 'beauty therapist'. From teenage magazines to your older sister's *Cosmo* that you kept under the bed, they all carry the same message: that sex takes meticulous preparation and calculated planning, whether it's learning how to 'do sticky eyes' (translation: staring at him sensuously before dragging your eyes away slowly as though they are bound to his with treacle) to attract that 'cute boy' or preparing your seduction 'two days in advance'. Never mind that you haven't even allowed him to unhook your bra yet – you might not even *have* a bra yet, let alone have worked out what it is you like sexually for yourself – it's about time you got prepped for a lifetime of consumerism via self-doubt.

Magazines love to claim that they're confidence builders, especially in terms of sexual exploits, but what they're actually doing is inserting their caustic world view into your mind so that it becomes inextricable from your sense of worth: this deodorant will make you more confident.

Dressing like Cheryl Cole will make you more confident. The latest dayglo body glitter will make you more confident. Reading these increasingly ridiculous sex tips will make you more confident, because every other woman is out to steal your boyfriend, and what sort of a man would he be if he wasn't naturally attracted to the woman who exudes the desire to please him the most? Ultimately, this is what the 'sexual confidence' touted by magazines is all about. Whether it's '1000 ways to please your man' or 'The seven kinds of orgasm that you absolutely must be having right now' (believe us, *there is only one – maybe, sometimes, two*), sex, and all that surrounds it, takes work. And more often than not, it's women's work. Female sexuality is all about man-pleasing, man-teasing, manipulation, deceit and insecurity. Male sexuality 'just can't help itself': it's excitable, spontaneous, clear, direct and easy.

PLEASING YOURSELF

Female masturbation is a normal, healthy part of adolescence and personal development and teenage girls learning to explore their bodies should be viewed in the same starkly simple terms as teenage boys, and yet the issue is cloaked not only in a scary amount of complexity, but also with a certain gross-out, 'cringey' vibe that women feel long into adulthood. US mother Gail Horalek, for example, was so uncomfortable with the masturbatory passage in Anne Frank's diary that she wrote to her daughter's teacher asking that it be removed from the syllabus on the basis that it was 'pornographic'. Perhaps Horalek, too, had been taken in by the widespread and damaging belief that masturbation is only for certain women, doing it in a certain way, in order for men to get off on it on PornHub.

Women having sex – or, even worse, *enjoying* it – has caused great consternation since the dawn of time. As Christopher Ryan and Cacilda

Jethá point out in *Sex at Dawn: How We Mate, Why We Stray, and What It Means for Modern Relationships*, men the world over go to great lengths in their attempts to restrain female sexuality, whether through female genital mutilation, corsetry, diagnosing women with 'nymphomania' and committing them to mental institutions, burning them as witches, or labelling them 'sluts'. And yet, despite this urge to repress the female libido, the message that women don't really enjoy sex anywhere near as much as men do (and that those who do are to be scorned and feared) is still being put about. As Ryan so wisely asks, 'Why the electrified high-security razor-wire fence to contain a kitty-cat?'

It could be argued that the female enjoyment of sex is most threatening when it's with ourselves. Thought you could take your orgasms into your own hands? Think again. Having decided that women were unstable and emotional creatures liable to suffer from 'hysteria' (which in the past was thought to mean that your womb had become dislodged and gone for a wander), kinky Victorian doctors found that 'pelvic massage' – or what your local charmer hanging around outside Oceana might call 'a cheeky finger' – was a great way of magically relieving it. This led to the downright bizarre fact that strait-laced male Victorian medical professionals *actually invented the vibrator*. Tiring of having to 'massage' these women back to happiness themselves due to painful RSI (we're not kidding), they put together a handy machine – and later developed it for home use. One of the originals even had a motor that doubled as an attachment for a sewing machine (that one had us in stitches . . .).

From then on, masturbation (by various euphemistic names) was considered a cure for all kind of female ailments, and by the turn of the century magazines such as *Women's Home Companion* were running advertisements for vibrators (one tells how the 'pleasure of youth . . . will throb within you . . .' – ooh-er!) while *Good Housekeeping* went so far as to review different models in 1909. By the time the Rampant Rabbit made its debut appearance in *Sex and the City*, vibes came in assorted sizes (from 'bullet' to 'bazooka'), ran on seventeen different settings and were available in several respectable high-street stores. Nowadays, if you're not sharing a two-way vibrating probe from Ann Summers with your latest squeeze or sitting on an inflatable chair with a plastic erection attached, you apparently haven't even lived.

Men invented the vibrator when the female orgasm was taboo, women perfected it when sex became an open discussion point, and now that we live in an age where sex sells faster than hot cakes, marketers have convinced us that it's all but a sexual necessity. The thing is, vibrators are still often featured in books and magazines as sex toys to be used alongside partners in the bedroom, but, while they might have you believe that masturbation is all about 'finding out what to do with your man', we all know that alone time can sometimes be just what the doctor ordered. Unfortunately, magazines still limit discussion of masturbation to within the bounds of heterosexual relationships. How many sex tips have you seen that incorporate self-love into some kind of for-his-eyes-only ramped-up bedroom lap dance? And, on the other side, how many have you seen advocating the Sarah Silverman method, as popularised by her wildly successful YouTube hit 'A Perfect Night', that is, in other words, to 'stay home, order in, watch a movie and masturbate'? Exactly.

We recall a boundary-pushing issue of *J-17* which instructed girls how to masturbate, facing the issue with the tact and poise so often lacking in the stuttering, embarrassed delivery of sex ed teachers, who would undoubtedly be dealing with a pretty dry disciplinary hearing were they to instruct their female pupils, as *J-17* did, to 'Mount a pillow. It feels good.' Young women in their mid-twenties always seem to remember this particular feature, not only because it was the first time many of us saw the word 'clitoris' in print, but also because that article was followed by a protracted eerie silence in magazines as far as stroking the bearded clam was concerned. In this sense, *J-17* was a true pudenda pioneer; the topic of masturbation for many of us was hardly raised again until magazines for older women picked it up and rebranded it as 'me time'.

Now women's magazines make the whole endeavour of rubbing one out a high-maintenance affair. Your Tuesday-night wank has now been rebranded as expensively scented, ritualised 'quality time with number one', as though it was some kind of luxury spa treatment for your genitals. Just how many women out there actually rely on whale music and aromatherapy to get off? And why aren't the men being told to stock up on Diptyque scented candles, rose petals and lavender bubble bath when getting down with their bad selves?

Although female masturbation has become a lot less frowned upon in the last couple of decades, there's still a long way to go. TV might regularly nod towards teenage boys' sheets cracking in half, but hardly anyone ever talks about the creaking and gasping sounds coming from the bedrooms of a nation of teenage girls. Whenever female masturbation does appear in visual media, it is usually presented as penetration-centric, presumably because a male audience would be dumbfounded if they were presented with an honest depiction of clitoral stimulation. Take the female masturbation scene in beloved comedy film of 2001, *Not Another Teen Movie*. The young girl in question takes out her gigantic dildo and inserts it into her presumably cavernous vagina – so far in that when her entire family walks into her bedroom she can't remove it, and instead has to lie there in the throes of penetrative ecstasy as they talk at her. Give us a break.

Whether you do it with a lipstick-shaped bullet vibe in a footed bathtub surrounded by candles and musical accompaniment by Enya (as recommended by *Cosmo*, though such ritualising is possibly more reminiscent of an exorcism) or with your index finger while watching back-to-back episodes of *Question Time*, just go with it. Lady love isn't about prepping for a man or 'treating yourself to romance'. Most of us just really like to come, and can handle the job pretty proficiently ourselves, no steam-powered sewing machine motor required (but hey, if you want or need a little help from time to time, all power to you). Suffice to say, it's depressing that teenage girls are reading magazines which tell them that there are umpteen different orgasms they need to master (not to mention umpteen different positions that they can reach them in), before they've even worked out the straightforward ways in which they can access their own sexual preferences. Perhaps it would be a good idea to start by telling them simply that it's perfectly OK for them to give themselves one.

LOSING IT

It is a truth universally acknowledged that women lose their virginity and men gain experience. The supposed purity and innocence that comes with not having had a dick inside them is still fetishised in girls, whether this manifests itself as compulsory premarital hymen checks and a creepy religious chastity ball that you're forced to attend with your dad, or an abundance of 'barely legal babes' in schoolgirl outfits on the front page of *Zoo* magazine, ripe for visual deflowering by their readership. A woman exchanging her sexual services for various benefits is a classic paradigm, and nothing's more of a commodity than purity. In our ruthlessly capitalist society, we can now cash in on such misogynistic assumptions by selling our virginity on eBay when the going gets tough, or 'empower' ourselves by offering lap dances to strangers on sugardaddie.com for a top-up on university tuition fees. Selling patriarchal idiocy back to men may well seem like payback – but however you dress it up, you're still buying into the same steaming pile of fetid, sexist crap. And let's not forget the age-old double standard waiting to catch you out: the option to 'empower' yourself sexually as a woman may exist from the moment you open your very first magazine, but don't bet you won't get called a slut in the process. Just because we are now much more in charge of our own transactions doesn't mean that it's liberating to conduct these transactions on a foundation of sexual doublethink.

Thanks in no small part to the popularity of 'barely legal babes' in porn, your purity is indeed a commodity, but only insofar as it can get you on the cast list for 'Naughty Schoolgirls Gone Wild 2: Siege of the Virginity Bandits'. As soon as it looks as though you actually want to hold on to it, the media don't want to know. While mothers may be engaged in a constant cry of 'I can see your knickers!' as their 12-year-old daughters roll their eyes and hitch up their school skirts, the younger generation are wondering where their teenage idol got that sequinned crotchless leotard from and pinning it to their 'Saturday night' board on Pinterest. This is a society where 14-year-olds can buy thong-attached skirts with 'Easy Access' emblazoned on them, and baby dolls come equipped with Babygros that rather terrifyingly ask 'Am I fit or what?' (Holly has photographic evidence of the latter, if you're curious.) And it's also one where those very same girls become social pariahs the minute they express a genuine interest in sex – they become 'sluts', 'whores', and 'not girlfriend material'. In many ways, it seems like you just can't win.

On the one hand, then, the ubiquitous emphasis on sex implies that every young woman should aspire to becoming sexually active ASAP, but on the other, relinquish your purity at her peril. Of course, the whole notion of a woman's 'purity' is one of those things that many of us view as 'total sexist bullshit' – the idea that you transform into a different kind of woman entirely just because you've had a cock inside you is, of course, ridiculous, but that doesn't stop our culture perpetuating it everywhere you look, and that includes teenage magazines. Don't be put off by the fact that no one in the history of the world has ever put forward a convincing explanation for why women who have sex are somehow worse than women who don't. What, is it because they're slutty? Sinful? Aren't willing to buy into paternalistic conven-

tions of ownership? What is 'sluttishness' other than a woman simply showing consent and agency in her own sex life? Purity isn't even a real thing, rooted as it is in the idea that female desire is unnatural, dirty and corrupting. Either that or nonexistent, so you must just be faking it to get something, or to manipulate men. The existence of the myths surrounding women and sex just shows how a significant proportion of the population still don't believe you have ownership of your own sexuality, but that men do.

This idea is borne out again and again by the advice given to teenagers about sex. Whether it's in a magazine, a lesson plan or a teenage soap storyline, boys are taught when and how it is appropriate to express the sexual desires they are experiencing, while girls are taught to resist them. In other words, boys are taught to say, 'Ohhh, yeah' and girls are taught to say, 'Whoa, no'. As many of you will no doubt recall when thinking back to your teenage years, the experience of being a sexually curious virgin involves the constant walking of a 'reputation' tightrope stretched between 'slutty' and 'frigid'. And it's even worse in the twenty-first century – one minute you're reading 'Ten steps to your first kiss' in *Shout* and the next you're expected to Snapchat Darren from 8E a photo of your 'newly shaven pussy'. Yet despite all the naked selfies that are doing the school rounds as we write, losing your virginity is still often portrayed by the media as a defining moment in a woman's life, with heavy emphasis on rose petals and romance.

No wonder, with all the pressure coming from every angle, the actual first time can fall spectacularly short. To cite an example, one of our readers described her first sexual experience at a peer-pressure-laden 'party' that her friend held while her parents were away one weekend. Arriving at a supposed sleepover laden with her toothbrush and a pair of flannel pyjamas at the age of 14, she was instructed by her best friend to 'take your clothes off', and, after minor protestation, was assured: 'It's a blow job party. All grown-ups do this.' Kneeling on the floor in her Tammy Girl knickers and starter bra, she delivered a spectacularly bad BJ with the help of two of her childhood friends. 'At that point, I didn't even know semen existed,' she told us. 'Needless to say, I only realised recently that this essentially counts as the only orgy I will probably ever have.' Judging by what we've heard from the Vagenda's readership, this is by no means an unusual story.

If you manage to sidestep being labelled slutty for ditching your purity and test-driving the car before you really drive it, then you enter headfirst and relatively unscathed into the ritualistic world of dating. Sexual politics, as we know, are alive and well in this arena – in fact, they're especially feisty. And there are all sorts of questions posed to women that, conveniently, men aren't really expected to give a shit about. For instance: should you have sex on the third date? Should you 'make him wait', since the man horn is real but the woman horn is a mythological female ploy; a unicorn horn, if you will? Should you take the Pill? Should you lick his balls? Should you apologise if you're on your period? Would you rather have a cup of tea?

Despite this bombardment, you can't step away from the shelf for long enough to realise that the magazines are doing what they always do: identifying a problem, making you feel bad about it, and then 'providing' you with the solution (all for the £2 cover price plus £39.99 for the satin body-stocking), like the good little consumer that you are. And you fall for it hook, line and sinker because you've been conditioned to perceive yourself as lacking and the magazine as all-knowing. The doublethink culture really comes into its own here, because the media beast would have it that, yes, you lose something precious (read: something a dude would really like to take off you) when you sleep with someone for the first time and thus render yourself a questionable can of used goods; but then again, once you're in a sexual relationship you need to behave like a squeezing, gyrating, permanently up-for-it nympho pixie in order to 'keep the magic alive' and prevent your boyfriend from straying. If you're not dyeing your pubes red and shaving them into a heart shape for Valentine's Day so he'll get a nice view as you perform your latest striptease for him, forget it. If you haven't invested in the latest deal from Agent Provocateur on fluffy handcuffs and tingling lube you may as well write off your shared love life as less meaningful than a quickie grope at the youth club under the sweet table. And if he doesn't get at least one apologetic blowjob every time you dare to selfishly bleed out of your vagina for an entire week? Well, then you're just so unreasonable that you're lucky to have conned some poor bloke into bed with you in the first place. In other words, once you've lost your sacred virginity, Magazineland swoops in with a whole new range of things to worry about.

PLEASING YOUR MAN

There was a time when sex was just you, your 17-year-old boyfriend, and a twenty-minute grope for the right hole culminating in a lot of commiserative cuddling. But in the twenty-first century, sex is complicated. Walk into an Ann Summers shop and you're faced with a range of S&M testicle clamps and some awful contraption called the 'dildo tree', neither of which makes a particularly welcome addition to 'date night'. In a world where you get a space of only about five years in between learning what the word 'uterus' means and getting your head around the fact that even your old best friend from the playground might now self-identify as a dominatrix 'cumslut' with a foot fetish, it's not surprising that a large chunk of the population chooses to sit at home and log in to YouPorn with their left hand rather than venture into the scary realm of single people and all their possible oddities.

There's no doubt that the experience of sex has changed dramatically over the last hundred years, and not in isolation from women's rights. You only needed to contrast the pages of recently defunct *more!* magazine (1988–2013) to the chaste virgins of 1920s romantic magazine fiction to know that things have become a lot more adventurous in terms of where things are being put and how. *More!* was particularly famous for its 'position of the fortnight' feature, which invariably involved recycling the same five sex positions and giving them increasingly ridiculous names ('the dolphin', 'the robot cuddle', 'the upside-down wheelbarrow') while illustrating them with Barbie and Ken dolls. It is fondly remembered by those of us who hadn't even had sex yet, but were nonetheless fascinated by the mechanics of the reverse cowgirl.

Betwixt teenagehood and womanhood something odd begins to happen. You've grown out of your teenage weekly read and into the strange *Cosmo* Girl universe. The advice of agony aunts, doctors and counsellors begins to wane and in its place you get 'His steamy sex fantasies' and 'Clever tricks to drive him wild'. In other words, women's magazines ramp up the raunch and the focus shifts away from female sexual pleasure to 'the secrets of the male orgasm'. For magazines written by women and for women, there's certainly a lot of cock-centric editorial, and it would be foolish to think that 'raunch culture' doesn't play a part.

Cosmopolitan, a magazine which 90% of young women in America reportedly look to as a significant source of sexual education, has spent the last two decades reserving the upper left-hand corner of its cover for a raunchy headline, which almost always features the appetite-whetting word 'sex' in giant capital letters next to the cover girl's face. A quick flick through their back catalogue reveals a smorgasbord of shagging know-how, including: 'Win the sex factor', 'Sex Q&A', '75 sex moves men crave', 'All new 60 sex tips', 'Sex survey results', 'Men, sex and you', '1000 true sex confessions', 'How normal is your sex life?', 'Be a sex genius', 'Sex uncensored', 'Best. Sex. Ever', 'His 6 secret sex spots', 'Guys rate 50 sex moves', and the exhausting-sounding 'Sex truths we learnt from 2000+ men'. *Glamour* also got in on the action with the 'What men think of sexual things you do' trend; examples include: '25 things you do that guys secretly love' and '12 little things every guy wants in bed'. Every one of these features, unfortunately, will be identical to the last, because, let's face it, there are only really about ten sexual moves in existence, and human beings have had them down for centuries now.

The fact of the matter is that most sex that you see or hear about in the media is not just boring, generic and stereotyped, but also geared almost entirely towards pleasing a man – and yet it claims to be proof of our sexual liberation. Sure, it's just great for guys that boobs are now on show at eye level in every local newsagent's via such bastions of decency as *Playboy* and *GQ*, whereas in times of yore you'd only find them on the top shelf – with the nudie calendars and the cardboard holders for packets of pub peanuts. Yet the 'boobs' we see peeking out of these lads' mags and the porn that influences them are more often than not plastic, sculpted appendages bearing very little resemblance to the fat-packets we usually carry on our chests. Likewise, the infantilised women in submissive poses appearing in videos online, who act theatrically the moment a man points his chapseye at them, tell us as little about actual, real-life sex as the saucy stories our great-grandmothers read. The characters are just more naked, is all. We're told this is liberating, and perhaps it is for those who enjoy being aggressively rammed in flat-pack bedrooms while a pumped-up himbo tugs on their pigtails. For those women whose tits have a natural droop and who have the audacity to get their kicks from clitoral stimulation? Not so much.

While magazines such as *Cosmopolitan* once sought to liberate and empower women by allowing them to take control of their own sexualities, they now seem to envisage their readers as a troop of performing sex monkeys. Whether it's recreating a strip club environment in the bedroom or dressing up as a sexy nurse complete with phallic syringe, much of the advice doled out to readers in need of 'spicing up their sex lives' contains an element of performance that would not be amiss in your average, workaday porn film. And a low-budget one, at that. So why not do it like a pornstar? Well, first of all, men still comprise the major audience for erotic film in its current form. We are fed the same stale line again and again about how the demand for visual erotica just isn't there from the female side: apparently women prefer Anaïs-Nin-style literature (or *Fifty Shades of Grey*) and when they do watch porn, they want a candlelit view of romantic coupledom where the man cries a little on climax. ('Tissue to wipe your spaff away, babe?' 'Thanks, sweetheart – but let me get my tears of happiness first.') As much as that is all fine and dandy, if you actually want to see a real woman having a real orgasm, then there are very few places for you to turn.

In other words, women aren't staying away from porn in 2014 because they don't care for sex and 'just aren't visual creatures': they're staying away from it because it's just another tiring male-dominated sphere that has absolutely nothing to do with female pleasure. If you're a randy woman perusing the internet for wank fodder, you're going to find either the dirty scenes from a cheesy chick flick or a barrage of doe-eyed, finger-licking girls who get their most powerful orgasms from the sheer pleasure of licking up the pizza guy's swimmers from the kitchen floor. A world of plenty it may be, but in the catalogues of pornography, where 'needle fetish dwarf porn' is genuinely out there for your viewing pleasure, it's difficult to find a single accurate representation of a woman having sex in an enjoyable manner. The same is true of magazines – all too often, women are expected to plan, conform and perform, rather than enjoy the ride. His pleasure comes first: hers is always secondary.

Just as in porn, in the fantasies pulled straight from the pages of *Cosmo* and *Glamour* the male gaze has primacy. Where there is a focus on female pleasure, it involves howling and screaming in ecstasy as soon as the tip of his member touches your vaginal walls, whether or not you feel like it. Often, you're seen as little more than an object to enhance what one of our readers sarcastically termed 'his wank into your vagina'. The cult of being single and in search of a sexual partner generally revolves around transforming oneself into this sort of man-pleasing man magnet (indeed, Helen Gurley Brown is frequently quoted as having said, 'If you're not a sex object, you're in trouble').

This notion of the 'sexy single girl' is *Cosmopolitan*'s *raison d'être*. The *Cosmo* Girl is also 'liberated'. She can have sex whenever and with whomever she wants, is economically independent, confident, consumerist, and has a handful of filthy sex tricks up her sleeve. All these sex trips are, naturally, gleaned from *Cosmo* itself. The *Cosmo* Girl can drive a man wild in bed and hold her own in the boardroom. She can shop at Agent Provocateur without feeling embarrassed, owns an admirable array of sex toys, and is adventurous and experimental in spirit. And she'd never, ever admit to having a bad lay.

Except, of course, none of this single girl sexual experimentation can happen on the first date. Kinky sexual exploration is all very well, but you can't expect a man to marry you if you're whipping out the handcuffs the first time he walks you home. Amidst all of its efforts to make you into a slathering unpaid prostitute, *Cosmo* also reminds you, with the double standard that only someone who truly loves you would hold, that it's just not a good idea to get *too* liberated. Don't go bandying about your reverse cowgirl technique on the first date or anything.

Cosmo is having a virgin–whore personality crisis. It wants kink, but kink within limits. It tells you that you should be having sex with whomever you want, wherever you want, but follows it up with a load of articles telling you exactly what it is you should be doing. For instance, '8 new places to have great sex', examples of which include, honest to God, 'shedlike structures usually placed in remote areas' (aka the set of a teen slasher movie), in the fridge, and in a rowing boat.

The contradictions in *Cosmo*'s outlook are amplified by the fact that every sexual proclivity is now catered to by that filthy behemoth that is the internet. Whether you like to wear a nappy, indulge in a bit of 'bum fun', or get jiggy with it in a full fluffy animal costume, the internet has it covered. Of course, women's magazines could never feature any of this stuff without kissing goodbye to their advertisers. No one at Clinique is going to want to see their moisturiser advertised next to a feature on bukkake (for a start, the visual references are too reminiscent), and last time we checked, none of them were down with the brown (got to keep Cadbury happy, after all). As a result, magazines are constantly searching for new ways to appear to whet the readers' appetite without undermining their own financial interests.

This 'pushing of the boundaries but within limits' strategy is how you end up with ridiculous sex tips such as the 'doughnut nibble' from *Cosmo*'s '31 Days of HOT SEX' feature: 'slip' a hot doughnut around your man's penis then slowly nibble it off? (This suggestion caused some consternation among our Vagenda readers. The hole in the doughnut is, wel . . . rather *small*?).

In order to avoid the repetitive recycling of sex tips (which nonetheless seems to make up much of the content), journos are finding themselves having to be all the more inventive within more and more stringent boundaries – with hilarious, and sometimes disturbing, results.

RUBBISH TIPS

The magazine sex tip is a long-standing institution, ranging from the sticky to the impractical, the ridiculous to the sublime. Here are some of our favourites.

> Cook dinner topless, apply a little tomato sauce to your nipple (make sure it's not too hot), and ask your man if it's spicy enough.

Follow this tip and – *voilà!* – the normally tedious task of cooking dinner becomes a saucy masterclass in eroticism. If you ask us, said writer hasn't gone far enough. Men love beef. Men love boobs. Why not dump the whole lot on your naked body and allow your man to frolic in your beefy bolognaise boobs to your heart's content? That'll get his juicy tomatoes really throbbing.

> Incorporating food into your passion play is a classic carnal
> activity. Take a few of your favourite erotically appealing
> flavour combinations, like peanut butter and honey or
> whipped cream and chocolate sauce, and mix up yummy
> treats all over his body.

Sex tips will vary as to whether it's your body providing the buffet or his, but surely having that many sticky substances in your various orifices cannot be good for you (and indeed, they're usually the kinds of foods that the magazine would advise its dieting readers to avoid). And what if you have allergies, not to mention the issue of your partner's possibly copious chest hair? When one coeliac sufferer complained about the clear gluten bias in *Cosmo*'s food sex strategies (and doesn't she sound like a hoot!), the magazine responded by suggesting that she surround his, ahem, love salami (read: penis) with cold cuts of meat for her to nibble on. Sadly, she was also a vegetarian.

> Sprinkle a little pepper under his nose right before he
> climaxes. Sneezing can feel similar to an orgasm and
> amplify those feel-good effects.

Why not give your boyfriend a sneezegasm? First you let him come on your tits, now he's phlegming in your face. But what's one more bodily fluid, eh? Three litres of water and a bottle of syrup of figs and you'll have completed the set!

> Sour Belts: While you're making out, use the belts to
> playfully whip each other's butts. Spanking releases
> feel-good endorphins and dopamine, which up the
> pleasure factor and increase arousal and excitement.

Sour belts are those sweets which look like extra long frogs' tongues dipped in sugar. This sex tip is from an entire creepy article about how to get your rocks off using candy from your childhood. This one's for you, Herr Freud.

Try Some Naughty Props

Do something unexpected with toys you already have lying around the house.

Hairbrush: A hard-bristled hairbrush is perfect for gently scratching his skin.

Rolling pin: Run this baker's basic over his back and thighs during an erotic massage.

Blush brush: Skip the pricey feathers you find at sex shops, and use this to tickle his neck, chest, arms and package.

More ways of transforming domestic drudgery into sexy fun play! And using tools which some hard-line feminists would regard as objects traditionally associated with female oppression – bonus! We especially like the rolling pin – why not kill two birds with one stone and roll the pastry out on his naked back before wrapping it sensuously around his member to create a real-life sausage roll? It looks funny *and* it's yummy, too – plus, you're performing two wifely duties in one fell swoop. Multitasking is just another talent that a woman brings to a sexual partnership, and why stop there? Those Marigold rubber gloves are the perfect accessories for digital anal exploration. And that fish slice is a perfect BDSM prop when slapping his bare bottom.

During intercourse, you're all wrapped up in each other. So extend that carnal concept even further by literally tying yourselves together. Take a really long piece of sturdy

> plastic wrap (long enough to fit around your body about
> eight times). Then fold it in half, twist it into a long rope that
> fits snugly around both of your bodies twice . . . you won't be
> able to move more than a few inches from each other.

Another inspiration from the animal kingdom. Did you know that foxes can't physically extricate themselves from each other for up to half an hour after sex? That one's all about sperm protection, but this one's all about fun times – though they don't mention how you detach yourselves afterwards. What if you end up stuck like that for ever, unable to reach the telephone, until one of you starves to death and your only sustenance, bar human flesh, comes from the tiny globules of spaghetti sauce left over from the last sex tip you tried? They *really* haven't thought this one through.

> Forget about just stroking your man with a simple pair
> of satin panties! For a real treat, pop those silky numbers
> in the freezer a day before you're ready for action. Then
> loosely wrap the icy fabric around his package and gently
> slide it up and down.

Freezing temperatures generally have an adverse effect on the male member's . . . ahem . . . turgidity. But the same is not true of your vagina. Instead of using the 'panties' (and doesn't that word immediately bring to mind a creepy old man?) to wrap around his penis, why not don the knickers straight from the cooler? It's the perfect antidote to that burning cystitis you've been battling all week.

> Don a wig. It will transform your looks and, consequently,
> your sexual personality.

Ah, a classic women's magazine assumption wrapped up in a helpful hint: your looks have changed and so, 'consequently', has your personality, allowing you to play out the classic 'sex with a stranger' fantasy (as long as it isn't an *actual* stranger, obvs, you big slag).

> Shave each other's pubic hair into pretty patterns: a heart, for instance.

His friends in the rugby club changing rooms will love you for it.

> Sneak Up Behind Him
> Blow his mind with this *sneaky move*: stand behind him and stroke his penis.

We have now definitely entered Creepytown. Walking up behind someone and grabbing his genitals while he's brushing his teeth or dreamily looking at the clouds, whether you yell 'Surprise!' or not, is unlikely to pan out the way that you wanted. It's not only unnerving but also deeply impolite. Men are keen to protect their nads from potential attackers at all costs, so following this advice may lead to his accidentally putting you in hospital.

> Start by stacking six scrunchies on top of each other over his package. Then remove them one by one using your lips and tongue . . . as each piece is removed, it releases a little bit of pressure in his penis, which will make his orgasm more intense when it happens. Plus, the movement of the fabric will feel wild on his skin.

We knew the nineties were having a resurgence. Who says those glittery butterfly hairclips don't make excellent nipple clamps? Then again, if you're going to have nineties sex why not just crimp your hair, drop an E, whack *Now 42* on the CD player and let him touch you over your clothes?

> Late at night, light off, phone off the hook. Make the atmosphere as spooky as possible. Watch a horror film to psych yourselves up even more. Then, dress in a skimpy outfit that makes you feel vulnerable, make him count to 100, then hide. When he does find you, it takes a woman with nerves of reinforced steel not to scream, wriggle, and half-heartedly try to escape.

There are no words.

WHERE ARE THE FLAPS?

Despite all the weird, wonderful and downright terrifying ideas that magazines have for spicing up your sex life, one thing you may have noticed is how none of their 'moves' are actually *that* kinky. Take an article that US *Cosmo* ran online in June 2013 on the difference between making love and f*cking (their asterisk, not ours – the presence of which, incidentally, leads us to question their suitability for giving sex advice in the first place – they can't even *say* the word). The 'making love' segments involved such romantic endeavours as 'tossing a sheer scarf over a lamp', gentle kissing and 'languorous oral sex' (which will at least leave you feeling fully sexually sated before you die in a blazing scarf-related inferno). Fucking, sorry, f*cking, meanwhile, involves incorporating some garden-variety filth, including handcuffs, thigh-high boots (which they describe as 'totally out of character' – because you're a good girl, not a hoebag), stroking his 'backdoor', and telling him – WITHOUT CRACKING UP – 'I'm gonna give it to you good'. 'Make some noise,' you're also told. What? Just any indeterminate noise? Or can it be the sound of you walking out of the house while slamming the *actual* backdoor in frustration? Because even the most soft-core genuine erotica at least has the gumption to use the word 'arsehole'.

We should also mention that most magazine sex articles are deeply heteronormative: women's magazines will only suggest lesbian love if it's in the context of giving your boyfriend a sexy treat. One women's magazine even suggested that, if you are uncomfortable with a threesome (or, to use their words, find it 'too racy'), then you can simply 'pretend someone else is there when you get it on'. Because initiating sex while pointing at thin air and saying, 'Mike, this is Martha. She wants to suck you off while I read the paper' looks completely normal.

Ridiculous sex tips aside, what is it about women's magazines that makes them so, well, vanilla? At risk of sounding like *Mean Girls*, there's something about them that is just so very . . . uncool. We think we've worked out the reason for this, and it has something to do with their soft-focus, rose-petalled, white-knickered concept of sex being so alienated from the actual, real-life experience of shagging that it's almost as though they are two completely different activities. Which, in fact, they are. Real sex is dirty, sticky, occasionally awkward, and lots and lots of fun. Magazine sex, meanwhile, is illustrated by stock photographs of clean-cut, smiling men and women tossing and tumbling on pristine Egyptian cotton sheets as a precursor to the 'soulful climax' they will both undoubtedly achieve *simultaneously and while making eye contact*. Very occasionally, one of them will get out a dildo but only as a prop, and, as no one in Magazineland has bodily fluids, it's never going to be much of a lark for either party. You don't need us to tell you that the sex in these magazines bears absolutely no relation to the sex that millions of people engage in, in their houses, every night. As human animals we sweat, we grunt, and we heave as we clumsily try and arrange our respective flaps of skin in a way that is pleasurable for both parties. Making the beast with two backs is an often cack-handed endeavour which, to an outside observer, looks like slapstick comedy.

Yet a magazine will never tell you this because it ruins the glossy airbrushed façade it is touting: that perfect, candlelit epiphany where you both see stars and no one gets semen in their hair. Everything about magazine sex is plastic: the models are plastic, the act is plastic, and the cock ring *Cosmo* told you to buy and which your boyfriend is now inching away from with a haunted look in his eye is, you guessed it, plastic.

What effect does this plasticised version of sex have on its female readership? Well, if you're a teenage girl, chances are that your first confrontation with an angry, red, throbbing penis is going to be something of a shock. Penises are, in our humble opinion, somewhat lacking in inherent aesthetic appeal, so chancing upon one unprepared for the first time is likely to be a little alarming. No one tells you this. And they never, *ever* talk about fingering. The fact that contraception is also conspicuously absent hardly prepares you for the awkward condom fumble of your first, second, third, and let's face it, probably twentieth sexual experience.

Sex involves flaps and fanny farts and foreskins and sometimes, yes, even fisting, but most importantly, it should be with someone you want, when you want, and how you want it, not how some media conglomerate *thinks* you should want it. It's important to relationships, whether you're in a fetishistic polyamorous triad or ushering in the golden anniversary of your blissfully happy monogamous marriage, so why have the media packaged it in a smooth, shiny silicone box and served it up to the teenagers of today with an extra-large helping of bullshit?

The sad truth is that, once we become alienated from sex, we become alienated from our bodies too, and rather than seeing them as physical entities to be explored, enjoyed and experienced, we start to compare them unfavourably with the shiny fakeness in the media or in porn. Despite the best efforts of many teenage magazines to counteract this effect (they have what can almost be described as a preoccupation with crabs, discharge and toxic shock syndrome), it almost seems that we're becoming even less comfortable with our bodies, which certainly isn't something that tallies very well with our so-called 'liberation'. As anyone who's been thoroughly rummaged in by a gynaecologist knows, talking about this stuff isn't easy. In fact, it can induce full-on vagina panic. We're increasingly told by the media that our genitals should be as smooth as a peach, as well as tight, white and out of sight, so a trip to the clinic for an exhaustive STD test or a Pap smear can seem very daunting. Granted, no one actually enjoys mounting a speculum while a doctor commands the nurse to 'get this girl some lube', but it is, to an extent, part and parcel of being a woman, which is why it's so weird that we clam up (pun intended) at the very mention of our fannies. It's not until something goes wrong down there, say an abnormal smear, a bout of chlamydia, or pain during sex, that you realise how alone you can feel. But on the plus side, it's not until your vag hits a medical speed bump that things tend to, er . . . open up. Suddenly women you barely know are matter-of-factly discussing their cervixes and telling you you'll be fine, and we have it on good authority that once you've had a baby (if that's your jam), you'll be so used to having other people poking around in there that you'll be jumping up on that medical table and spreading your legs quicker than your doctor can say, 'That's really not necessary for tonsillitis.'

The culture of shame surrounding female sexuality is alive and well. That, rather than all of this razzmatazz involving whips and handcuffs

and anal beads, is why we need more frank and honest communication on the subject (the handcuffs can come later). Sex is, after all, a
relatively uncomplicated rhythmical movement involving two people's
genitalia, and despite what the *Cosmo Sutra* may tell you, there are
really only a handful of possible bodily contortions you can manage
while keeping a penis inside a vagina (we once saw a position that
involved a woman sucking off a man in a deckchair elevated to the
status of 'beach blowjob' – oh, *more!* magazine, how we miss you).
Strip away the leg restraints and the dirty talk from any porn that's
going and you'll see the same thing: an in-and-out motion involving
your naughty parts. Let's not get too carried away; it is, after all, just sex.

5
Underwear That Gets on Your Tits

BURNING OUR BRAS

Underwear: ever since your bra's underwire melted in the tumble dryer for the first time, we're pretty sure it's been the bane of your life. All right, perhaps not the bane, but definitely a permanent annoyance that cuts into the skin under your arms and disappears up your crack far oftener than any sane human being could possibly enjoy. High-street stores seem permanently in competition to come up with the least viable form of undergarment, often charging an eye-watering sum for a pair of knickers that doesn't even have a crotch and so could presumably have been sewn by anyone with a strong piece of thread and a length of PVC. Meanwhile, it's fairly commonplace to find balcony bras and thongs in tweenage sizes, sometimes complete with cutesy little slogans to really hammer home the nasty. Every now and then, a little bit of controversy rears its head in the (mostly right-wing) press about how the sexualisation of children takes place mainly because of these slogan-patterned shorties – and who could forget the unwise decision of Asda to market *High School Musical*-themed knickers in 2008 with 'Dive In' written across the front? – although it has to be borne in mind that the newspapers peddling this outrage have usually also been fetishising the latest celebrity's four-year-old child since her conception.

Every woman remembers her first bra, just as she remembers the first time she saw the 'Hello, Boys' Wonderbra ad starring Eva Herzigova, looked downwards at her own breasts, and thought, 'Bollocks'. The realisation that breasts are thought to carry totemic mystical powers (especially to men) comes incredibly young, probably at just around the time that yours have started growing. Teen magazines are full of questions about sore nipples and tender flesh, as well as stories from girls who have written in to share their 'embarrassing moment' – such as when the scrunched-up tissues used to stuff a bra popped out in front of that 'cute crush' in French class.

Suddenly you're 12, and you're wondering why you haven't got a bra yet, what sort you should have, and whether or not the straps are pingable. From what we remember, there was no greater embar- rassment than having a lad in your class reach out to ping your strap and find nothing there, except maybe a glimpse of nipple beneath your school shirt. We both came of age at a particularly cruel time – the tit-obsessed nineties, era of the lads' mag, Page Three, and Geri from the Spice Girls – when not having the pneumatic boobs of Melinda Messenger was an unspeakable sin, even at age 11. The bra-related anxiety of the young woman comes before she even knows what all-important boob camp she falls into (for there are only two camps, of course). It isn't long, however, before we all find out.

It's true that, when held up and scrutinised with the benefit of booby hindsight, our teenage bras can seem almost laughable. Most of us started picking out bras with cartoon dogs on them from Tammy Girl way before there was any visible need for support in the chest area; little did we know then that the lingerie section is fraught with controversy.

Yes, women's magazines – and, even more often, girls' magazines aimed at the teenage demographic and below – tend to concern themselves with tits and arse just as much as your average lads' mag. Of course, for those publications aimed at young girls, it's what's covering up your tits and arse that's on the menu, rather than straightforward ogling. But the idea that someone *will* be ogling is almost always implicit in the articles they produce and the tips that they give. Make no mistake about it: prepping for a lifetime of underwear paranoia starts early.

'The dos and don'ts of wearing a bra', an online feature courtesy of *Seventeen* magazine, perfectly encapsulates this. 'DON'T wear a white bra under a black tee (*like, ever*)' they preach, illustrating their point with a picture of Taylor Swift doing it all wrong. 'DON'T suffocate yourself with a too-small bra!' (Demi Lovato). 'DON'T wear a full coverage bra with a low-cut shirt' (AnnaLynne McCord). 'DON'T wear a white bra under a sheer top' (Ashley Tisdale). 'DON'T let your bra lines show through your dress' (Jessica Simpson). You only have to look below the line of this article at the Facebook comments to know what teenage girls themselves think of such breast regulation: 'God forbid anyone see my bra strap or a white bra under a white shirt [. . .] The world CAN'T KNOW I WEAR BRAS – they must believe my boobs are just held up by gravity,' says one. Another concurs, 'Yes! Boobs are a HUGE SECRET. No one should know you are wearing a bra! Secret bra, secret boobs. No one should be aware of bodies.' 'This is lame – I'm sorry but I'll wear my bra how I want to,' grouches another (quite rightly) frustrated teenage girl.

How exactly you're supposed to have the confidence to 'work the underwear as outerwear trend, just like Pixie [Geldof]' – as young teen mag *Shout* suggested to its readership in 2011 – at the same time as being up to date with all the possible ways in which your underwear can turn on you is beyond us. Of course, you could follow American *Elle*'s 'After-school special' fashion feature of the same year, which used the teenage actors from the US version of racy drama *Skins* to illustrate how exactly to do 'innerwear as outerwear' ('These teens do spend more on-screen time out of their clothes than in them. Who better, then, to model one of spring's sexiest trend [?]'). Or you could go rogue and pop down to your local supermarket, where padded or 'cleavage enhancing' bras for prepubescent girls appear like clockwork on the shelves every year. They'll cause a brief ruckus (in 2008, when Tesco was found to be selling £4 'bust booster' bras for seven-year-old girls under their Cherokee label, even the NSPCC stepped in), only to reappear once again when the seasons change.

The fact is, when you're a girl, your bras and knickers seem to be everyone's business, and those in the know like to get the process of moulding you into a lifelong consumer started nice and early. As the school-age girls' magazine *Bliss* put it in their fashion section of June 2013, 'You don't just need a whole new wardrobe, you need a whole new load of underwear too!' Lingerie remains a touchy subject for us all: the relatively quick graduation from Hello Kitty 'boy shorts' to polyester crotchless thongs is worth at least a passing glance, and the fact that at least half of us have experienced the 'fortnight of thrush' effect from the toxic combination of 'sexy' underwear and skintight jeans is nothing short of an international scandal. All of which leads us to question just who exactly this lacy lingerie is actually intended *for*. Not us, surely? Oh, that's right: it's for men.

Much like men, feminists have always stood accused of concerning themselves with women's underwear, although, it has to be said, their interest is believed to lie in an altogether more incendiary direction. The 'bra-burning feminists' myth came about during a 1968 protest outside the Miss America pageant, an event revolving around a woman's seemingly innate ability to model lingerie under the guise of the 'swimwear heat'. In fact, the alleged 'bra-burning' never happened, and was in fact a journalist's attempt to draw comparisons with the Vietnam War protests where young American men were burning draft cards. Never mind. Turns out that we *do* have something to say about bras anyway, although since our own are flame-retardant and composed mostly of fume-producing plastics that even a glue-sniffing bully off *Grange Hill* would balk at, we won't attempt to conduct our own radical bonfire in the back garden just yet.

Funnily enough, most feminists (with the exception of Germaine Greer, who called them a 'ludicrous invention', and fair play to the woman) haven't seen the bra itself as inherently oppressive. Unlike the corset, which in 1874 American author Elizabeth Stuart Phelps Ward quite rightly called to be burned (because only then could emancipation truly begin), most women recognise that, rather than being 'instruments of female torture', bras perform a vital function for any well-endowed woman who is planning on doing anything more vigorous than walking at a brisk pace. The shrinking of the corset to become more bra-like is probably why the latter still carries a whiff of restriction. Going bra-less certainly represented a special kind of (naked) freedom in the 1960s and '70s, though look at the cone-shaped contraptions that had been doing the rounds and you can see why. In fact, there are still those who claim that bras are bad for you: in 2013 *France Info* quoted 'research' by Professor Jean-Denis Roullion of the University of Besançon that suggested that your breasts might actually become saggier from long-term bra-wearing. However, considering this was also the man who said that 'an overweight, 45-year-old woman with three kids has no business not wearing a bra' (read: by all means ditch your bra and let your nips be wild and free, but YOUNG AND HOT LADIES ONLY, *s'il vous plaît*), we suspect he may have a vested interest. And therein lies the nub of the feminist beef, of course: if bras are primarily garments for women, then why so much male involvement?

To an extent, Greer was right. There do exist ludicrous bras, the sort that you rip off the minute you step through the front door, or pull through your sleeve in the ladies' toilet like a conjuror's assistant, and they're not so different from the kind that our feminist forebears were wearing. Perhaps they had never experienced the religious epiphany of having their breasts properly sized up, courtesy of the joyfully supportive Marks & Spencer fitting service, let alone Rigby & Peller. In which case: who can blame them? We'd want to set fire to those bras, too. On the one hand: if you're in the market for torching stuff, is there not a better symbol of modern femininity than the underwired boulder-holder? On the other, let's face it: the absence of a bra only ever feels like freedom if you've got the kind of boobs that can stand on their own two teats.

HOW TO MAKE YOUR BOOBS LOOK AMAZING

Women can have a strangely complex relationship with their breasts, and just owning a pair has become politicised. Those with big baps can feel that they are condemned to a lifetime of impertinent comments, attention from the 'wrong kind of guys', and the sort of frumpy support bras that cost upwards of fifty quid and look like something Mrs Doubtfire might wear to the Tory Party conference. No dainty straps and paper-thin lace for you, my friend, say the high-street stores. Nope, you get the polka-dotted heavyweight option, made from the kind of steel usually reserved for suspension bridges. Meanwhile, the likelihood of seeing a pair of jugs on the catwalk, wibble-wobbling seductively as the model does that weird stampy giraffe trot, is practically zero. As previously mentioned, any female celebrity with a pair is condemned to a life of being referred to as 'curvy', 'womanly' or 'shapely', unless she's in a tabloid of course, in which case it becomes, 'Cor! Look at those TITS!', or, if you're fresh out of childhood, a creepy leer along the lines of the *Daily Mail* article about Selena Gomez in February 2012 which proclaimed: 'The fresh-faced teen who got her break on the Disney Channel has been replaced with a cleavage-bearing young lady just months away from her 20th birthday.'

And yet, despite their marked absence in fashion spreads and women's mags, your boobs are often described patronisingly as 'assets' that you should 'make the most of', in the same way that a bloke might have a couple of houses in the Canary Islands and a few hundred shares in Google. The appendages resting against your chest are often described as though they're the only things you've got going for you, so it's no wonder many women with big boobs confess to worrying that anything they think, do or say may be viewed as secondary to their mammaries. While the cliché of the lecherous man who is unable to look you in the eye can sometimes be true, it's a major bummer once you realise that the entire media are doing it too. Articles like the aforementioned '50 great things to do with your breasts' (*Cosmopolitan*) or '10 easy ways to make your boobs look amazing' (*Glamour*) could have been written by an editorial team consisting entirely of masturbating teenage boys. You know, the kind of lads who say things like, 'If I were a woman, I'd just stay at home and play with my tits all day' (which, btw, you totally wouldn't, because trust us, matey: if you were a woman you wouldn't have TIME). Posho magazine *Tatler* even ran into trouble in 2013 when its 'Titler' feature attempted to rate 'the most marvellous and magnificent breasts in all society'. (Incidentally, google 'Titler' and you'll notice that the feature in question is practically eclipsed by a swathe of images of Adolf Hitler with tits, or, tits that have been painted to look like Adolf Hitler. The internet is a strange place.) Unfortunately, the person who decided to call out *Tatler* on its 'sexist' boob gallery was none other than ex-Conservative politician Louise Mensch, who would have been one hell of a lot more convincing if she didn't work for National Booby Bible *The Sun*.

Having a pair of marvellous and magnificent breasts is all very well, but if you're big-boobed because of breastfeeding, you can forget about glorying in your mammary glands; the media all too often take a similar stance to the Stagecoach driver in Australia who infamously told breastfeeding mother Lauren McKenna in 2010 to 'put them away or get off', or the kindly member of the public who, in March 2014, labelled breastfeeding mother Emily Slough a 'tramp' on Facebook. Breasts-in-action, being used for the milk-providing purpose that they exist for, and the nursing bras they usually need, are still regarded with embarrassment, or simply don't exist as far as the media are concerned. As the powerhouse parenting and politics commentator at the *New Statesman*, Glosswitch, put it, 'Sexy breasts are for the men, lactating, stretch-marked breasts are for the women.' You're unlikely to find red lace bras with leak-proof breast pads built into their cleavage-enhancing frame in the nearest naughty lingerie shop (unless you buy them from the entertainingly named 'sexy maternity wear' outlet Hotmilk.) But a lot of lactating women *do* want to get jiggy with it, whether or not they accidentally squirt their sex buddy in the eye while changing positions, so the relative invisibility of maternity wear in the naughtier stores is disappointing. After all, we don't all have to accept the false dichotomy of 'sexy vs lactating' just because a few men might be struggling with the idea of their favourite toys getting 'spoilt' by a baby's taking a liking to them.

As it is, big and bouncy boobs are only media-friendly when they don't have a baby attached to them, and outside of the fashion press, which we all know has a penchant for what the journalist Camilla Long describes as 'Chanel tits', those of us with flat chests are equally unappealing. You'd think that having tiny tits that are no good for motorboating were a disability, rather than simply another body type which comes with the undeniable benefit of rarely requiring the services of a chiropractor. A very small amount of comfort was lent to the smaller-chested amongst us when a popular T-shirt appeared in the noughties (courtesy of tshirthell.com) that stated: 'Who needs tits when you have an ass like this?' but, let's be honest, it was short-lived. We're taught from a young age that the grass is always greener, and all those perfectly rounded surgically enhanced fuck-balloons from porn haven't really helped matters.

Even if you possess the holy grail of boobage (a set of criteria which changes randomly, according to public taste but currently seems to centre around 'natural perfection' – basically meaning 'looks like a boob job but isn't'), you can't help noticing how your breasts are used to define you. No wonder, in the quest for better boobs, we spend a fortune on bras: whether they're for norks small and perky enough to model tiny scraps of Chantilly lace held together with wisps of unicorn hair, or plumptious, creamy breasts undulating from the sweetheart neckline of a 1950s basque, you can't deny that a good bra can work wonders. Take it from two girls who've spent enough time risking puncture wounds in the tit by an underwire gone rogue. But that's not to say that underwear is, as the magazines would have you believe, inherently 'empowering'. Yes, modern bras are so advanced that the effects can be transformative: balcony bras that resist the gravity pulling on larger breasts, for instance, or gel bras that create the effect of a well-endowed pair for the flat-chested amongst us – to the extent that certain douchebags amongst the male population will bemoan feeling 'conned' once the things come off. Yes, these guys are invariably dickheads, but just why is it that so many of us feel that we need to literally embody these booby stereotypes anyway? Furthermore, when we've forked out close to a hundred quid on pants and paraphernalia, and are standing admiring ourselves in the mirror, whose eyes are we actually seeing ourselves through?

SEXY SMALLS TO DRIVE HIM WILD

At some point or another, perhaps inspired by an Agent Provocateur ad (that one with Rosie Huntington-Whiteley and the striptease in the trench coat comes to mind) or a *Cosmo* sex tip, most of us have attempted to embody the character of the lingerie-clad vixen, the saucy, sensual seductress of popular culture. Not that it works every time – going to meet a lover in a negligee and a trench coat isn't particularly exciting when you're sitting on the 29 bus, as one of us will happily confirm if asked. Perhaps it's because we're constantly told that we need to 'spice up' our sex lives, and are so frequently exposed to women in their scanties in newspapers, on billboards, and in music videos. Ever since Christina Aguilera upped the ante and teamed those red knickers with a pair of crotchless leather chaps, MTV has begun to resemble some kind of naked sex party, except, of course, that all the men are wearing clothes. It's become practically a given that there'll be a striptease or lap dance taking place, from Beyoncé's burlesque-inspired video for 'Naughty Girl', to Gaga's avant-garde 'fashion bitch' jewelled pants routine in 'Bad Romance', culminating with Rihanna's latex dominatrix antics, or perhaps the stripped-down girls with bums wrapped in transparent plastic riding toy animals next to suit-clad men in the video for Robin Thicke's runaway 2013 hit 'Blurred Lines'.

In other words, female sexuality has become almost inseparable from our ability to make our bums look good in French knickers. Perhaps it's because women spent so many centuries trussed up like turkeys in layer upon layer of petticoats that the thought of the removal of those constraints has become so erotic. It must have taken hours to undress a woman, so it's no wonder that we're still expected to behave like presents waiting to be unwrapped, sometimes literally (see Ann Summers Christmas collection).

While good underwear can make you feel sexy and powerful and, ironically, ready to kick the universe in the nads, we need to question just why, exactly, our ability to look good in our pants has become so culturally important. And these are words from two women who *love* underwear. Whether it's a pair of frilly silk French knickers that actually do make your bum look great, a vintage slip with a delicate trim that skims the tops of your thighs, or a pair of lace-top stockings teamed with feather-light nightwear, most of us understand that underwear can feel confidence-building. And though the right lingerie can enhance all the right bits and give you the kind of assurance that you could only have dreamed of back in the teenage years of mum-bought triple-pack M&S briefs, we have to question why it is that that confidence so frequently comes from being an object of the male gaze. More and more, we're seeing ourselves through men's eyes, and, unfortunately, although underwear seems an intrinsically feminine endeavour, much of it only appears to exist for their pleasure and enjoyment.

Just take a look at the way underwear is marketed. With the exception of a 2000 Gossard advert that bore the tagline 'If he's late, you can always start without him', implying that you'd find yourself so damn hot in your new pants that you just wouldn't be able to resist, well, fucking yourself, most adverts for lingerie tend to depend on the tried-and-tested method of making you think that a £50 bra will magically turn you into a man-eating sex bomb. While early adverts did initially focus on the confidence-boosting aspects of underwear (if only by making you feel like shit – one example of a girdle ad featured the tagline 'I hated to face a full-length mirror'), as the twentieth century progressed, more and more lingerie adverts were geared towards the importance of being sexually desirable to men. A 1964 ad for girdles asked 'Why do men who hate girdles like girls who wear Warner's?' The answer being that other girdles, which 'flatten what they should mold' are 'anti-woman' (if there was ever a more cynical attempt to hijack the women's liberation movement then we haven't seen one). Ads such as these, with their focus on male enjoyment, paved the way for the full-on raunch-fest that was the late 1990s, a decade which saw probably the least comfortable item of lingerie in history, the thong, reach the height of popularity.

We bet some of you remember the adverts from around that time, verging as they did on soft-core porn and channelling an unmistakably male vantage point. Sloggi were particularly guilty of such tactics, with their early-noughties thong adverts containing three perma-tanned women with perfectly peachy, plastic arses appearing in teen magazines to inform us that 'It's string time!', as the one holding a butterfly net looks cheekily over her shoulder as if to say: 'Oooh, busted! Looks like you caught us hunting butterflies in our thongs and stilettos; now I suppose we should have a threesome on this plastic grass.' If you need any more convincing, just look at any underwear advert from the last decade. More often than not they rely on the same 'gotcha!' stolen snapshot cliché, as though you've just accidentally suprised an international supermodel masturbating and decided to take a picture. Even the aforementioned Gossard ad, with its knowing (and, admittedly, taboo-busting) wanking reference, makes you see things through the eyes of a man who has just walked in on an intimate moment. This voyeuristic trope reached its squalid, tasteless conclusion with American Apparel, whose boundary-pushing (read: pervy) ads feature models in various stages of undress, including the infamous image of a woman spreading her legs accompanied by the words 'Now open'. However, you'd be mistaken if you thought this marked the low point – they've now reached the stage where they barely bother to show the model's faces, instead focusing on giant arse, tit and crotch close-ups, or naked ladies in knee socks, touching themselves. Yet photos of naked hipsters are about as likely to get us buying pants as the infamous 2004 advert for underwear brand Lejaby, which shows an Orlando Bloom lookalike *sniffing* a pair of red lace knickers accompanied by the immortal words 'Remember me'. Ew.

As many lingerie adverts show, part of the innate sex appeal of lingerie is to do with concealing and revealing, and as society has become increasingly sexually liberated, the layers have been coming off. In Helen Gurley Brown's day, having a half-slip that 'peek-a-boos a bit beneath [your] short sheath skirt' when you sit down was considered the height of sexiness, while nowadays the wank-fodder that is the Victoria's Secret Fashion Show leaves so little to the imagination that you can almost cop an eyeful of what the model (hasn't) had for dinner. Meanwhile, the covers of men's magazines such as *Maxim* and *GQ* show that the minute any female celebrity has anything to promote she's expected to strip down to her pants while her male cover star counterpart gets all dressed up in an expensive tux.

Undergarments have always existed for the benefit of men, of course (no one but a sadist could ever argue that the organ-crushing properties of the corset were in women's interests), but living as we do in a world where everything can be commercialised means that even putting on a pair of knickers has become a loaded concept. While it used to be that you'd change your pants on the off-chance you'd get hit by a bus (or so your nan would say), we're expected to be shag-ready at a moment's notice, having donned one of the pieces from 2012 *Glamour*'s '50 shades of lingerie'.

Magazine articles warn us of the perils of cohabitation, most of them following the line of online lifestyle magazine *Apartment Therapy* that 'moving in together means getting rid of all the ratty old granny panties'. We should never leave our greying period knickers out to dry, they tutor us, lest our beloved realise we have bodily functions and immediately and permanently lose his boner. Strangely enough, you don't see similar articles in men's magazines, advising against allowing your girlfriend to wash your pants lest she discover your skidmarks and leave you in disgust. As far as scummy smalls are concerned, it's very much a one-way street.

Yes, despite there being nothing less sexy than a lass having to rummage in her bum crack every few minutes to retrieve a missing gusset, we're told that we should be wearing the smallest, teeniest pants possible because that's what men like – and they won't be able to cope if they find out that 75% of the time that's not what we really wear. Of course, we all know that big pants are the most comfy – most of us own at least one pair that would be capable of sailing the *Mayflower* to the New World were they given a chance – yet we persist in donning the kind which make cystitis look like a satisfying round of foreplay in comparison. That so much of our lingerie is foisted upon us by boyfriends and advertisers often serves to add insult to injury, especially when you see articles such as 'What your bra says about you'. COME ON. Think about it for a second: what your BRA says about YOU. Jesus. Unless your bra can actually speak (and you're not on an acid trip), it's not saying anything about your personality at all. Small sexy knickers are supposed to denote beautiful, smooth, well-kept ladyparts, while Big Pants basically mean you're the great unwashed. Of course, we all know that the kind of mock-satin static-inducing pants the article is advertising would have your vag steeped in crusty discharge faster than you can say 'pH imbalance', yet somehow an understandable resistance to trashy (but 'sexy') underwear has been made to appear unhygienic. Better to continue feeling as though you're being rimmed by a floorboard sander than admit to anything approaching a need to be comfortable (and don't get us started on the dreaded frontal wedgie, a condition which Caitlin Moran once infamously described as the feeling that your knickers are 'sitting on top of your clit like a little hat'). Oh, if only we could return to the 1970s, a time when disposable knickers (then known as 'Paper Panties') were briefly popular, though we dread to think what they thought a pair of those might indicate about your inner soul (probably that it's slutty).

Most underwear available on the market is a nightmare to wear and almost always entirely incompatible with the simultaneous wearing of clothes, not to mention your everyday routine, as anyone who has unwittingly bent over in a communal changing room while wearing a pair of transparent pants will no doubt tell you. It's the dishonesty of it which bothers us the most: that this is an industry which exists for the benefit of women; that 'National Cleavage Day' (much like 'Steak and Blowjob Day' and the 'Diamond Boobilee') is a fun outing for us all to enjoy – in the ironic words of the *Metro* in February 2013, 'It's the one day of the year that fundamentally reminds us girls that we are worth so much more than the sum total of our breasts. We are worth the sum total of our breasts squashed together.' To celebrate the 2013 National Cleavage Day – a holiday which, naturally, it had created – Wonderbra asked women to send in pictures of their cleavages for the perusal of the internet. But they needn't have bothered, when *The Sun* had already taken the time to compile a gallery of celebrity women's cleavages and invited their readers to 'celebrate National Cleavage Day by voting for the best of the breasts'. If that's not empowerment, we don't know what is.

Not forgetting those bullshit 'scientific' surveys we have to endure every so often, such as the widely reported University of Manchester 'research' that equated a push-up bra with female happiness ('First scientific research into uplifting lingerie proves push-up bras make women 75 per cent more confident,' trilled the *Mail* in March 2012). And no, don't try and kid us that we need to purchase 'Valentine's Lingerie' or 'Christmas Lingerie' or 'Halloween Lingerie' or 'Birthday Lingerie' for anything other than his sexual gratification, because pretending it's for us while telling us to 'do like professionals do and give him a lap dance in a G-string and heels' (*Cosmo* again) is just taking the piss. As are the articles such as *Lingerie Insight*'s July 2012 piece 'Lingerie star reveals top 5 styles loved by men', featuring a young woman modelling various kinds of lingerie with a cold, dead look behind her eyes, accompanied by captions such as 'Men love a girl with a wild side – animal print underneath it all is a perfect way to express it', and, 'This [nylon lace body-stocking thing] exudes pure sexiness and is a guy's dream come true'. Before we wander off to vomit into the nearest drain, let's make it totally clear that we're under no illusions that lingerie of this kind is made for our personal enjoyment. Nor that sticking a couple of bows on our knickers will magically communicate anything about a woman's person-ality; after all, surely the only reason that a man would try to decode our inner traits through the patterns on our undies is if a startlingly similar male version of *Cosmo* existed, and had convinced him through another useless quiz that that was the done thing. In reality, most boob-related articles in *Cosmo* would make him run away screaming: consider '25 ways to be boobilicious', the magazine's stand-out article of January 2011 that included the tips 'Trace your nipples with minty lip balm, and have him blow on them', 'Request that he slip on a pair of ultraluxe cashmere gloves before running his hands over your bare breasts', 'Dip your breasts in edible body paint, and use them to sponge paint his entire body', and 'Tickle his feet with your nipples'. Ultraluxe cashmere gloves, of course, being the stalwart of every modern woman's underwear drawer.

Unfortunately, the idea persists in women's media that underwear can be seen as a statement, and teen media know this well: take the scene in adolescent box-office smash hit *10 Things I Hate About You*, where innocently owning a pair of black knickers is seen as an indicator of future sexual activity. In the spirit of such revelations and their connection to a film that is aimed squarely at teenagers, we have taken it upon ourselves to put together our own list, inspired by this moment.

10 REASONS TO JUST GO COMMANDO

1. *The assumption that your knicker drawer says whether you're going to have sex or not*

Remember that bit in *When Harry Met Sally* where Sally reveals how her boyfriend broke up with her because the absence of 'Sunday' amongst her days-of-the-week underpants made him think she was cheating, when really it was because they don't make Sunday 'because of God'? Well, that. In other words: never set too much store by your drawers.

Unless it's hiding seventeen Rampant Rabbits, a ball gag, some hog ties, and the phone list for your nearest swingers' club, your underwear drawer probably says very little about your sex life, and even less about the possibility of your *future* sex life. When Holly was 12, almost every pair of underwear she owned was from Tammy Girl and had a cat motif on the front (she was too young to note the – probably unintentional – 'pussy' connotations that would later turn her stomach). If underwear actually has anything to say about possible spinsterhood, then that fact would surely have consigned her to the feline-infested bedsit of every stereotypical bachelorette's worst nightmares. Despite this huge initial setback, she has somehow managed to trick at least a handful of men into fairly alternative intercourse (even while *owning* a cat at the same time), which just goes to show that even the least promising knicker drawers can give rise to the most colourful sex lives.

2. *The assumption that thongs = sexy*

An April 1975 article in *Cosmo* entitled 'Thin enough for a thong?' announcing the invention of the 'garment' (perhaps too strong a word), implied that without a 'rigorous exercise programme' we could kiss any thought of revealing our bare buttocks goodbye. Of course, any woman worth her salt knows that, no matter how skinny you are, that mofo is going to cut into your hips like cheese wire, yet there was a time when seeing one poking out of the back of a pair of jeans was commoner that a *Grease* medley at a student night. Thongs lost their allure for us when one of our medically trained friends referred to them in polite conversation as 'thrush factories'. Yep, a tiny little sliver of material that spends most of the day stuck to your sweaty private parts is more of a perfect breeding ground for unfriendly bacteria than a celebration point. (Pair with pleather leggings for special effect.) Unfortunately, no matter how many times you play admittedly catchy nineties hit 'The Thong Song' by underwear enthusiast Sisqó, it's not going to lend any street cred to your overgrowth of candida.

3. The stuff you're supposed to wear on Valentine's Day, and how it's apparently sexier than being naked

There really is no word for this myriad of madness except 'stuff'. It hangs there in the naughtier shops, all stringy and elasticated and hook-and-eyed, and nobody seems to know exactly how to get in or out of it, not to mention how much it costs. Whenever it's featured in high-end magazines such as *Vogue* and *Harper's Bazaar* it's always accompanied by the ominous acronym 'POA', meaning 'price on application', or 'dream on, hobo'. Valentine's Day is the day when, apparently, you're supposed to spend a good few hours figuring out how all of this works for your partner's pleasure, despite the fact that he or she will probably come home, attempt to take it off you for a 'steamy' fifteen minutes, and then freak the hell out. Men spend years bemoaning the difficulty of the lowly bra strap, and then a shiny swimming costume made of string is supposed to turn them on? Surely nothing says 'boner killer' more than a plastic corset that squeaks when you move and only comes off once you've lubricated its vice-like grip with tears of frustration. Plain white knickers don't look so bad now, eh?

4. The twenty-first century paradox of 'shapewear'

If you're not fluent in Lingerie Department Speak, 'shapewear' is the all-over 'smoothing out' tool used underneath awards-ceremony dresses – and now everyone's dresses – to make women's figures look flawless. As Sara Blakely, founder of Spanx, once said (while we threw up into our handbags), 'I always say that Spanx is the canvas and your clothes are the art.' Bear in mind this is the woman who proudly retells the story of the 81-year-old woman who got stuck in her pants and refused to let the emergency services cut her out of them 'because she loved them so much'. Lord knows what they did with her. She's probably still in there.

And the purpose of that Spanx canvas? To stop you 'spilling out', obviously. As an article in *Woman & Home* illustrated, there are myriad places that you could be 'spilling out', whether it's 'over the top', 'underneath', or merely 'out of the sides'. Whatever the question, the answer is always 'shapewear'.

There are different levels of 'shapewear' according to how much you hate your body, so you can choose to just 'boost' your bottom (seriously), 'flatten' your stomach, 'streamline' your thighs, or 'de-sag' your breasts – or, indeed, all of the above. That you're pretty much only allowed to have sex in the modern world if you're fully boosted, flattened, streamlined and de-sagged is in direct opposition to the fact that you're supposed to be permanently prancing around in jet black French knickers with bows on the back from a celebrity's new fashion line in Harrods. How on earth are you supposed to sport these completely unsexy perfection aids *and* wear the lingerie of the cheeky minx that you're expected to?

The truth is, of course, that no woman enjoys the feeling of her gall bladder migrating halfway across her body as she waddles through the room in a giant stretchy body sock (something to bear in mind next time you're watching the Oscars). Beneath the magnificent Dior

Couture and Oscar de la Renta, the red-carpet princesses all resemble a tapeworm inside a popsock. No wonder so many Hollywood actresses and pop stars opt to go commando when out for a night on the town, and all power to them. From experience, we're able to confirm that it is impossible to get out of a taxi without flashing your flange, even if you try it headfirst and there are no paparazzi in the bushes waiting to get a money shot for the tabloids.

5. The expectation that your boyfriend has better taste in underwear than you do

Undeterred by the knowledge that £100 million a year is wasted by men on unwanted lingerie, designers seem intent on foisting upon us the trashiest, cheapest, most uncomfortable smalls ever seen outside of a 'barely legal' show in Vegas. It's all very well dreaming of silk and satin scanties, but the fact of the matter is that a man's mucky mind is much more likely to conjure up a hot pink diamanté thong rather than anything from La Perla (just ask Rhiannon, who once made the mistake of going underwear shopping with an Italian man, and came home with just that), which is perhaps why so many of them find the whole lingerie-shopping experience so embarrassing (to the point where Victoria's Secret has had to install a special private room to help those who blush at the sight of a gusset). Meanwhile, women who might want to dress their men for bedroom antics are treated to rows and rows of 'comedy elephant trunk' pouched thongs and luminous mankinis, à la Borat. Talk about an unlevel playing field.

6. The way 'scientists' get creative with our bras and knickers

Every so often, a new 'miraculous' contraption comes along that just so happens to fit snugly into your cleavage or along your knicker line because, like, science. Examples include the anti-rape underwear ('AR

Wear') of 2013, a crowd-funded project on Indiegogo that claimed to create 'an effective barrier' to prevent sexual assault, and the 'smart bra' developed by Microsoft (also in 2013) that 'detects stress' with a strategically placed heart monitor and therefore 'could help prevent stress-related over-eating'. Forgive us if we don't jump enthusiastically on to the 'solve all society's problems through interesting additions to women's underwear' bandwagon.

7. Suspenders and the misfortunes they inevitably cause

Suspenders are amongst the most bizarre examples of underwear paraphernalia, not least because, in the age of hold-up stockings, they don't even serve much of a purpose any more. And if you haven't hooked yourself to the back of a restaurant chair on a date and dragged your romantic dinner off the table at least once, then count yourself luckier than at least three women we know. Suspenders have a funny way of suddenly deleting twenty minutes of your life as you vainly try to figure out which clip goes where. And all for a sticky-backed stocking to fall down your leg in the middle of the street while your boyfriend laughs. Many unfortunate women know from experience that these instruments of irritation never, *ever* lead to the sensual bedroom gambol that you envisioned, but almost *always* lead to something more akin to a sideshow sketch in a *Carry On* movie.

8. The apparent crimes of camel toe and VPL

Just when you'd discovered that VPL wasn't a sexually transmitted disease or a new kind of technological advancement, and had been instantly convinced that it was the most heinous crime since culpable homicide, camel toe came along. We were supposed to be anxious enough about whether or not anyone could see evidence of us actually wearing underwear, but then the age of going commando (prompted mostly by Paris Hilton and Lindsay Lohan getting out of taxis) meant that the shape of your fanny flaps might freak everyone out at the water cooler. Did everyone just chill out and maybe make the 'private-parts-covering' piece of women's clothing a little bit chunkier to avoid such fashion faux pas? Did they hell. This is where a staggeringly stupid invention like the SmoothGroove comes in: basically a plastic gum shield for your fanny lips, whose makers claimed that '55% of women will experience camel toe at some point'. The company even created a Pinterest board of camel-toe celebrity situations called 'Should have come to SmoothGroove'. Because there ain't nothing sexier than a giant plastic maxi-pad in your Spanx, and you don't want to be caught out with a VLL on your first date (visible labia line – what, you hadn't heard of that?). That old 'worrying rise in labiaplasty' had led to the demand for this vagina shoehorn, according to the SmoothGroove press release, which seemed to *kind of* imply that actually, if you're not on board with hiding your VLL just right, then you're going to be the odd one out any day now. The downside is that you're guaranteed never to be able to negotiate peeing while you're drunk in a nightclub again. Good luck out there, girls – at least no one will see your flaps through your leggings, even if there is a suspect puddle on the floor.

9. 'Subtle' bras that aren't really subtle, and 'matching sets' that only allow for one shape of woman

Stick-on cups, tit tape, transparent plastic backs and/or straps ('invisible', HA!), 'gel bras' or anything that calls itself an 'instant boob job': none of this so-called subtlety ever really works. Ever. Try getting yourself a matching set and you'll find out pretty quickly that big bras come with big pants; small bras come with small pants. If you have the audacity to want to pair up big bums and itty bitty titties, or massive ta-tas with very little junk in the trunk, then no dice, lady.

10. The way boxer shorts are comfortable, and pretty much everything on-trend for women makes your vagina feel sad

Everyone's extremely concerned about sperm count – in 2010, the media had become so hysterical about swimmers being destroyed by ball warmth that Holly's boyfriend was brought to tears by her inconsiderate decision to place her laptop in his lap – but nobody talks about the dangers of a perpetual wedgie. Have you ever picked up a particularly pretty piece in the lingerie department and exclaimed, 'This looks great. *And* really comfortable,' the way you might about a solid but beautiful pair of shoes? Of course you haven't, and that's because you know you're going to spend the next ten hours trying to dig those pants out of your arse crack without Matt from Accounts noticing. The same goes for anything from American Apparel. Much like that venerable country's politicians, they seem to just pick a side and stay there. Sperm are sacred, but the pH balance of your 'vajayjay' is something that can be brazenly altered as part of Ann Summers's sadistic games.

Of course, behind these nitpicky reasons for literally getting our knickers in a twist are a lot of historical reasons why we should keep talking about the material in which we clad our boobs and behinds. From those Victorian corsets that regularly rendered their wearers unconscious, to vending machines in Tokyo where girls can sell their used knickers to local businessmen, our underwear has always had to stand for something. It turns out that even bowing out of the game and dedicating your life to shapeless and sensible cotton hip-riders counts as making a statement. More than anything, however, this state of affairs draws attention to a huge collective feeling of boredom amongst moneyed capitalist societies with everything to market and nothing to say – therefore your bra must speak for you. And if you needed further proof of the conflation of your identity with your smalls, look no further than the 1978 magazine advert for a Warner's bra, which bore the infinitely depressing tagline 'It's not just a bra, it's you.'

6
Fashion and the Shoeniverse

GETTING IN WITH THE 'FASH PACK'

Shoes and shopping. From the evidence of billboards, fashion mags and sundry television programmes ranging from *Sex and the City* to *America's Next Top Model* to *Gossip Girl*, you'd think they were the twin pillars of female existence. We're surrounded by media implying that, if you're a woman, it's what you wear and not what you say that ultimately matters, and boy, do they start you young – just look at little Harper Beckham in her toddlership, hailed as a 'fashion icon' by *Grazia* before she had even mastered bowel control. That's right, folks: she may be shitting her pants but at least she's doing it in head-to-toe Gucci. While at its best fashion can be transformative, inspiring, and huge amounts of fun, you only need to take one look at catwalk shows and their accompanying displays of fashion designer one-upmanship to realise that the shoeniverse is also little bit off its head. And for an industry run largely by women *for* women, it can often feel as though it isn't really all that female-friendly at all. Especially when you're in a changing room trapped inside a sample-sized dress in an upside-down contortionist's pose with hot tears running down your face. Especially then.

As a privileged attendee of Fashion Week, you can witness all kinds of madness: young and beautiful people modelling mermaid-themed collections while being basically waterboarded on a transparent sheet of tarpaulin; trussed-up women dragging 400 lb puma skin evening gowns up and down escalators or through tube trains packed with commuters, and teenage girls in vertical shoes and bustles attempting to navigate impossible runways that are more akin to obstacle courses. One designer, undoubtedly popular with his employees, even set his models on fire for a 2008 fashion show. And you thought you were angry with your boss for that rubbish Christmas bonus.

Away from the eccentricity of the catwalk, there is a lot of money to be made in fashion, especially for the magazines that make it their USP. MediaGuardian 25, a survey of Britain's most important media companies, found that the magazine winners of 2013 were those touting high-end fashion: *Vogue* came storming in at the top, enjoying its most profitable year ever with the highest number of pages since the financial crash in 2008. Needless to say, most of these pages were filled with advertising – which explains why *Vogue* is doing so well financially, despite declining sales. Elsewhere, Hearst Magazines proudly announced that the total ad volume for *Elle*'s bumper March issue in 2013 was 216 out of 412 pages, meaning that over half of its content consisted of adverts. Hearst's other fashion baby, *Harper's Bazaar*, 'broke all records in its recent history' in 2013 by exceeding advertising revenue by 6% year on year. In other words, advertising is a major part – if not *the* major part – of reading a fashion magazine. As anyone who's spent twenty minutes trying to get to the contents page of *Tatler* will tell you, the sheer volume of advertising packs a punch in these mags. And apparently, we like it that way: 65% of readers view magazine adverts as essential to their reading (*Media*

Values, IPC), and research shows that magazine advertising is more likely to be used as a buying guide than advertising in any other media (*Ten Reasons to Advertise with Magazines,* PPA).

So if it works, and we like it, then where's the (hand-massaged, lean-cut) beef? For us, it's the message that, if you're not already worrying about your body, you'd better bloody be worrying about the garments you're using to hide it. Most fashion magazines offer up the kind of luxe status porn that provides a lovely, albeit brief, daydream of style and affluence, but which is nonetheless always followed by a sickly bitter aftertaste following the realisation that most of us will never, ever have that life. And yet they send the message that unless you fart Chanel No. 5, own the latest styles and drift around in a cloud of expensive chiffon, behaving as though you've just stepped off a Monaco yacht, then you just haven't got this 'being a woman' thing down. Though fashion itself is as old as the hills. Ever since cavepeople competed over who had the softest furry loincloth (probably), human beings have been using their clothes to express their personalities, wealth and social standing – it's hard not to notice how modern consumerism has perverted it to such an extent that we're all being told to look, think and act exactly the same way.

A woman in her eighties who approached us after a speaking event said exactly this. When she was a young woman, the biggest fashion faux pas she could imagine was turning up to a party in the same dress as a fellow guest. These days, everyone's got exactly the same 'must-have' Topshop jumper that *Glamour* told you to buy – or, if you went to private school and sport a name like Appollonia, the latest 'must-have' Mulberry bag straight from the pages of *Harper's.* Furthermore, we're expected to aspire to dress and behave like the women we're constantly exposed to in the media, whether it's 'style icons', socialites, celebrities or, most recently, fashion bloggers. Let's be honest: 'stealing George Clooney's style' isn't really an activity many men are encouraged to pursue. Nor are they informed in grave tones that Kanye's leather jogging bottoms are a 'must-have'. But from an industry that supposedly values women's individuality and creativity, everything looks suspiciously the same, and we've become a nation of style sheep running blindly around a field while the farmers sit back and enjoy the evening's entertainment (before fucking us). It makes you question just how much of your style can be attributed to personal preference and how much of it has been determined by advertisers and magazine staff who'd never dream of following suit.

It's ironic, considering how homogeneous everything has become, that we're still being encouraged to wear some seriously freaky stuff (those flesh-coloured Prada boots designed to look like legs come to mind), possibly dreamed up by people too weak with hunger to get to the end of their sentences. Hence the fash pack's 'totes pretensh' penchant for abbreviations and its use of the moniker 'darling'. But ravenous loons aside, fashion can, to the average woman, seem to be a dizzying mix of glamour and mystery; glamorous because the champagne parties are appealingly endless (not to mention free), and mysterious because you can't quite work out why anyone would go outside wearing moon boots, a swimming costume and a Cossack hat, or why everyone in the front row (sorry, 'frow') looks stylishly impassive as opposed to pissing themselves laughing.

Fashion can be many things, but it very rarely has a sense of humour, as demonstrated by Anna Wintour's permanent facial expression and anything Karl Lagerfeld says about anything, ever. Maybe this is why models such as Cara Delevingne – quite frankly a breath of fresh air, in this regard – have been able to build whole careers around their ability to pull silly faces as well as pout.

Fashion has lost its grip on reality in ways more frightening than not being able to take a joke: its often warped perspective has impacted the way we think about and treat our bodies, sometimes through very sinister means. This is a multibillion-pound business, and one which, rather unusually, is run by women and gay men. Which is why it stings that these queens of style don't seem to be on our side all that much. When they're not trying to con us into sporting a fetching culotte/ leotard combo, then they're telling us our cankles (a portmanteau term which reportedly originated in a 2003 issue of *Glamour*) are too big for their skintight suede jodhpurs, or that £5,000 on the latest (sh) it bag is a sensible investment. There's nothing wrong, of course, with being a feminist and liking fashion. Believing in gender equality and wanting to express yourself through clothes are not mutually exclusive. It's that sometimes, just sometimes, it can seem like the editorial staff, designers and PRs of the fashion world are actively conspiring against you, whether it's by making you look (and feel) like a twat, or by taking every last shred of confidence you had, cutting it up, and turning it into a size-zero jumpsuit.

Yes, the fashion industry and its advertising cronies have an alarming tendency to screw with your priorities, to the point where when asked, 'What's better in life than a new handbag?' (FYI this is a genuine question from the *Marie Claire* Twitter feed) you answer 'NOTHING!' rather than the real answer, which is of course, 'World peace, gender equality, and a nightly audience with Ryan Gosling.' Take it from us, once a wide-eyed waif of a fashion assistant has critically eyeballed you from head to toe as you chow down on your blueberry muffin before hastily gabbling 'I'm not judging you!', you stop bringing food into the office. After only a matter of hours in the industry your self-confidence has plummeted as low as your blood sugar (although at least you can comfort yourself with the knowledge that a diabetic coma provides a handy excuse for you to be fed via a drip without anyone asking too many questions).

Even when you're an intern, having someone yell: 'WE NEED SHOULDER PADS, NOW!' in your face with all the seriousness of a Foreign Office civil servant announcing the outbreak of war (and in such proximity that you can practically taste their herbal laxative tea) is something that, after a while, begins to mess with your head. It feasts on your brain in the same manner as a flesh-eating zombie (except, of course, this brand of zombie has the self-control to merely chew and spit you out afterwards in accordance with their latest 'mastication diet'), and eventually you start waking in the night, sitting bolt upright gasping for air and shrieking, 'CONTROL PANTS!' while your irritated boyfriend rolls away from the fleshless dagger points of your emaciated elbows and asks yet again when you're going to quit. Rhiannon, having spent her early twenties interning at fashion magazines, can testify to the fact that, alongside the genius artistic visionaries, undercover feminists and GNPs (genuine normal people), you will inevitably find the appearance-obsessed husks of human beings that, thanks to films such as *The Devil Wears Prada*, we have come to expect.

When she was allocated the task of locating a missing boot while at a photoshoot (as the model stood hopping and photo-ready while wearing its counterpart – no pressure), she spent the next two hours having a panic attack because a fashion PR exec had placed the boot on a scooter heading for the opposite side of London. And if the absence of one single accessory reducing a room full of adults to blind panic wasn't enough to put her off, there was always the colleague who complained that her addiction to chai latte was bankrupting her. 'Why not get a thermos?' Rhiannon asked, innocently. 'Oh, I have,' she replied, 'It's just that my bus route includes the King's Road and I don't want everyone to think I'm a chav.'

As someone who can't go without food for more than a couple of hours without turning into a raging bitch-monster, Rhiannon realised pretty sharpish that a fashion career wasn't for her. She emerged from the experience underweight, destitute, battle-weary, and subject to recurring nightmares in which she was ejected from Fenwick's for being too fat for Chanel (hand on heart, this is actually a frequent occurrence). She maintains that she loves fashion, but there are just too many things that drive her up the (Farrow & Ball) wall about it to make it a central part of her existence. From the size-zero epidemic and 'heroin chic' to the prepubescent and ever-younger 'fashion icons' who are emerging, photo-ready, from the womb rocking this summer's latest magenta placenta, the industry's gone badly wrong, and before we all get sucked into the lace-lined black hole and spat back out again as perfectly accessorised kindergartners, it's worth pointing out some of the more ridiculous notions it has bequeathed to us. Hold on to your A-line skirt suits, ladybros.

TOP TEN FRUSTRATING FASHION FAUX PAS, AS EXPERIENCED BY TWO AVERAGE SKINT YOUNG WOMEN WITH NORMAL-SIZED ARSES

1. I'm sorry, but I don't speak 'fashion'

Flick through a magazine such as *Look* (always a particularly good example of utter vapidity) and you'll notice how most of what they say is expressed in a kind of girlie gobbledygook indecipherable to your average woman (we like to call it 'twig Latin'). When the fash pack aren't busy spaffing on about how everything is 'totes amaze', 'delish', 'fabulous' and 'fierce', they're using baffling phrases such as 'tonal separates' and 'capsule piece'. *Grands dames* such as *Tatler*, *Vogue* and *Harper's Bazaar*, thankfully, always maintain a certain level of aristo-cratic detachment. It's the magazines lower down the food chain, such as as *Grazia*, *Glamour*, *Company* and *InStyle*, that talk about fashion in tones of breathless reverence or squealing enthusiasm (OMG! WANT!) that imply clothes actually *mean* something profound.

Hence a pair of leggings becomes an 'investment piece', a T-shirt is a 'wardrobe staple' and a skintight pleather graphic print catsuit becomes a 'must-have' or even a – shudder – 'lust-have'. And let's not forget the tendency of fashion journalists to use singular terms for plural items, so instead of 'statement heels' and 'casual trousers' you get 'statement *heel*' and 'casual *trouser*', and all the while you're sitting there thinking: 'WHAT ABOUT MY OTHER LEG, GODDAMMIT?!' and wondering if you've entered a twilight zone of idiocy. Which, of course, you have. In fact, part of the reason so many women love the actress Jennifer Lawrence is her absolute refusal to inhabit that twilight zone by speaking twig Latin. When a TV presenter asked her at the Oscars what 'pieces' she was wearing, she innocently retorted, 'What do you mean? Like, this is the top, and this is the bottom.' Our kind of woman.

2. Bond Street is not a high street

Don't you just love it when a magazine or newspaper supplement shows you a picture of a gorgeous dress, only for you to note that it retails at an eye-wateringly expensive three grand? And that's when they've bothered to show the price tag. The higher-end magazines often just put 'price on application', which we all know means 'Not for the likes of *you*, plebeian scum.' It bags costing enough to feed a small family for a week will still be hailed as a 'bargain' because hey, it's not like you need to eat, is it? Is it? And that's before you even get to the next level; Hermès bags have their own waiting lists and cost upwards of ten grand. To quote the incredible Nora Ephron, author of such seminal essays as 'I Hate My Purse': 'On the waiting list! For a purse! For a $10,000 purse that will end up full of old Tic Tacs!'

Then again, the more you spend on clothes and accessories, the less you spend on carbs and therefore the more likely you are to fit into those tiny silk hotpants that the Rich Kids of Instagram are wearing this season. What do you mean you need to pay rent? You can sleep under your fur in a supermarket skip, darling. 'Hey, it's OK that your only investments are hanging in your wardrobe!' squeals *Glamour*. But is that really OK?

What's more, any fashion magazine claiming to be putting out a 'high street' issue will still only feature the most expensive shops, such as Reiss and Whistles, and a few pages later will inevitably get distracted and start gushing about Miu Miu again. Because although they claim to listen to their readers, they still seem to assume that you're reading their rag from a yoga retreat in the Maldives, or, having it read *to you* in the sauna by your personal secretary/slave while he or she brings you to orgasm with a solid gold loofah. What's even more hypocritical in this mindset is that most of the journalists writing the content are being paid shockingly low wages – if they're being paid at all. We all know how fashion loves an unpaid intern: *Company* magazine once cajoled their fashion writer into producing one of the most insulting articles of all time, entitled 'How to be a good intern', which cautioned readers to think of lengthy unpaid internships in fashion and fashion journalism (technically illegal but prevalent, we might add, in the good old UK) as 'free training, rather than, say, slave labour'; this in the same breath as recommending that the intern learn how everyone in the office has their coffee and file this vital information next to their individual phone numbers. Knowing who has their decaf soy latte at 4 p.m. hardly seems like training you couldn't get for minimum wage at Starbucks, so *Company* pretty much shot themselves in the foot with that one – not that we're likely to see them change their payment policy any time soon. As a friend of ours who recently quit fashion to become an estate agent said, 'I'd like to actually be able to afford the clothes.' Which brings us to our next point.

3. *They don't actually wear the clothes*

You know that ugly lilac coat the fashion people are constantly telling you to buy? The faux fur one with the metal studs? They'd never wear it in a million years. The only reason it's been featured in their 'ten hot items' section is because the hack owed the PR a favour. Sometimes they'll even acknowledge that a trend is slightly dubious and start tittering, 'We know it's wrong, but we want it anyway . . .' (Subtext: Buy the knee warmers, you gullible fool, I want more freebies.) The dishonesty of it all is palpable: nowhere is it more obvious that what masquerades as content for women is really just a dumbed-down pamphlet heavily influenced by marketing than in the fashion media. It's the same with those annoying 'Street Style' features (we're looking at you, *Grazia*) which imply that the whole country is populated by designer-clad, stylishly casual trust fund twiglets ('Oh, we just *happened* to bump into Arabella Whittington-Starley-Moncrieff looking effortlessly chic in Croydon of all places'), when in reality it's a stupid, fake set-up engineered by journalists to give their overprivileged young friends and relatives another little nepotistic thrill. And that's because . . .

4. *They think you're an idiot*

Thought you could dress yourself? Think again, shitmuncher. From that 'How to wear' feature (see: every fashion magazine ever) it's obvious that fashion editors think you can't even put on a pair of trousers without their assistance. If they could have their way, they'd break into your house and burn all your clothes, because they basically think you're a baboon in a dress. This is why they'll show you a picture of a celebrity wearing jeans and a T-shirt and tell you to 'get the look', with appropriate replacements from the high street helpfully attached. Consider that online clothes retailer ASOS's market dominance stemmed from its marketing of celebrity looks (it stands for the long-forgotten 'As Seen On Screen'). And, if the celeb isn't wearing the industry-approved ensemble that advertisers want you to buy into, there's always the clothes-shaming feature where fashionistas pick apart some poor celebrity's red-carpet appearance because she dared to pair a navy necklace with *clearly aquamarine shoes. Grazia* is a great one for this. Its weekly bitch-fest 'You, the Fashion Jury' sees a panel of experts and one reader annihilate a woman in the public eye because of her fashion choices, damning her with faint praise and words such as 'unflattering' and 'frumpy'. Examples include such bitchy 'witticisms' as Florence Welch being described as looking like 'a doll that's been dressed by a child in clothes made from a duvet bought in a house sale', Heidi Klum being slated for failing to match her genetics to her dress ('a pity Ms Klum has hazel and not azure eyes') and Rita Ora being told that she looks like she's starring in 'the new Harry-Potter-inspired video by Prince' (er, sounds awesome to us). It's all part of this myth that fashion is an exclusive club as well as being an esoteric, difficult-to-master discipline in which one must try hard to become an 'expert'.

Because of your fashion ignorance, magazines think it's their job to mummy you through every conceivable scenario you might experience – from what to wear on a date (red, tight), to what to wear for a 'meet the parents dinner' (three-piece suit to demonstrate your serious side; dominatrix heels to show that your bedroom skills are up to producing the family's next heir). And yet, while they'll always tell you what to wear on a spa retreat or a show at London Fashion Week, they'll never tell you what to wear at times when some wardrobe advice might actually be pretty useful, such as giving evidence in court, going up the job centre, or attending the funeral of someone you didn't know well because of their very attractive and newly single grieving spouse. And that's because they're too busy trying to convince you that 'shopping' is a leisurely pastime we're all supposed to bond over. But the fact of the matter is that . . .

5. Shopping is not a hobby

When they're not berating you for owning the wrong kind of plain white T-shirt, fashion magazines are busily engaged in trying to convince you that fashion should be your life, and that your life, in turn, should be fashion. Choosing which on-trend leather flying jacket to 'invest' in this season is pitched as a decision akin to Sophie's Choice with serious, potentially life-threatening repercussions (despite the fact that by next year it'll be totes passé). This capitalist correlation between what you wear and your very existence – the clothes you wear become, on some level, you – goes some way to explaining the strange phenomenon that's emerged in the last few years of treating shopping as a hobby. What once used to be more of an everyday errand has now become a worthy pastime in which women can engage. This is no thanks to lifestyle porn such as Sophie Kinsella's novel-turned-romcom *Confessions of a Shopaholic*, structured reality shows such as *The Hills*, *Real Housewives* and *Made in Chelsea*, and that pesky, persistent notion that one has to look 'fierce' at all times of the day and night (we blame supermodel TV mogul Tyra Banks for this – a crime on a par with the myth she perpetuated that it is possible to 'smile with your eyes and not your mouth', or 'smise').

Yes, shopping can be fun, but as most women will tell you, it can also be a tedious, stressful experience that tests your mental health and self-esteem to the limits. Enough of us have returned home with armfuls of shopping bags and collapsed into an armchair breathing heavily, a traumatised look on our face to rival that of a veteran who has seen action in 'Nam, to know that shopping is by no means a constant merry-go-round of super-fun funsies, nor a form of therapy, nor a replacement for more meaningful cultural activities such as going to an art gallery or bitching about your job over pastries. Indeed, trying to find a pair of the latest velvet jeggings in Topshop on a Saturday afternoon is more akin to Dante's vision of Hell than a chilled-out weekend excursion. Meanwhile, we've all managed to convince ourselves at least once that a jaunt down to Primark will be perfectly lovely, never mind that it usually ends with a near fist-fight in the queue for the last designer-copycat crop top: the opening of a new Primark store on Oxford Street in London in 2007 saw 3,000 people stampede into the store at opening time. When the carnage couldn't be controlled by the fifty security staff already hired to quell the chaos, police officers on horseback rode in to help shoppers who had been thrown to the ground and trampled by their fellow bargain-hunters.

Just as strangely, magazines have started treating shopping as a formative experience akin to losing your virginity or graduating college; a feature in *InStyle* called 'My life on the high street' even had celebrities indulging in misty-eyed, nostalgic reminiscence about the first pair of jeans they had ever bought. Seriously.

6. Clothes maketh not the woman

When you're not being reduced to tears of joyful reminiscence by the thought of your first ever trouserskirt, it's important to be constantly aware of what message your clothes could be revealing about the inner workings of your personality. (Does that kaftan say 'charming ingénue' or 'member of the Manson family?') It's a good thing we have articles such as 'What your party outfit says about you', then, to show us the ropes. *Not*. And delightfully for us, the sage advice of style 'experts' has increasingly been replaced by exactly what young men in their twenties think about the top you squeezed your knackers into on a Saturday morning when everything else was in the wash (because we dress completely for men – didn't you get that memo?).

Said young men take to this daunting task of contributing to features with such erudite titles as 'Men vs fashion' with all the seriousness of a Booker Prize judging panel, pontificating needlessly on some poor victim's outfit choice and psychoanalysing her tit tape without even giving her the courtesy of a right to reply. 'You can tell from her cleavage that this girl likes to party and is wild in the bedroom,' Jason, 23, from Husbands Bosworth will grin, when in fact Mandy is a virgin who hates social gatherings and simply paid too much attention to *Elle*'s assertion that 'the nineteenth-century French courtesan trend is really in this season'. Of course, you'd never get a bunch of feckless twats commenting on some poor bloke's sartorial choices in the same way in a men's magazine, probably because the statement 'The fact that he is wearing bootcut jeans means he must be excellent at cunnilingus' is not something that anyone would say, ever.

7. They want you to buy into bizarro trends

Whether it's 'luxe military', 'geisha oriental' or 'nautical seafarer', fashion magazines will try to convince you to buy into some (probably offensive) trend or another, despite the fact that, in reality, they run in five-year cycles and if you hold on to your old shit long enough then those space-age shoulder pads will eventually look up-to-the-moment once more. The fact that fashion is tediously predictable remains, amazingly, one of its best-kept secrets, even though spring inevitably means florals, while anything hitting the shops around Christmas will have so much blingy diamanté attached to it that it will look as though its been spaffed on by Liberace. Fashion constantly tries to disguise the formulaic nature of its output by throwing in the odd 'statement piece' and disguising the trend with a different name. Last year's 'glam goth' becomes this year's 'Victoriana', 'utility' becomes 'military', and 'masculine' becomes 'lesbian' (we're not kidding: according to Style.com, 'lesbian chic' was all the rage in August 2012. Who knew what you did with your genitals could hold so much cachet on the fashion circuit?).

8. They have the tact of a dead donkey

As the ongoing 'lesbian trend' demonstrates, fashion is known for many things, but its sensitivity to political correctness is not one of them. While telling us to 'channel our inner 1950s housewife' (presumably by popping a Valium and screwing the milkman with the lights off) can't be seen as too 'ridic', sometimes the names of these trends can be a real kick in the teeth for ethnic minorities (see the aforementioned 'oriental') who, weirdly, may take offence at their entire culture being reduced to a fashion stereotype. Just look at the Navajo trend. Every time a magazine describes a trend as 'Red Indian' while offering up the latest fringed moccasins by Kurt Geiger, they are essentially taking a dump from a massive height on thousands of people with Native American heritage who suffered and are still suffering at the hands of colonial settlers, and all because some socialite heiress put a feather in her hair when she was coked up at Soho House. If you think that's bad, then allow us to present you with Exhibit B, namely that occasion in 2011 where Italian *Vogue* tipped 'slave earrings' (normal hoop earrings to anyone else) as the hot new trend. And while we're on the topic of fashion's failure to speak to anyone who isn't Caucasian, can we please address the 'nude' trend? As one of our Twitter followers pointed out: 'YOUR NUDE DOESN'T NECESSARILY MEAN MY NUDE.'

American *Vogue* in particular has a reputation for tone-deaf editorials, perhaps most famously with their Hurricane Sandy 'Storm Troupers' photo spread, which showed real members of the emergency forces posing with models in couture. Other tactless turkeys include Italian *Vogue*'s 2007 'Make love not war' story, which attempted to sex up the conflict in Iraq by showing models straddling topless soldiers and was described by a British broadsheet as looking like 'prostitutes brought to an army camp as entertainment'. That's before we even get to discussing *Vogue* Germany's infamous attempt at 'homeless chic', French *Vogue* putting Lara Stone in blackface, and US *Vogue*'s 'Rose in the Desert' shoot with Syrian dictator Bashar al-Assad's wife, Asma al-Assad.

Of course, it's important for any art form to push boundaries, but, for a magazine industry that already fails to represent the racial and physical diversity of its readers, these examples of cultural insensitivity don't give us much hope for the future. Nor does the glamorisation of violence, disaster and oppressive regimes. Is it only a matter of time before *Vogue* announces that it's 'channelling political prisoners' and that 'this vintage trench coat and complementary furry hat are the perfect attire for when you're trying to escape from the Eastern Bloc while being chased by the Stasi'? Still, never mind – provided you keep hold of them, you'll be bang on trend come the next Ice Age and *Elle*'s spin-off 'Climate Change Apocalypse' issue.

9. *The clothes make you look bonkers*

Of course, to our eternal credit, most women dismiss 90% of these fly-by-night fashion trends out of hand, which is why you hear so many of us shrieking, 'What kind of bell-end would wear that?' in the middle of River Island. You may recall the fashion industry's conspiracy to get us to wear floral trousers and 're-imagined' neon platform trainers a while back, trends which had such little uptake that the only people wearing them were teenage fashion victims who looked like 1980s children's TV presenters on the run from a Channel 5 documentary about people who form meaningful relationships with inanimate objects. And although you'll occasionally spot the odd fashion victim fearlessly working a pair of gingham knickerbockers, despite what fashion magazines might think, most of the population aren't dense enough to buy something that makes them look totally crap and/or entirely lacking in self-awareness.

It's a hard truth to learn that something built to look good on a 7-foot-tall Russian 15-year-old probably isn't going to look good on you. Fashion magazines will tell you to 'celebrate your curves' before making you flick through a shoot comprised solely of painfully thin models, and they are *always* trying to 'teach' you how to dress for your shape by categorising you as an apple, a pear, or a sodding butternut squash (and that's the polite ones – one issue of *Jackie* bluntly asked its readership, 'Are you a skinny, a normal, or a fatty?'). Despite this need to divide and conquer, the simple fact remains that if you're in possession of tits, then what they'll tell you to wear, every single time, guaranteed, is a wrap dress.

Nevertheless, magazines such as *Woman & Home* and *Good Housekeeping* are intent on forcing you to 'flatter your shape'. 'Upper arms are nearly every woman's weakness in summer,' instructs the former, as you look at your perfectly normal sized arms and, trying to hold back tears, head for the 'bikini cover-up' (the summer equivalent of the wrap dress) aisle.

And even a boring old wrap dress is likely to be subject to some kind of wacky fashion influence. We've lost count of the times that we've heard women in shops sighing heavily before uttering the words, 'Well,

I could always just cut out the shoulder pads', or being forced to buy jeans with diamanté studs on the pockets which they'll then pick at for weeks, all the while hoping that the bastard things will just drop off the trousers and hopefully the planet.

10. You're never really comfortable

When you're a teenager, and therefore precisely the person the fashion industry is targeting 99.9% of the time the ridiculousness of a fashion trend isn't really a concern. The more impractical your mum thinks it is, the better. In fact, if the whole fashion industry were controlled by teenage girls then those 'winter wonderland' shoots in which a bare-legged model poses seductively in a pompom hat while failing miraculously to contract hypothermia would make a lot more sense. Examples from our readers have included persistent thrush from the 'shorts, tights and French knickers' trend (an unholy trinity if ever there was one); a 'genius' stick-on bra falling off at an extremely posh charity ball; and a pair of 32 in. flares wrapping themselves around one woman's legs as she crossed the road, tripping her over and propelling her into the pathway of an oncoming car (which stopped just in time).

And let's not forget high heels, or tools of the patriarchy, as Ms Greer would have it. They're becoming more and more impossible to walk in, and at their worst can cause you to trip and fall to your death in a stairwell. They're not great when you need to get anywhere fast, either, and, in Holly's case, they damn well ruined a country walk by reducing her to the unwitting prisoner of a cattle grid. And that's without mentioning those women who recommend taking two ibuprofen before hitting the town to offset the pain of particularly punishing heels. Yet the fashion industry is especially keen for us to continue wearing them. We're supposed to stand by and nod sagely as study after study is vomited out by the bulimic world of fashion PR asserting that women can't get respect in the workplace unless they're six foot tall. Or we're expected to pour our money into such ridiculous concoctions as the Tamara Mellon 'Sweet Revenge leather legging boots' being pushed by Net-a-Porter in the winter of 2013, described as a 'standout creation' where the 'thigh boot pulls right up into a legging'. Yes, these are high heels with trousers attached. And FYI, they cost £1,595.

Elsewhere, let's not forget that tabloids took great delight in 2011 in reporting what Christian Louboutin reckoned to women wearing heels. Apparently, by slipping your dainty little foot into a delicately arched frame, presumably as you let out a little moan of ecstasy at the supple qualities of the reindeer leather (sorry, Rudolph), you are putting yourself 'in a possibly orgasmic situation'. Clearly, Christian has never been over at ours on a Saturday night, when we've grunted, sworn, and used frighteningly large plastic implements to bring ourselves to the painful stiletto climax of *just getting the damn things on*.

So, while of course you can be a feminist and wear high heels, it would be quite nice if they could be made a little less impractical and a lot more comfortable. Matters are not helped by the market appeal of It bags, which you're supposed to hang stiffly on the crook of your arm – despite the fact that they get heavier each season, and now rival blinged-up baby elephants whose brass addenda just add to the likelihood of one losing one's balance. As the aforementioned Nora Ephron pointed out, a bag like this 'immobilises half your body' – a body which should be free to do all manner of other things, like dancing, running, collapsing on the floor in fits of laughter, and hiding from your friends in large super-markets while getting them to announce that 'Mummy's waiting by the customer service desk' over the tannoy.

But then, that's fashion: totally useless when it comes to everyday life, even when it comes to getting off (and we're not counting those vibrating knickers that connect to your iPod). If you took serious notes, you could easily end up shivering in the corner of Mahiki with a cheap version of Lady Gaga's 'meat dress' attached to your huddled frame with a tired roll of tit tape, wondering why no one wants to join you on the dance floor. The truth is, shedding ragged bits of bacon rind into a hot guy's champagne probably isn't going to get you a second date with him (or your girlfriends). Nor is accidentally sending a sausage flying off your necklace during a particularly enthusiastic fist-pump. So why do the powers-that-be in the fashion world keep insisting that what's totally incompatible with the reality of anyone's life (not to mention potentially regrettable) is also totally cool? And if fashion is so fun then how come it causes us so much grief?

Not that we haven't been victim to funny flights of fashion fancy ourselves. You, like us, might find your way to a pair of disco knickers one day, reclining seductively in a prominent display. 'These seem, in context, to be items of actual clothing,' you might then think to yourself 'I could saunter off to the changing rooms and give them a cheeky try.' But have you ever tried on a pair of disco knickers? Holly has, and her mother's rather candid response – 'I like them. I mean, I like the fact that they'd look great if you had longer legs, a tan, and no fat on your thighs' – was pretty much par for the course (and marginally nicer than the follow-up, a few months later: 'I was beautiful at your age. I looked just like your cousin'). Disco knickers are almost guaranteed to look bad, and that's because they are basically Pampers Easy-Ups with sequins stuck on, implying that the fashionistas of this world have found it necessary to prepare you for an imminent second babyhood. Alongside the re-emerging trend for playsuits, you could be forgiven for believing that there's an industry-wide regression conspiracy going on. Hold on to your disco nappies, because shit is about to get creepy.

THINK OF THE CHILDREN

Oh, the 'fashion icon': that woman in our lives that every magazine imagines 'inspires' our 'look', and who never, ever exists. In every insipid quiz, the question about your 'fashion icon' will inevitably arise. She is the idol that feature writers suppose you have. It's par for the course that you'll have a spiritual affiliation with the way some unsuspecting celebrity 'rocks a trend', and it's supposed to say something deep about your personality. While it's true that fashion can be a means of creative and personal expression, it's also a hell of a lot of pressure to live up to an 'icon' with an entourage of professional stylists and a habit of being photographed on the red carpet after about seven hours' collaborative preparation, rather than in the student union after seven hours of 'mystery shots'. And that's before you even get to the benefits of Photoshop which, let's face it, could work wonders on that hangover if you had it at your disposal, feminism aside. (We sympathised when Tina Fey wrote, 'I feel about Photoshop the way some people feel about abortion. It is appalling and a tragic reflection on the moral decay of our society . . . unless I need it, in which case, everybody be cool.') If you lack your icon's access to Photoshop, however, you can kiss goodbye to popping down the corner shop in trackie bottoms for a bag of junk food.

Disturbingly, fashion icons have become younger and younger as time has gone by, and the five-page spread on the celebrity's toddler isn't a figment of our imagination: it's something that we've seen with our own eyes in magazines intended for grown-up women. Meanwhile, one quick search of the *Daily Mail*'s infamous online catalogue of celebrity stories shows a vomit-worthy amount of 'all grown up' or 'coming of age' photos – mainly child stars who have just turned 16 and are now officially legal to perv over, in case you were wondering – but also an unnerving number of 'jailbait' photographs of scantily clad girls who are still technically children, accompanied by icky descriptions of how some supermodel's eight-year-old daughter has 'lithe limbs just like her mother'. (At the time of writing, the *Mail Online* boasted 1,060 articles about Suri Cruise, the eight-year-old daughter of Tom Cruise and Katie Holmes.) When they're still being potty-trained, however, they feature instead as fashion accessories or 'mini me' accompaniments to stylish celebrities: a 2013 Givenchy campaign ran adverts with model Mariacarla Boscono clutching her baby daughter in lieu of a handbag, while *Grazia* ran an article in October 2013 titled 'Kim Kardashian says North's designer wardrobe is as big as hers'. This was when her daughter North was four months old.

Outside of tabloid paradise, tweenagers now often turn up in catwalk clothes and heels during 'tasteful' mag shoots, photographers pursue the children of celebrities as much as the celebrities themselves, and the clothes we wear have started looking more and more as if they were bought from Barbie's Princess Fairy Dust Magical Sparkle Super Girlie Unicorn Palace. Considering that young girls are often brought up on a media diet of *Disney Princess* magazine (the 'how to be a princess' manual with a target demographic of 3–10 years old), followed by *DYOU* (Disney's follow-up mag for 10–14-year-olds, promising 'Celebs – Gossip – Fashion'), and then are catapulted headfirst into the land of *Teen Vogue* and its eye-watering price tags, it should come as little wonder to us that the lines between childhood and adulthood are some of the most blurred you'll ever come across in fashion. One day you might walk in after work, wearing your kitten-print tutu with a bow in your hair, slip off the ballet shoes and skirt to reveal your entirely hairless body as your boyfriend calls you 'baby girl', and start wondering if it's all gone a bit Benjamin Button in here.

If you're modelling your look on the latest addition to Celebrity X's perfectly manicured brood, then you couldn't be any closer to setting yourself up for a fall. While it's well known that the fashion industry has a chronic fear of ageing – rumour has it that some Hollywood starlets have been advised to book in their 'preemptive Botox appointments' by the age of 18 – the focus on youth at all costs has gone positively fetishistic in the last few years. The popularity of child models prompted Condé Nast International to release a statement in 2012 that *Vogue* would stop using models under the age of 16 (one of their most contro- versial shoots had featured a fashion spread with ten-year-old French model Thylane Lena-Rose Blondeau sprawled seductively across a leopard-print bedspread in heels and lipstick). And New York fashion week promised in 2011 to leave the under-16s off the catwalk, but many designers flouted their own bans. A friend of ours who worked as a model was scouted at 13, and told at 15, when she developed hips, that she no longer had 'the right look'. That is not uncommon within the industry. Elsewhere, model Lily Cole posed, pigtails and all, in a Lolita-esque photoshoot for *Playboy* which had her hugging a giant pink teddy bear on the cover and seductively licking a giant lollipop inside. Whether you think it's a disgusting sexualisation of children or a disgraceful infantilisation of women, or a little bit of both, it ain't good news for the ladies. Ten-year-olds need a childhood, and twenty-, thirty- and forty-year-olds need examples of actual womanhood to get on board with. After all, the iconic billboard of David Beckham in his smalls didn't feature him draped across a SpongeBob SquarePants poster with an Action Man dangling from his boxer elastic.

Fashion's childhood-chasing epidemic can be seen as part of the reason why 'size-zero chic' became 'totes cool' at the turn of the millennium, when LA based stylist Rachel Zoe pioneered the 'boho- bird' look epitomised by waifs Nicole Richie and Mischa Barton, relying on supersize accessories such as bug-eyed sunglasses and enormous handbags to make the stars in question look even tinier and more bird-like. The sight of those sticklike limbs protruding from billowing sleeves, those brittle wrists and protruding ribs, led some of the more enlightened media moguls to start questioning whether enforced starvation might count as bad workplace etiquette and even to begin petitioning for boring old health standards. As Alexandra Shulman, the editor of UK *Vogue,* pointed out, part of the blame lay with designers, who made the sample sizes of their clothes so small that fully grown women with normal bodies were unable to fit into them. But if these clothes barely fit anyone at all, why *are* they being made that way?

Take a glimpse at any beloved piece of artwork from the Renaissance onwards – Rubens is a prominent example – and voluptuous women are the definite epitome of beauty. The 'perfect ten' wasn't really on the menu before the twentieth century, back when everyone lazed around not giving a shit about their thunder thighs or bingo wings, clearly *hoping* that their bum looked big in this. Adverts as late as the 1950s even encouraged women to gain weight, carrying slogans such as 'If you want to be popular, you can't afford to be skinny' (an endorsement ad with actor Linda Peck claiming that 'so many Hollywood girls depend on' a weight gain supplement called

Wate-On), 'Skinny girls are not glamour girls' (this for Kelp-A-Malt tablets, which promised to 'add 5 lb of solid flesh in a week'), and 'Men wouldn't look at me when I was skinny . . . but since I gained 10 pounds

this new, easy way, I have all the dates I want.' Admittedly, these aren't exactly positive messages in themselves. However, they do illuminate how strange it is that the second half of the twentieth century saw the media pursuing fat cells with the fervour of a torch-carrying mob chasing out the resident Frankenstein's monster.

Why did the tide suddenly turn? The generations who stood in ration queues and subsisted on thin, bland food during the Second World War and immediately afterwards knew that being called 'round' or 'filled-out' was a compliment because it implied you could could afford better portions and expensive cuts of meat. Their legacy lived on during the careers of models like Marilyn Monroe and Sophia Loren, but it began to die when their children – the baby boomers – came into power. Baby boomers had known lives of plenty, and thinness soon became a badge of sophistication and restraint, rather than poverty and hunger. A delicate woman was expected to prove her self-control by picking at tiny plates of walnut salad and was supposed to look like a beautiful, precious, tiny doll next to her burly husband. The age of Marilyn was long gone; Twiggy became the new ideal.

Of course, those least likely to be in possession of fat cells are prepubescent girls. Fashion insiders will argue that an extremely lithe frame 'makes the clothes hang better', which doesn't make much sense when you consider that *they made the clothes that way in the first place*. Clothes designed for thin women are going to look better on thin women, but this is an industry that is supposed to be catering to *all different kinds* of women, and if a large proportion of them are being excluded on the basis that their bums and boobs are incompatible with the wearing of clothes then something has gone badly wrong.

If you don't think that's dark enough, consider what the models themselves have said about the industry that made them. Kate Moss famously admitted in a candid *Vanity Fair* interview that she wept after being coerced into posing topless for style magazine *The Face* early on in her career, saying, 'I see a 16-year-old now, and to ask her to take her clothes off would feel really weird. But they were like, 'If you don't do it, then we're not going to book you again.' So I'd lock myself in the toilet and cry and then come out and do it.' She also detailed a breakdown she suffered at age 17 after her famous Calvin Klein campaign, which featured her semi-naked on top of a male model, admitting, 'It didn't feel like me at all. I felt really bad about straddling this buff guy. I didn't like it. I couldn't get out of bed for two weeks. I thought I was going to die.' Moss's interview is one of the most disturbing indictments of the modelling industry to date, yet the incidents she describes happened at the same time as male journalists were holding her up as a symbol of the euphoria of the 1990s. They certainly don't come across as all that 'euphoric', nor does a scared child who was bullied by powerful people at her most vulnerable fit with the media ideal of Mossy: a strong, hard-partying goodtime gal from Croydon who made it big and got to shag Johnny Depp.

While national papers and fashion rags alike will tell you that they condemn this sort of behind-the-scenes behaviour, their protestation often rings hollow. A *Guardian* investigation into the presentation of girls in fashion mentioned a child beauty pageant that had been 'covered enthusiastically by many of the tabloids', with editorial that paid lip service to criticising the parade of made-up babies placed alongside lots of close-up photographs. A subheading from *The Sun* on a heavily illustrated piece summarises the situation pretty clearly: 'CAVORTING provocatively in a tiny pink swimsuit and clutching a cuddly stuffed kitten, little Ocean Orrey struts her stuff in a British beauty pageant – aged just FOUR.' The *Mail*, meanwhile, campaigns against child sexualisation while simultaneously publishing photos of tweenage girls in their swimming costumes, seemingly seeing no contradiction in the fact that it loathes child porn but is at the same time providing what could be argued is an instruction manual for perverts. We're now in the age of fashion accessories for, quite literally, baby girls – which perhaps is a natural progression from media frenzies over the coveted 'first baby photos' of celebrities' children. Products like 'Girlie Glue' (strapline: 'It's never too early to be Girlie!') encourage you to glue felt flowers to your baby's head. Yes, really. Perhaps it's only a matter of time before we switch their nappies for control pants. After all, baby fat has no place in fashion, does it?

ONE SIZE FITS ALL

Over the past three decades, the fashion industry's obsession with youth, and the slimness that goes with it, has become increasingly noticeable, as has the number of pro-anorexia or 'pro-ana' websites (a term which refers to a cyber-movement encouraging starvation behaviour and sharing tips on how to hide eating disorders from friends and family) inspired by it. While fashion designers snapped their tape measures and slyly told some models that they were bordering on 'plus size' if they dared to balloon to a size 12, 'eating is cheating' became a well-known mantra. The toothbrush down the throat in a high-society nightclub became so openly acknowledged that it was parodied in a music video by P!nk called 'Stupid Girls'; meanwhile, tales of models eating tissue paper to fill their stomachs and scouts targeting anorexia clinics in search of new meat were leaked to the media. After this baptism of fire, it's fair to say that we were all dragged kicking and screaming into an awareness of the shady world of thinspiration and exploitation.

If you've ever lost a vicious battle with a pair of American Apparel's size-small high-waisted leggings, or bitten back tears in a changing room because the sadistic bra-sizer insists that you're a 36A rather than a 32D, we hear you, sister. You may have just mastered the art of looking your naked body square in the areolas with pride, unflattering lighting and all, after years of thigh/bum/calf/boob/shoulder/neck anxiety (yes, neck anxiety. Holly once even googled 'neck liposuction' at a particularly low point), but a trip down the high street probably won't make it all better. Shop sizing no longer makes any coherent sense whatsoever: while designer gear tends to err on the small side (surprise, surprise) and budget stores conserve their fabric, many high street names practise 'vanity sizing', so a Dorothy Perkins size 10 might end up being a Gaultier size 16, and all the while you probably look about a 12 but your confidence is constantly yo-yoing between 'sky-high elation' and 'torn to shreds'. Men's sizing is generally far more predictable – it's hard to manipulate a 32 in. leg – whereas women's sizing can feel like an act of psychological warfare. The UK and US don't have standardised female sizes, so it opens the gates for pretty much anyone to play merry hell with your head while you're desperately trying to work out if your bum is too big (diet) or too small (implants, padded knickers) in that pair of drainpipes. And amongst this plethora of mixed messages, it's apparently a mystery why so many young women suffer from body dysmorphia.

Anorexia has the highest mortality rate of any psychiatric disorder, from suicide as well as health complications, so it's obvious that fat is a feminist issue – and at least some of the blame rests with the fash pack. Ex-supermodel Janice Dickinson, of *America's Next Top Model* fame, has been controversially candid about her management techniques, saying, 'I've got 42 models in my agency and I'm trying to get them to lose weight. In fact, I wish they'd come down with some anorexia. I'm not kidding. I'm running into a bunch of fat-assed, lazy little bitches who don't know how to do the stairs or get their butts into the gym.' Meanwhile, it was Kate Moss who popularised the phrase 'Nothing tastes as good as skinny feels', so beloved of pro-anorexia websites. It doesn't take a genius to realise that if girls under the age of 18 enter an industry where knees that you can inflict stab wounds with are prized over roast dinners, they're vulnerable to developing unhealthy eating habits – and if the rest of us attempt to base ourselves on their waif-like bodies, we are likely to develop unhealthy eating habits ourselves. While fashionistas are quick to remind us that a definitive causal link has never been established between their industry and psychological problems in society, many women who have suffered from body dysmorphia and eating disorders have said otherwise, and admitted to actively using images in the media as a stimulus for starving themselves. On thinspiration and pro-anorexia websites, pictures of fashion models abound; their precarious frames and delicate bones are decorated with slogans such as 'Eating isn't very Chanel' (nor is being hospitalised, though). A young thinspiration blogger who was interviewed by *The Atlantic* said that the majority of the images come from modelling portfolios and fashion adverts for brands such as Victoria's Secret. The link between fashion imagery and eating disorders is clear.

In 2007, the late model Isabelle Caro committed herself to a campaign across Italy called 'No Anorexia', which showed her naked, emaciated body in painful detail on a giant billboard, making a powerful statement about the portrayal of women's bodies during Milan Fashion Week. Controversially the campaign was banned because of these harrowing images, but Caro's legacy remains, including her assertion that the fashion world had in part contributed to her demise. 'I thought this could be a chance to use my suffering to get a message across, and finally put an image on what thinness represents and the danger it leads to, which is death,' she said. She wanted 'to make people react, for young girls to see this and think: Oh, so that's what lies behind the beautiful clothes, the hair, the image that we are shown of fashion'. The industry, with its demands to emulate a singular ideal, had literally handed Caro herself a death sentence, and she succumbed to her eating disorder at the end of 2010, aged just 28.

The lack of body diversity in modern visual culture hardly reassures us that there's more to life than a washboard stomach, especially when images of extremely slim women are juxtaposed with features on dieting, 'natural weight loss pills' in the supermarkets, cult exercise DVDs, and, of course, endless stock photos of women laughing their heads off while eating salad. It's time to put the record straight here: no one's ever collapsed in delighted hysterics at the home-made fat-free, dairy-free, fun-free, water-thin balsamic dressing dripping off a cherry tomato, regardless of how many times a day they look at 'Reasons to Lose Weight' on Tumblr (reasons which include, incidentally, 'So he can pick me up and spin me in a circle', 'So as not to be the big bridesmaid', and, most upsettingly, 'To be somebody else's thinspiration').

Thankfully, we're starting to see attempts to fight against the onslaught of thinspiration madness, from websites such as Tumblr and Instagram endeavouring to ban the related hashtags to designers introducing health checks and *Vogue* UK signing Equity's models' code (which amongst various employment rights includes being entitled to food and drink and not using models under 16 to represent adults). A recent anorexia campaign in Brazil placed idealised fashion illustrations side by side with painfully thin models and the slogan 'You are not a sketch. Say no to anorexia.' Meanwhile, *Vogue*'s focus on 'ageless style' has seen women of varied ages and backgrounds grace its pages, Spanish *Elle* ran the plus-size face of H&M's 'Big is Beautiful' swimwear line on their front page in 2013, and Kerry Washington appeared on the cover of *Vanity Fair* in 2013 after a campaign that pointed out the relative invisibility of black models in the pages of fashion magazines. All these developments represent a step in a more healthy direction, but more often than not, they're tokenistic gestures that fail to make a lasting impact on the magazines' editorial. Like commercials that use 'normal' women rather than models but then airbrush the hell out of them, these publications often remain rife with hypocrisy and essentially committed to one single, homogeneous ideal of womanhood. If we don't continue to fight the uphill battle against this ideal, then the problem of self-starvation doesn't look as though it will go away any time soon.

Ultimately, fashion should be fun, female-friendly and empowering, not an exploitative madhouse staffed by fat-phobic fascists. As long as we don't bat an eyelid as we flick past another photo of a naked model on all-fours, covered in handbags and shoes (happened), we're opening wide and swallowing the tainted bodily fluids of one of the most sinister industries we have. It's impossible to avoid: the guilt after the spaghetti bolognese, the children being bullied by grown women into taking their clothes off, the competitive thinness, the ridiculous novelty trends posing as art, the smarmy, condescending tones of the fashion feature writers. Serious campaigns for ethical standards in fashion have a long way to go, and we're on board that train more than we've ever been on board with a gladiator sandal. Maybe it's time to kiss the fashion dream goodbye because if you look *really* hard at the po-faced fash ensemble, carrying bags made of boa constrictors and including the occasional 'models on fire' incident, it starts to look pretty hilarious – even self-satirising – as you back further and further away. We still love clothes, but we're also laughing our bloody heads off. Because if you didn't laugh, you'd cry – and if you don't look fashion straight in its glassy, vacant eyes and see it for what it really is, it might one day literally be the death of you.

7
Boyfriends, Break-ups, and Breakdowns

ALL THE SINGLE LADIES

According to women's magazines, being single is a right old lark – provided you're savvy enough eventually to 'bag that man', of course, at which point you'll graduate from their dating tips to their month-by-month relationship guide, complete with constant allusions to whether he may or may not be thinking about 'breaking it off'. One minute you're the epitome of Magazineland's sassy single woman stereotype, flashing your cash and hitting the town for cocktails with 'the girls'; the next, you're made to feel like a shrivelled-up spinster because you're not cosying up with 'the boy' on the sofa for a 'dreamy night in'. Or, if you're a teenage girl, 'locking lips with that luscious lad' is the highest of priorities, because, even if most of your class have moved on from kissing to the old handjob through the bottom of a popcorn bucket in the local cinema routine, romance is the name of the game. Forget homework – you'd better be learning those '10 steps to your first kiss' off by heart, baby girl.

While assorted lifestyle guides may laud the idea of female independence – 'fun, fearless females' are, after all, their main advertising

target group – it soon becomes clear from much of the content that, even in these modern times, being a single woman still isn't A-OK. You'd think that choosing to be footloose and fancy-free would be nobody's business but your own, but as we're about to show you, even in these wanton days of Ann Summers parties, Tinder fucks and sperm-donor-fuelled pregnancies, we're as defined by our relationships with men as we ever were. In the world of dating advice, much of what's doled out is geared towards pleasing men, and not yourself, and this remains a constant whether you're currently shagging one or not.

If, it turns out, you're actually not, then people are fascinated as to why. Much like incurable diseases or something Kate Middleton's worn, 'the single woman' is constantly wheeled out as debate fodder by newspapers, magazines and television shows in need of a quick angle. Does she count as a spinster or a bachelorette? Is she a lesbian, and is that anyone else's business? Can she 'have it all'? Should she delay 'settling down'? If she has babies, is she one of those 'feckless single mothers' they talk about in right-wing newspapers? Is she responsible for the moral decay of society? Or, if she doesn't want children, is she, in the words of one particularly enlightened soul we once came across on a Vagenda night out, 'one of those feminists who refuses to get married and have babies out of spite'?

Life as a singleton can be idyllic (lots of sex with nice people, weekends beholden to nobody but yourself) and at times slightly tougher (lonely Tuesday nights spent giving yourself a dead arm so it feels like it's someone else's hand). And the same thing can, of course, be said for relationships. Despite what *Cosmo* and its bitchy friends might tell you, there's no such thing as a 'perfect' relationship, nor is there really such a thing as 'the One', so dedicating your single days to finding it and him will more than likely end in disaster. Having both spent prolonged periods being single, as well as having experienced our fair share of boyfriends, break-ups and associated breakdowns, we've learnt the hard way that most of what the media have to say about the dating game is complete and utter unadulterated BS. But then from the looks of all the emails we get, raging about terrible magazine advice drawn from dating manuals with titles such as *Why Men Love Bitches* (Sherry Argov, 2000) and *If You Want Closure in a Relationship, Start With Your Legs* (published in 2007 by a male author known only as 'Big Boom', who got his big break as a 'celebrity bodyguard'), we'd hazard that a fair few of you already know that.

Despite the proven existence of 'career women'; the efforts of our foremothers to smash through the glass ceiling with a diamond-encrusted hammer; the gradual and overdue death of referring to a woman as 'Mrs John Jones'; and an assortment of other social progressions, it's still par for the course to define a chick by her relationships. Filling out a simple form can tell you as much: a shrinking but significant amount of official documentation asks a woman to define herself as 'Miss' or 'Mrs', as indeed it has done for hundreds of years. Of course, that's progress compared to what Rhiannon's great-grandmother, who apparently at age 21 married unacceptably late, had to put up with when her marriage certificate thoughtfully included, 'Occupation: Spinster'. But why it's of any relevance to your local gym whether you've legally committed yourself to another person or not is beyond us (we're big fans of the Ms, in case you hadn't guessed). Women have always been damned if they do and damned if they don't, stuck between the equally unpalatable stereotypes of spinsterhood and wifehood, and with magazines still running articles like 'Kate vs Kate – what's your wifestyle?' (in this case it was 'perfect wife' Middleton vs 'lazy boozer wife' Moss), things look unlikely to change soon.

It's sad but true that one of the 'top tips' circulating amongst women applying for jobs twenty years ago – sometimes even resurrected today – was to remove your wedding ring before you went in to the interview, lest your potential employer spy it and immediately realise that you're a hormonal, coupled-up baby-machine-in-waiting, rather than a competent, well-qualified human being. There's certainly a hard core of fetid old farts who still think that way, not that being labelled with the alternative cliché of 'cat-owning, desperate gin-drinking old maid' is preferable (apart from the gin-drinking, obviously. And the cats. We love cats). The assumption that everybody, male or female, must aspire to a relationship is all around us, leading inevitably to the even more poisonous one that if you're single, there must be something wrong with you. But where there is room for the cool, committed bachelor who 'just can't be tied down', double standards dictate that there is still something desperate about the perpetually single woman: the lonely thirtysomething shovelling ice cream down her throat, or, as Bridget Jones has it, the lizard woman in disguise. Women's magazines are acutely aware of this – and are particularly happy to exploit it.

CATCHING THAT MAN

They say your life is not complete until you've found that special someone, and thankfully women's magazines have long considered it their role to help you find him and (this part is key) entrap him like a fly in your sticky male-munching web. 'The One', or 'Mr Right', is out there, they will assure you, and if you're still single it must be because you're fat, or just not looking hard enough. The only thing to do is read articles with titles such as 'How to meet men' and 'WLTM: a smart, funny guy' and follow their advice on new ways to corner complete strangers in increasingly inventive scenarios while manipulating them into spending time with you. Why they find the trusty, traditional way of meeting guys (aka drunk at a bar, which is far too sluttish) so unappealing has very little to do with success rate and a lot more to do with a prudish and surprisingly conservative notion of how relationships should pan out, resembling as it does the classic movie formula of boy meets girl, boy loses girl, boy gets girl. Women's magazines would much rather you joined an evening class or went to a museum in order to perfect your pulling, although clearly not the kind of museum the pair of us like to visit regularly (locking eyes over a pickled foetus in a jar is hardly the gold standard of Hollywood 'meet-cutes' – which is a shame, when you think about it).

When magazines do suggest relatively modern ideas, such as 'multi-dating', there'll always be what we like to call the 'slag caveat' (namely: 'I may be dating lots of men, but I'm not *sleeping* with them. I'm not a *slag*'). Take this example from an article in *Grazia* in March 2012 entitled 'Why settle for one man when you can have THREE?' Despite the writer's displaying some pretty predatory man-hunting tactics ('I would identify my prey, track him at length – sometimes even years [years!] – then launch an assault, usually with enough alcohol to render him defenceless'), she isn't actually shagging these men, admitting that she favours an 'options open, legs closed' approach. Which begs the question: why bother? You may call us a pair of slappers (actually you may not), but it sounds like a hell of a lot of effort to go to when you don't even get an orgasm at the end of the night (or decade). Nonetheless, if you're ever going to find that man, you'd better sit up and start assessing whether every man of your acquaintance is boyfriend material by reading books like *The Gaggle*, which recommends that you viciously exploit all the men in your circle in order to find TBP ('The Boyfriend Prospect').

Once you've homed in on your potential prey and are waiting to pounce like a lioness stalking a simple but loveable wildebeest, all you have left to do is 'persuade' (read: manipulate) him into falling in love with you through a succession of coldly calculated and impeccably timed body language gestures or stock scenarios such as visiting a theme park (the adrenalin from rollercoaster rides will fool him into thinking you're hormonally bonding, FYI), which was pitted as a sure-fire way to make love by magazines and women's websites in 2012. It isn't the first time this theory has done the rounds, either. In reality, it's a fairly well documented psychological phenomenon that bears the sexy moniker 'misattribution of arousal': the idea that when your heart rate increases, your blood pressure rises, you begin to sweat and release adrenalin, you will unconsciously associate these feelings with the person you're with and conclude that you are attracted to them. Before you know it, you'll be heading off into the sunset together, right? Wrong.

These magazine articles place the responsibility for instigating – and afterwards, maintaining – a relationship completely on the woman's shoulders. And boy, does it take a lot of reading up. When magazines aren't bursting into your bedroom mid-shag to inform you that your love life isn't *Fifty Shades* enough, they're bombarding you with a confusing array of tips on what to buy your latest squeeze for his birthday or Christmas or the anniversary of his guinea pig's death, according to his hair colour and/or how long you've been together. 'Man facts' and 'boy analysis' features pour out of magazine special editions like a pair of 36DDs out of a Page Three bikini, usually cloaked in pseudo-scientific psychobabble. While *J-17* (God rest its soul) dubbed this complex area of study 'boyology', *Cosmo* went for the more social-science-graduate friendly 'manthropology'. Their eminently sellable commodity is 'top secret' information about men, information that will unlock the key to their hearts and 'make you his'.

Editors are quick to commission articles on how to tell whether he's 'in it for the long haul' or whether his body language says that he wishes you would make his cups of tea like his ex-girlfriend did, and they'll illustrate it with pictures of celebrities holding hands awkwardly or blinking in the cameras of a million paps chasing them down the street. One *Mail Online* article titled 'What his body language means' (December 2013) advised that you should 'hesitate before a second date' with a man if he 'puts his hand on your shoulder' as this means that 'he's very interested, but he's also territorial and can be dominant' and that if he answers the question 'How do I look in this dress?' with 'You look absolutely stunning' then 'chances are he's not even looking at the dress – just feeling amorous'. Meanwhile, if he says 'I honestly love you' rather than 'I love you', or says 'I love you' while smiling slowly or with his pupils contracted, then he probably isn't being truthful either. A US *Cosmopolitan* online feature from the same month, called 'What he's really thinking – revealed' suggested that you conduct conversations without eye contact because 'men don't do eye-to-eye very well' ('A man knows that if someone is looking him in the eye, that person is (a) about to take a swing at him, (b) his mother, (c) a divorce attorney'). You should also avoid using 'trigger words' like 'finished', 'future', 'needs' or 'sorry'. 'You'll get much better results', apparently, 'if you don't ask him how he feels. Instead, ask him what he thinks about it, thereby appealing to his inner cocktail-party bore.' Hear that, chicas? Women feel; men think.

REASONS WHY YOU'RE NOT MARRIED

Unfortunately for dating advice peddlers, romantic encounters usually involve another conscious human being with a mind of his or her own, an autonomous person who can only be controlled or tricked on to a rollercoaster a limited number of times (despite what many a Japanese website will tell you, scientists have yet to invent the sentient sex robot). Not that it stops magazines from trying, and they've been at it since time immemorial. Read Helen Gurley Brown's *Sex and the Single Girl* (1962) and you'll notice how it stipulates everything from your manners to your outfit to how your apartment should look, and all for a bit of cock. Contrast it with more modern (in time alone) dating manuals such as *How to Make Anyone Fall in Love With You* (Leil Lowndes, 1997) or *How to Make Any Man Want You: How to Be So Irresistible You'll Barely Keep from Dating Yourself!* (Marie Forleo, 2008), and you'll see that very little has changed since then.

We may think that we have moved on from Gurley Brown's advice circa 1962 that a single girl shouldn't leave underwear lying around because 'she wants her apartment to be sexy, not necessarily to encourage *rape*'. But the onus is still on the woman to primp, prime and usually change herself and her habits in order to tempt, then keep, a boyfriend. After that, it is her responsibility to take charge of the relationship by being a 'dream girlfriend' or a 'perfect wife' – meaning that if abuse happens, it should also be seen as a female failure, an invitation she accidentally left lying around in her pile of dirty socks. You would hope we had moved on from this, but the odd magazine still claims that a messy bedroom means 'he will think you're easy'. Even features such as 'Clothes to make him love you' (*Women's Weekly*, 1965) are not as dated as you might think; the aforementioned *How to Make Any Man Want You* actually has a chapter called 'Perfect packaging, or how to be a delicious, scrumptious, knock-his-socks-off, take-me-home-now gorgeous gal 24–7'.

Even the ostensibly feminist magazines of the seventies and eighties didn't quite succeed in shaking this male-centric relationship agenda: *Company* ran a cover feature in November 1978 entitled 'How to meet men now you are liberated', for example. Meanwhile, in the same issue, a pro-woman article called 'How to be a millionairess' was later undermined by a piece on sexual signals saying 'don't put it on when you want to put off' (i.e. don't be a cocktease). Unfortunately, by 1981 *Company* had abandoned any attempt at pushing a feminist agenda, with such stories as 'Nice girls DO marry for money' gracing the pages. Although less brazenly 'desperate' in language, modern 'what to wear on a date' spreads and studies about how anyone with a penis is 'evolutionarily predisposed' to start humping your leg the minute you put on a red dress are essentially the saying the same thing as their predecessors.

While the notion that there must be something wrong with you if you're not shackled to your ball and chain already (or as we prefer to call male partners, 'him indoors') might sound distinctly 1950s, we assure you that it's alive and well. In 2011, the *Huffington Post*'s Tracy McMillan nearly made the internet explode with her article 'Reasons why you're not married'. The reasons were as follows. 'You're a bitch' ('men just want to marry someone who is nice to them'), 'You're shallow' ('if you were looking for a man of character, you'd have found one by now'), 'You're a slut' and 'You're selfish' ('a good wife does not spend her day thinking about herself'). Way to make a girl feel good about herself, Tracy (you total cow). This accurately demonstrates the view most publications are pushing: being single is a sad state to be in, and the problem is always you. Tracy's article has been echoed by features such as 'What's destroying your love life? Um . . . it could be you' (*Glamour*), features which bombard you with questions ('Do you confuse sex with intimacy?' 'Do you take the fun out of it?') that are likely to leave even the most self-assured of us feeling slightly shitty. And all of them assume that every woman (unless she's bitchy or slutty or has something else wrong with her) wants to be in a monogamous, committed relationship all the time.

Sure, magazines do sometimes pay lip service to the naughty notion of casual sex, but it will always be followed by an article entitled 'Step away from the penis!' or 'Don't be a first-date slapper', telling you to stop before you do something reckless like have some actual fun, even though one night with no strings attached is often eminently preferable to sitting in a Café Rouge listening to some bellend with too much gel in his hair talk about his marketing job, an experience made all the more unbearable by the advice in dating guides like *The Rules* that you shouldn't drink on a first date, *at all*. *Cosmo* did a feature in November 2012 on this, claiming that you should never have sex drunk because 29% of women get an STD after a night out drinking, but then later on in the same magazine there's a picture of a happy couple with the headline 'I asked him out . . . after 50 mojitos' (presumably from her coffin). What their crazy, seemingly self-contradictory stance actually *is* is anyone's guess. Forget enjoying sex, too: dating books such as *Not Tonight, Mr Right: The Best (DON'T GET) Laid Plans for Finding and Marrying the Man of Your Dreams* (Kate Taylor, 2007) go as far as telling you to refuse to have sex with your man until at least six months after you have started dating, while girls in their late twenties or early thirties should preferably wait for an engagement ring. The 2012 US box office smash hit *Think Like a Man* (based on the 2009 dating manual *Act Like A Lady, Think Like A Man* by Steve Harvey) managed to make an entire movie out of the idea that women should stick to 'the 90 day rule' to hook the serious interest of a dude. Needless to say, in the film it works flawlessly, but in reality it's a ridiculously old-fashioned prospect that not only assumes the guy is willing to spend months overlooking his massive erection, but more importantly makes no allowances for female sexual pleasure (not to mention female sexual frustration) at all.

The notion that women are either mentally unsuited to casual sex (i.e. sex without love) or shouldn't engage in it if they want a long-term relationship is one of the most popular fallacies of our time. Notwithstanding the fact that shagging someone is an excellent way of working out how much you like them, that old 'third date' or 'X day' rule (or, in *Not Tonight, Mr Right*'s case, the SIX-MONTH RULE) buys into the ancient notion that a woman is either a Madonna or a whore, depending on her sexual behaviour (and, spoiler alert, it's the former who gets the ring on her finger). Part of the reason we're warned off a one-night stand is, sadly, because of the mantra that women are crazy and hormonal and romantic, while men are practical and serious with a stiff upper lip and little time to discuss love because they're busy running the country (darling). Everyone insists on believing that once you've had a man's throbbing member inside you, you will automatically want to be his girlfriend, if not marry him and have lots and lots of babies. Which, of course, you won't be able to, because you're the First Date Slapper.

Books such as *The End of Sex: How Hookup Culture is Leaving a Generation Unhappy, Sexually Unfulfilled and Confused About Intimacy* (Donna Freitas, 2013) are enthusiastically covered by the media, adding to the myth that young women are just too sensitive and emotionally vulnerable to handle a meaningless shag or a fling. If you're a woman, the need to ascribe meaning to sex is everywhere, from columnists saying that after ten sexual partners it 'stops meaning anything', to male chauvinists accusing sexually liberated women of being 'loose'. Tales abound of shag partners who eventually saw the rose-tinted light and settled down together (see innumerable magazine features), and Hollywood movies such as *Friends with Benefits* and *No Strings Attached* perpetuate the myth that a woman is incapable of swapping bodily fluids with any man without secretly falling madly in love with him – probably because she releases 'love hormones' during sex that make her feel superglued to the man she just had inside her, like some kind of fox–woman hybrid. We all know that sex only has as much meaning as you ascribe to it, and the idea that you turn into an intimacy-craving, desperate bunny boiler the minute you hook up with a guy is not only condescending, but can also feel a bit, well, embarrassing.

FOLLOWING *THE RULES*

If you do manage to meet someone whose presence doesn't make your vagina shrink and close up shop, the next step is finding out if he likes you or not. God forbid you should actually do something as outré as *asking him*. Instead, you're supposed to consult a *Cosmo* flow chart entitled 'Is he looking for a hook up – or more?' to 'reveal' his true intentions' (if he tells you that you have a great body, then he just wants to sleep with you; if he puts his face close to yours, then he's a player; if, however, he shows very little interest in you, then he's 'in it for the long haul'). You're not allowed to simply say to a man, 'I'm into you. Let's make this a thing.' That would be too easy. And when it's that easy, you stop needing the magazines. Their lists and rules rapidly cease to mean anything to you.

The central ethos of 1995 dating bestseller *The Rules* by Ellen Fein and Sherrie Schneider is that (and we quote) 'as unfeminist as it sounds, a woman should do absolutely nothing to start a relationship'. Unfeminist? Sure. But also complete toss. Some of the 'rules' listed include: never asking a man to dance, never calling a man, being 'honest but mysterious', and never initiating conversation. *The New Rules* (2013), meanwhile, tackles digital communication, and states that women are 'over-texting', apparently by replying too quickly. Well, show us one person who ever got laid from not texting back and perhaps we'll eat our words, but as it stands, your physical presence during the act is generally a must. It's as though these authors forget that a relationship involves two people.

Traditionally, yes, women have been the chased rather than the chasers, and yes, once upon a time men did line us up like cattle at the market and pick the one with the fewest whiskers and the best childbearing hips. But we'd like to think we're beyond that now. Depressingly, the need to sit pretty and laugh at his jokes remains as important in Magazineland (and the books which feed into it) as ever. Advice like 'dry wit may work with friends, but sarcasm is a bad idea when dating' is still doing the rounds. Utter bollocks, of course, for if it were true we'd both be perpetually single (although, come to think of it, a guy did once inform Holly that she had what he called 'too many opinions'. She still wishes that she'd pointed out there were also 'too many hairs on his back').

Because women are still not really allowed to be themselves when it comes to the dating game, magazines rely on a terrifying combination of underhand seduction tactics and hyper-awareness. Hence features such as '4 signs he's hiding something' (*Cosmopolitan* online) containing an array of possible indicators, none of which are ever 'Maybe ask him?' Granted, there are men out there who dedicate just as much time to analysing women's dating behaviour – google 'pickup artists' at your peril – but even the internet's creepiest NLP-toting pickup creeps are outnumbered by the media coverage that is given to looking 'inside men's minds' at the expense of being yourself.

God forbid you be overly forward or initiate anything. It's paramount that you play a convoluted cat-and-mouse game that's confusing for everyone and tends to result in your either sitting there silently, or behaving like a teen movie stripper on MDMA who's suddenly decided she really, really needs a boyfriend, because you're following advice such as 'You should touch him five times within the first fifteen minutes', or 'Simulate oral sex using a beer bottle', both tips given by the *Cosmopolitan Ultimate Sex Guide* and which would have most *people*, let alone men, running for the hills. And even if both parties are determined to have an equal relationship, you're still in a media environment that insists on portraying men and women as two different species.

If you're a lesbian, or bisexual, then you're just ignored. The status quo has been 'men take charge' for so long that magazines tend to avoid the topic of non-heterosexual relationships completely. The publications we consulted in our teenagehood would often dismiss same-sex curiosity as a phase. In her book *Gender and the Media*, Rosalind Gill cites a *J-17* agony aunt's response to a letter titled 'I fancy my friend', wherein the confused teenager is told, 'It's common to experiment sexually with each other, but I have to ask where it will lead. What happens if one of you finds a boyfriend?' before concluding, 'If my hunch is correct, you'll both agree that your make-out session was fun while it lasted, but the cost of going for the gusto again is way too high.' That was in 2003 – the climate that we, and many magazine writers, grew up in – but the absence of even the slightest nod to same-sex relationships indicates that we're not out of the woods. Those woods are still right at the back of the closet, in Narnia. Maybe lesbianism and bisexuality are just too confusing for the hacks to handle. You can sort of picture a staff writer for a women's glossy, sitting there chewing her fluffy pen late into the night, unable to defer to a body language expert or astrologer, contemplating the balance of power in same-sex relationships and wailing, 'BUT WHO IS THE BOSS?' at their computer screen.

Negotiating straight couplehood is hard enough, and being bisexual or a lesbian in a world where 'the boyf' or 'the hubby' seems to be a prerequisite for most mainstream media conversations can be even more so (while we're at it, can we please have a moratorium on adult female columnists referring to their partners as 'the boy'?). Unfortunately, it's incredibly difficult for a woman and a woman to be taken seriously as a couple at all; lesbians are usually expected to be porn fodder or those ugly butch cartoon feminists with their mullets and the vulva-sized chip on their shoulder – because male genitalia are so awe-inspiring that you must be mentally unstable or particularly masochistic to spend a lifetime avoiding them. Successful sitcoms that attempted to push boundaries back in the day by portraying one or more of their characters as gay – *Will & Grace* as the most prominent example – ended up taking a jab at lesbians as 'gross' or 'freaky' all too commonly, often through the mouthpiece of their gay male characters. And while some radical feminists have suggested that getting into heterosexual relationships is literally sleeping with the enemy, a worrying number of people stubbornly cling to the idea that women in same-sex relationships are somehow in it to spite men. In reality, most of us just listen to what our sex drive tells us, and act accordingly.

SIGNS HE'S CHEATING

Back amongst the glossy pages, where heterosexual conformity rules supreme, once you've successfully circumnavigated conflicting dating advice, learnt how to read men's minds, submitted to your crazy, crazy lady-hormones, and then ignored all that advice and told someone with whom you have a mutual attraction that you fancy them, chances are that you'll have got yourself a boyfriend. After you've emerged from your cloud of post-orgasmic joy, half a stone heavier and with chronic 'honeymoon' cystitis but still smiling, a whole other set of rules comes into play to ensure that you're kept in the same state of heightened confusion you were in as a single lass. In other words, the state which keeps you buying magazines. As Caitlin Moran pointed out in her 2012 book *How to Be a Woman*, you can tell a woman is in love when she responds simply, 'It's just . . . good. I'm really happy', to repeated requests for information (before later getting pissed and admitting that 'the size of his penis makes it a borderline medical emergency').

But as far as magazines are concerned, such a beatific state cannot last. Now that you're coupled up, you're either going to stop being their core market because you'll be too 'fucking busy' (and vice versa, as the amazing Dorothy Parker once wrote on her honeymoon) to go down the newsagent's, or things will start going wrong almost immediately, at which point it's time to consult the magazines again.

You're now bombarded with pointless questions from every magazine rack, news-stand and website that concerns itself with human relationships: should you earn more than him? Are you a 'feminist housewife'? What happens if he's not the primary breadwinner? Are stay-at-home dads trendy and open-minded or (more likely, by tabloid standards) beaten-down losers who couldn't provide for their partner? Is he henpecked or – the even more enlightened term – 'pussy-whipped'? Should you propose to him, or is proposing 'the man's job'? And if it is 'the man's job', then how come all the men's outlets talk about marriage being 'game over'? This continues right up until you're buying magazines like *Good Housekeeping* and *Woman & Home*, at which point adverts for vaginal lubricant and anti-ageing night cream are interspersed with articles on how to 'get the best out of your relationship by synchronising your diaries' or 'DIY your Divorce' (which, by the way, makes no grammatical *sense*).

More disturbing still are the articles that are bloody-mindedly determined that something is wrong with your relationship. Features such as 'How to tell he's cheating' always, always include the counter-intuitive theory that his wanting to have more sex with you, buying you flowers, asking you about your day, or bringing you thoughtful gifts are sure signs that you should be 'suspicious'. 'Signs of a cheating man', one such article in *Marie Claire* in February 2010, warns that you have to 'be careful not to appear to be paranoid' (emphasis on 'appear'). 'There's a problem if he's not laughing or seeming as passionate as usual,' it states.

'It's hard to spread love/passion between two people, so the person who used to have it will feel it slipping away if it's being given to someone else.'

Of course, your boyfriend could be depressed or suffering at work – but ever since you read a feature called 'Why guys want to be dumped', you've been convinced that he's plotting the end of your relationship in some heinously manipulative way, and besides, he's taking way too long to text you back and *you haven't even met his family yet.* Better watch how often his pupils contract for clues.

Everywhere you turn, as a proud possessor of two X chromosomes, someone wants to tell you how to conduct yourself with your partner(s). Worst of all is the obsessive need to find out exactly what type of man it is you're dating. Is he a high-flyer? A commitment phobe? Is he the Man Who Is Frightened of Intimacy? As short-lived nineties humour magazine *Bitch* asked in a spoof article entitled 'Living with a man with no *Cosmo*-label', *just what kind of bastard is he*?

This veritable toxic smog of unhealthy questioning is hardly ever intended to promote equality in our relationships. It's usually generated by a bunch of cynical content-peddlers, sitting around a minimalist table in a London high-rise, to create artificial problems for their readership so they can sell counselling and lipo advertising space in the back pages alongside 'Love Guru' psychic hotlines. Et *voilà* – more money for the worry-makers. Which is why it's so important to make sure that we collectively answer these questions with the only helpful response, which is: I don't give a tiny rat's ass.

Could the agony aunts shed some light on any relationship problems you might genuinely have? Unfortunately, they have a sizeable amount of bile to offer of their own. If your sex life is dwindling, for instance, it's often because you're just not trying hard enough on 'date night'. One of the worst examples we saw of this alarming trend was the case of a

Cosmo reader who had written in lamenting the fact that her boyfriend kept trying to pressurise her into (and there is no delicate way of putting this) putting her finger up his arse, even though, in her own words, 'I don't want to'. Instead of congratulating her on standing up for herself and reinforcing the notion that no one who cares about you would in a million years try to get you to do something you didn't want to do, *Cosmo* opted for the gung-ho 'stick your finger up his arse . . . go on, it might be fun', approach. Sort of like that one friend you have who's always full of terrible advice ('Babe, that boob tube makes you look like Cindy Crawford circa 1987' and 'No, only girls carry chlamydia'), and in your heart you know it's wrong, but you start to doubt yourself nonetheless.

Sometimes the broadsheets take his side, too. In 2012, a reader wrote in to *The Guardian* with the news that her boyfriend often jokes that 'he finds my vagina repulsive' in sexual situations. Rather than advising the young lady in question that she should be telling him to 'do one' as a matter of urgency, Pamela Stephenson Connolly recommended that they watch an educational vagina DVD together because 'your boyfriend's background may make it difficult to be comfortable with his sexuality, and your genitals'. Seriously? Surely the truth is that she should kick him out of bed faster than it takes to say, 'If you think my vagina is repulsive, then you probably need a boyfriend of your own.'

If that's not enough to make you impale yourself on the anti-pigeon spikes outside Clinton Cards, then you've clearly forgotten about Valentine's Day. The whole embarrassing charade of Valentine's Day can be enough to reduce the most hardened singleton to 2 a.m. tears over the second bottle of Sainsbury's Cava, and the most loved-up girlfriend to the sort of cynicism usually reserved for those who buy holidays to 'Paris' (Vatry) in the Ryanair sale. Restaurants suddenly become Tunnel of Love-esque labyrinths, where you're expected to battle your way through heart-shaped balloon missiles before you're allowed anywhere near a deep-fried Brie to calm your nerves. Previously safe retail environments become purveyors of toddler-sized teddy bears, all clutching huge red hearts emblazoned with 'I Love You' or, if you just can't say those special three words without feigning a speech impediment, 'I Wuv Yew'. 'Your man' is expected to 'treat' you to some of this crap, lest his resistance to teddies and Hallmark platitudes be wheeled out as evidence in the newest magazine's latest feature that he 'doesn't really love you'. Meanwhile, men's media give out annual advice on how to 'humour' your girlfriend on Valentine's Day, as if an all-female conspiracy to procure as many big-eyed puppy toys holding saccharine messages as possible were the reason that the holiday exists in the first place. Not that many men listen. Crappy Valentine's Day presents received by our readers range from a cookie that once read 'I'll be your slave' (the 's' and the 'e' had fallen off') to a steam carpet cleaner. OK, so crying with hunger because your boyfriend's bank card got rejected at McDonald's, as one of our readers did, or finding out he's married when he leaves the hotel room for wine and never returns (again, a reader) doesn't make for a great V-Day, but nor does being lumped with the blame for this most consumerist of holidays when it's not our fault. Welcome to the world of romance.

DISTRESS IN A DRESS

Congratulations! Your relationship has now reached a certain, arbitrary point, and there's only one of two ways that it can go. Either it's time for you to wave goodbye to your *Cosmo*s and your *Glamour*s in favour of the, quite frankly, terrifying world of wedding magazines, Pinterest boards and *Easy Living* articles with titles like 'Do his sperm hate your eggs?' or it's time to break up and take up your rightful place in the singleton sisterhood once again (do not pass 'Go.') Forget real-life heartbreak; inhabiting as they do a shiny-shiny world of happy capitalistic joy and shoes, magazines are pretty rubbish therapists when you've just had all your hopes and dreams torn out through your vagina, and at some level, they know it. Yes, they'll offer clichéd advice along the lines of 'Get rid of bad bedroom energy by investing in a new duvet set', 'Delete his number from your phone', and 'Take up Zumba to get the amazing body he never got to see', but none of that is any use when you're a pyjama-clad snot monster with an unstoppable urge to drunkenly belt out Carly Simon's 'You're So Vain' at a student karaoke night on the Euston Road for an audience of four. When you're in that kind of state, there's absolutely no way that baking is going to help heal your broken heart, and neither is a too-short fringe, cut as the result of a 'new you' makeover session. Because no matter what they try to say, there is no 'new you' in the painful few days following unexpected heartbreak: only old you, but sadder.

Perhaps this is why magazines tend to most often take the *schaden-freude* approach to break-ups, opting for the 'look how much more miserable this female celebrity getting out of a car is than you' distraction method. Whether it's 'Tragic Demi's Cry For Help', 'Rihanna Joins the Broken Hearts Club' or 'It's All Over Yet Again for Doomed Spinster Jennifer Aniston' – all examples from the covers of 2012 and 2013 *Grazia* – it's good to know that the celeb magazines are keeping our cockles warm by churning out dubiously sourced coverage of a small group of women's seemingly relentless relationship misery. One of our media insiders at the magazine told us that the covers are referred to in the office as 'distress in a dress'; they are depictions of neutral-faced, nicely turned out female celebrities invariably hailed as 'women on the verge'. 'Talk in Hollywood points to the fact that she has been exhausted and jet-lagged due to the extreme pressures she suffers at the hands of the global press,' the global press will report, without a hint of self-awareness. Because nothing makes you feel better more quickly than another woman's impending mental collapse. It shows that even when you have rock-hard abs, an entourage and a mink coat, you can still get dumped and be sad about it.

What rankles most about these 'distress in a dress' features is the expressions of faux-concern you imagine on the faces of the magazines' editorial staff, similar to your colleagues' faces when they tell you you look tired and put their head to one side in the dreaded 'sympathy tilt'. Yes, they pretend to care, but really they hate you and want your job. This is why you can never be a female celebrity and happily single. The laws of Magazineland dictate that you must be on the verge of a nervous breakdown at all times, because it suits their narrative better and, let's face it, 'Cameron Diaz, perfectly happy, says "No complaints here!"' just doesn't sell as well.

Of course, where break-ups are concerned, it's always the celebrity woman who is painted as a crazed, howling victim teeming with bitter recriminations and a lust for revenge, while the man just shrugs nonchalantly before being papped stumbling out of a strip club the very next night. Even if the woman is doing absolutely nothing to indicate that she might be feeling in any way affected by the break-up, and is in fact dealing with it all with stoic silence in the face of the glare of the world's media, celebrity magazines will still find a way to make her look like a volatile, suicidal mess for deigning to go to the 7-Eleven without make-up. Indeed, refusing to wear two inches of slap or get dolled up for the benefit of the paparazzi is often taken as a sign that Celebrity X has 'let herself go' post-breakup. Is it any wonder Britney shaved her head?

A MODERN FAIRY TALE

Long before relationship issues became regular public fodder, progression through four states – single, girlfriend, fiancée, wife (often closely followed by mother) – was fast, and the only realistic pathway for a 'woman of good character'. Women were often charmingly referred to as 'arm candy', a decorative addition to a man's real life. Of course, after those sex tips imploring you to wrap a candy necklace around his member while you lick his gobstoppers, a woman is wont to decide that 'candy' and relationships should rarely be mentioned in the same sentence, even in the context of 'he referred to me as his arm candy so I strangled him with a strawberry bootlace'. We've all grown up a bit since we actually believed that women were sillier versions of men, but with tits, whose specific functions were to be passed around as collateral between the guys, even if we do preserve some cultural ceremonies that are built around that idea, like being 'given away' by your dad at the altar to your future husband during a traditional wedding ceremony. And yet it's clear that there is still a lot of work to do before we retire into the equality utopia.

Take romcoms – or, as others might have it, chick flicks. These are films based on the premise of a 'modern fairy tale': the aforementioned formula of boy meets girl, they fall in love, some minor difficulties occur which are eventually overcome, and then they live together in eternal committed bliss. This is a tried-and-tested structure that has been exploited by Hollywood producers for decades, and, needless to say, it works, and many of us enjoy these films. Fairy tales, and their knights in shining armour, will always be popular. The modern incarnation could be said to be a *Sex-and-the-City*-esque 'Mr Big' figure with a gigantic salary and a luxury New York apartment, as in E. L. James's monumentally successful *Fifty Shades of Grey* trilogy. Christian Grey is a rich and powerful man of experience, who exists to educate one lucky young lady in the ways of business, love and anal beads. So far, so normal – Prince Charming may not have whipped the tampon out of Snow White's bits before taking her up against the bathroom sink in a Hilton suite, but she certainly hopped on his stallion when he was ready for her. Professional trolls have been quick to suggest that the popularity of such fiction must mean that women throughout the ages have continued to crave the fairy-tale prince, the knowledgeable (and usually rich) man who comes along to transform her into a princess and whisk all her troubles away, bar sandwich-making. But guys and gals, it's time to put the fairy tale to bed.

The fairy tale originated in a world where a woman could only hope to define her life by her husband, and where, in the absence of educational or career opportunities, jumping aboard an eligible husband's life was the best-case scenario. While we still suffer from pay gaps, judgmental remarks about maternity leave ('baby holiday', as it was once memorably described by a male character in *Friends* who was, to be fair, supposed to be a bit of an arsehole), and studies about what make-up to wear in the office to 'get taken seriously', it's safe to say that the modern world remains a fairly fertile environment for the fairy tale. Considering that women make up the majority of those in minimum wage jobs and that, according to the Equalities and Human Rights Commission, it will take seventy years before there is an equal number of male and female directors of FTSE 100 companies, the so-called 'gold-digger' phenomenon is arguably unsurprising. Websites like sugardaddie.com have enjoyed particularly high levels of popularity amongst female university students during the recession and have taken advantage of the fact that men are still more likely to be rich and women's bodies are often seen as the best commodity they have. The women involved in such transactions could argue that it is a savvy decision in a world where the playing field is hopelessly bumpy in the first place. It might be all open and consensual on sugardaddie.com, but it's still a bit depressing, adding as it does to the cultural stereotype of the old, rich man with the money-hungry post-pubescent beauty queen.

In reality, most of us meet boyfriends or girlfriends at school or university or the corner shop or the office, and live very similar lives to them. Snide speculations on the part of men about our motives persist primarily because society hasn't quite stopped thinking of girls as appendages to men, rather like extra penises with slightly prettier heads. So long as there are serious differences in power between the sexes, problems in our personal relationships will persist. But girlfriend, trust us – you are so much more than a spare willy with a comedy face painted on the end. Whether you're straight, gay, bisexual, trans, polyamorous, asexual, all of the above, or perhaps anti-definition, false statistics that we just made up in our heads show that 99% of you have suffered some sort of emotional fallout from a human relationship.

The only definite thing you can know about relationships is that every single one of them begins and ends. Whatever happens in between is never as simple as what he means by the colour of that bunch of roses, or whether his foot fetish indicates a propensity to be unfaithful. It can't be adequately illuminated by *Cosmopolitan*'s '55 things you can learn about a guy in 10 minutes', or the *Brand Guys* dating guide (a manual on decoding your boyfriend's personality by the brands he uses – one of the most depressing things to come out of capitalism since the pleather jumpsuit). And it makes no difference whether you propose to him, or he proposes to you, or you propose to each other, or you never want to get married at all, or not to a man anyway. It doesn't matter if he's a bank manager and you're a homemaker who brings up seventeen children, or you're in the army and he's a house husband, or you're both in a travelling circus and make money performing around the country in a colourful caravan. You know this, of course, but it's worth reiterating it every once in a while when we come under such sustained attacks from the publications around us. It's OK to have your own relationship which bears absolutely no resemblance to anything you've ever read in

Cosmopolitan, with whomever you want and however many people you choose. And if you want to have an eighteen-month meltdown after a break-up rather than 'getting out on the town' after a fortnight and a single tub of Ben & Jerry's, then that's OK, too.

Many women will maintain that it's a great loss that men are supposedly no longer 'gentlemanly' (although why a man can't hold open a door for all people, regardless of gender, is beyond us), and a few women we've spoken to have cited 'not being treated like a lady' as a reason to stay away from labelling themselves feminist. But appreciative, loving relationships between two people who respect each other as similar human beings are worth a thousand car doors being opened for you by someone who thinks you're too delicate to do it yourself and who is also probably allergic to swear words (at which point, we'd like to say: fuck. And also: cunt). Because if you want equality, it has to be equality in all respects – and that means ditching the dating advice and being willing to accept that the fairy tale will only let you be a princess if you get yourself a prince. In the eventuality that you find yourself chasing one, however, you'd do well to remember the fate of the most prominent princess of our time, Kate Middleton. 'K-Middy' has been presented to the media in a way that makes any yearning for a fairy-tale ending with Prince Charming wither and die: in the words of Hilary Mantel in the *London Review of Books,* Kate is supposed to be 'capable of going from perfect bride to perfect mother, with no messy deviation . . . without quirks, without oddities, without the risk of the emergence of character'. This is the world's version of an ideal fairy-tale princess, every slipper polished, every gown bespoke, every word policed. A princess has no personality and no agency – and there's just as little power in that as there is in following *The Rules*. Welcome to the twenty-first century.

8
Working Girls

INDEPENDENT WOMEN

All the way back in 2000, when Destiny's Child sang 'Independent Women' on the soundtrack of *Charlie's Angels* they were making a declaration, and that declaration was 'I bought it'. The central tenet of the song was that women could be financially independent of their men, and that their independence should be a point of ass-kicking pride. (How that quite fits in with the fact that all three of Charlie's 'angels' still ultimately answer to a male boss who technically 'owns' them, however, is another question entirely.) Ever since *Cosmo* declared, 'Cheers for the capitalist feminist!' in 1986, the idea of the woman at the top, dressed to kill and with a work ethic to match, has dominated the popular imagination. She is the 'career woman', workin' 9 to 5 with her trouser suit and her shoulder pads and her ballsy, assertive attitude. *Cosmo* argued that the way to female equality was through earning your own money, and, considering that it wasn't until 1958 that a lady could even have a bank account without her husband or father's permission, you can't help but agree that, to a point, the magazine was right.

In the 1960s, reproductive freedom, in the form of the contraceptive pill, gave women the reprieve they needed from being baby-making machines in order to focus on other things, one of which was to start trying to redress the balance as far as gender roles were concerned. The ability to choose if and when to become pregnant enables a woman to pursue certain careers that, previously, would have been constantly interrupted by that inevitable offshoot of procreation: being covered in a permanent film of shit and vomit. Being able to have your own career and your own money gives you a different kind of freedom: the freedom to buy your own shoes, the freedom from dependency, and the freedom to leave a relationship that has become unpleasant or violent, taking your children with you. This new freedom was initially what *Sex and the City* was all about. It portrayed a new kind of woman: financially and professionally successful, in control of her own romantic life as well as her career, and yes, very much able to buy her own shoes, too. Unfortunately, as the series progressed, it became less about those other kinds of freedom and more about the shoes, reaching its nadir with Mr Big's construction of a magical fashion cupboard for Carrie in the more-than-slightly disappointing 2008 film of the same name. Somehow, society had swung it so that female liberation had come to denote simply being able to buy more stuff. The fact that most of that stuff was wrapped up in traditional notions of what it meant to be a woman (looking pretty) was surely just a coincidence. Right?

Money was important to female liberation because, much like Esperanto but with a larger uptake, it's the language of the world. Suddenly, in the 1980s, women were speaking it for the first time. Authors such as Jackie Collins and Shirley 'Life's too short to stuff a mushroom' Conran captured the mood perfectly in their novels – the 1980s career woman was a force to be reckoned with, and her sexuality was completely tied up with her power. While previously the twin attributes of ruthlessness and assertiveness were universally perceived as male qualities, the 1980s saw the creation of a new kind of cliché: the office bitch and the foxy female boss, complete with stiletto heels, electric blue eyeshadow and aggressive sexuality. The 'Women of Wall Street' issue of *Playboy* from August 1989 depicted just this fantasy woman: a huge-titted lady clad in a suit jacket (nothing underneath) is the central image, looking seductively out of the photograph from behind her sexy glasses. It's pure porno professional – like a cast member from 'Dominatrix Headmistress Makes Cynthia Squirt 'Til She Cries' or 'Busty Librarians in Heat'. But the reality was very different, and rather than spanking naughty account executives with their trousers around their ankles in the boardroom, women were running themselves ragged trying to juggle the new demands of work and the old demands of home.

There comes a point, however, where there's a limit to the liberation that money can buy. Romance-novelist-turned-Conservative-MP-turned-journalist Louise Mensch once wrote an approving article in *The Guardian* about how right-wing feminism (that apparent oxymoron) is all about the pursuit of money. For her, financial equality was the only equality, and the way to achieve it was through selfish individualism, battling your way to the top without worrying about any social and cultural factors that might have been keeping you down. That might be the way to CEO for one woman, but it isn't the way to equality for all women. As coverage surrounding the death of Margaret Thatcher noted, there's no use making your way through the glass ceiling if you're going to pull up the ladder after you. But if you really do want that position on the company board in the City, it's worth examining how those rare female high-flyers are presented once they've reached the dizzying heights of the company boardroom.

A DAY IN THE LIFE OF A HIGH-FLYING CAREER WOMAN

It's not often that women's magazines concern themselves with your career, but when they do, they're pretty sure that it all starts with granola. 'I begin the day at 5 a.m., with a spot of Bikram yoga,' the standard 'life in a day' article will read. 'After that, I really need to set myself up for a hard day in air traffic control, so I make sure that I boil my semi-skimmed milk to exactly 35 degrees – the optimum temperature to complement my home-made multigrain porridge. I go out and do a bit of redirecting aeroplanes, which is stressful but I'm dressed for success. At midday, we eat jacket potatoes, which I know that I can work off at my 5k jogging class round Hyde Park in the evening. If I didn't look the part, then nobody in this male-dominated environment would respect me.

'Some days, there might be an unexpected occurrence; for instance, a plane crashes on to the runway, engulfed in a huge, searing fireball. I slip off my court shoes, don pumps, and get stuck in, clawing through the wreckage for possible survivors. My flotation therapy might have to be rescheduled on a day like that, if I really want to be home to pick up my two beautiful children from Gifted and Talented class by five. I don't beat myself up about it – after all, what's really important now is the precious "me time" I get while moulding my greenhouse-grown organic chickpeas into falafels for dinner.'

Ever come across this sort of narrative, smugly encased in a 500-word feature that's apparently intended to inspire the innocent reader? The problem is, it's very rarely a genuine source of inspiration. Take Nancy Dell'Ollio, a cross-disciplinary superwoman who lists public affairs, networking, novel-writing and TV production amongst her many talents, 'dedicates a lot of time to cleansing and moisturising' and is 'gifted to not need a lot of sleep'. Her descriptions of her afternoon acupuncture or her lunch meetings, fascinating though they are ('I have a lot of meetings,

You mean a woman can open it?

Alcoa
Aluminum

which I like to do over lunch at the Berkeley in Knightsbridge, ten minutes from where I live. Or Claridge's, or the Ivy Club. I don't know anyone who does as much as I do'), are unlikely to impart to the common reader much in the way of practical information.

Women at the top of their game are always presented as living lives that reflect their smart career choice: smart food choices, smart exercising regimes, smart clothes in a 'capsule wardrobe' that doesn't include one single gaudy item they once found in the bargain bin at Forever Vintage and convinced themselves was a period piece, rather than a dead person's worn-out cardigan that boasted an appliquéd sequin kitten motif and smelt vaguely of damp. No stinking cardis for the CEO! She's sorted, she's 'sussed', and she probably didn't need an epidural when she gave birth to little Johannesburg Esteban IV, either. She doesn't feel paranoid and guilty about paying for childcare rather than staying at home all day. She lost her baby weight by doing coordinated pushchair walks with other local mothers during her (two-week) maternity leave. It's not difficult to see why, all too often, this 'aspirational reading' becomes another reason why you can take your permanently hungover, yoga-illiterate, demonstrably untoned arse right back to the Sainsbury's checkout counter. After all, if you haven't even got your own herb garden yet, then how the hell can you expect to become a space scientist?

BUYING INTO BUSINESS

That's the thing with magazine career advice: it purports to give you a helpful leg-up into the business world, but really it's just another lifestyle story. Where some magazines used to include practical advice about building your CV, negotiating a wage review or the qualifications needed for veterinary medicine, in the last twenty years most of this has been swallowed up by sensationalist writing – mainly because of the agendas of advertisers who would rather see Dior lipsticks in make-up bags than ladies on the board of Dior. There is no guarantee that product-pushing can be included in a careers section, especially as job interview attire is generally so conservative that it can never really be reliably 'styled up'. They may tell you that Maggie T is this season's style icon, but ain't nobody ever looked cutting edge in a skirt suit. As we all know, any outfit that doesn't involve big 'directional' hair or a sheer-bottomed 'trouser' (yes, just one) isn't of any interest to the fash pack. Nor is your interview ensemble likely to feature a cheeky flash of 'underboob' for that candid front-page photo.

The word length for the average feature in a women's monthly magazine has shrunk demonstrably in the last decade (now averaging around 300 words, which is about how much a five-year-old can read before getting cranky), and the career section has all but disappeared from most publications. Look back at the magazines of the 1980s and you'll be surprised by how long and in-depth some of the writing about earning potential and career possibilities is in comparison to today's cursory input.

In the past, magazine professionals have suggested to us that because more women buy magazines featuring celebrities in bikinis than they do those containing references to female entrepreneurs or women in management or heads of socialist financial cooperatives on the cover, the female readership has spoken. According to their sales figures, we don't want careers advice – and even though sales figures are a fairly inaccurate and superficial way of judging how people respond to editorial content (there never seems to be a box to tick for 'meh'), we've been told to swallow the fact that they know best. This very narrow definition of 'women's interests' is almost always being decided for us, mostly by men (at the time of writing, six of the seven 'key people' in the Condé Nast boardroom are male, and yet they oversee a raft of female titles including *Glamour*, *Easy Living*, *Vogue* and *Tatler*). Screw that. In a world of stubbornly persisting gender wage gaps, bulletproof glass ceilings, and a dearth of female world leaders and high-ranking executives, content that speaks to us seriously about career opportunities is important, necessary, and socially responsible. How can we ever aspire to success in the workplace when the message that we're constantly being fed is that physical beauty is more important? We hate to say it, but the more you're told that your mind doesn't matter, the more the words seep in and start affecting your self-perception, to the point where your podgy earlobe obsession starts affecting your childhood dream of becoming a paediatrician. The fact that so many women end up succeeding despite the deluge of bullshit thrown their way every day should be an enormous point of pride.

This is exactly why articles praising fruitarian restaurant owners moonlighting as Zumba instructors, ex-City workers who've moved to the country and now make their own driftwood coat-hangers, or women who used their 'power maternity leave' (a phrase invoked by *Stylist* magazine to describe young mums setting up their own businesses, which was marginally better than the *Telegraph*'s 'time off work') to found their own raw food bar collectives – aka women that you'll never be – are so frustrating.

Perhaps they're supposed to be inspiring, but really these tales of abnormal success just make you sad because you know, deep down, that starting a knit-your-own-organic-veg-box factory when you can't even sign up to a £2-a-month charity donation for fear that the direct debit will bounce renders your business plan a distant and impossible dream. Like the 'celeb reports' which scrutinise what the most recent graduate of *The X Factor* eats and her exercise regime, these 'career profiles' have been morphed by a constant demand for sensationalism into 'true-life tales'. When the chief designer at Google spends 200 words of her 500-word article waxing lyrical about the fact that the Google canteen gives them *free food, every day* (seriously) right after some blatantly falsified 'morning regimen' (we're willing to bet she actually chows down on a bacon butty while checking her emails at 6 a.m., swearing about the waiting times on the tube and getting rubbed up against on the daily commute by a guy in an anorak with chronic BO), the virtue of the career section has gone down the pan quicker than a muesli lunch on a high-fibre diet. How are *you* ever supposed to find yourself in the Google canteen, snaffling up the last of the free fish and chips on a Friday afternoon? 'Try hard' at university. Get into wholegrains. Sign up to a Yogalates class, preferably with a pre-dawn start time. Beyond that, you could bleed a modern-day article on business dry and still only be left with the remnants of someone's 'ultra-healthy' vegetable soup and a facile admonition to 'just apply yourself to something that you love'.

So what's a girl to do if she's truly determined to become a 'career woman'? Well, first of all, the media conspiracy to continue on with the term 'career woman' should probably be swallowed by a black hole – unless 'career man' makes his long-overdue comeback. If you manage to mentally resist all the assertions that you should be properly versed in 'domestic goddessery' such as introducing probiotic bacteria into your own yoghurt, before you even set foot in an office cubicle, then you might be on your way. But there's nothing a women's magazine likes more than to stick another bright pink obstacle in your path, so be prepared for an altogether new onslaught once you're headed for professional success. This comes in the form of that grating, perpetual question: 'Can women have it all?'

HOW TO HAVE IT ALL

Now, if you're a female human being over the age of 13, you've probably become aware of this ubiquitous question. It got asked a lot in the 1970s, after women who had been housewives decided that if you're going to be at a man's beck and call for most of the day, you might as well do it for money. Then, for a while, all was quiet on the western front as equal parenting and attitudes to domestic work changed; it seemed as though we were witnessing the gradual evolution of stereotyping and prejudice into freedom and opportunity, where men's familial roles would expand just as much as those shoulder pads women were starting to wear in the workplace. Needless to say, we *have* progressed in leaps and bounds when you compare today's world to the days when a woman in a laboratory was assumed to have gotten lost on the way to the baby-changing facilities. But the granola-eating air traffic controller, with her two well-rounded children, her laidback but effortlessly wholesome lifestyle, and her adoring husband, is still never far from our minds. She is an unusual human being. She is a woman who 'has it all'. And you're probably nothing like her.

The twenty-first century has seen a resurgence in media interest in whether women can 'have it all'; in fact, 'Why women still can't have it all' by Anne-Marie Slaughter was one of *The Atlantic*'s most globally discussed features of 2012. But what exactly is 'having it all', and why do we never care whether men can? The question *appears* to be whether the woman in question can 'have it like a man', but the subtext is whether she can live her life according to a set of unrealistic expectations which almost never impose on her male counterparts. First, there's the assumption that she needs to be the primary caregiver to her children, almost entirely and solely responsible for how they are raised. Secondly, she has to be constantly available for work during hours that don't usually correspond with school times, since they were decided upon when almost every household had one partner (the woman, in case you hadn't guessed) permanently in the home. Thirdly, she should single-handedly uphold her romantic and sexual life with her husband, usually by pretending to be a lap dancer in the lounge on regular occasions; and fourthly, she should be the first port of call for any domestic issues whatsoever.

It's a rare publication that frequently calls for a male readership to examine whether 'you're doing your best in the kitchen, the bedroom, the nursery and the boardroom', and an even rarer one that asks him to consider whether his massive pay packet intimidates his girlfriend. While magazines present being a successful career women as an unachievable ideal, and then in the next breath question whether 'having it all' is possible (never mind whether you even care about 'having it all' – or, God forbid, might distribute those anxieties between you and your partner equally), they're edging us further and further away from that enviable salary. In 'Why women still can't have it all', Slaughter spoke of the 'genuine superwomen' who are high up in government or senior business positions – the ones who really *do* manage the porridge and 5 a.m. aerobics class – and how they are the only ones to break through the barriers because of the weight of these unrealistic expectations. These women have to be ten times more dedicated than their counterparts just to get a brief nod in their direction. And a lot of them, having been told relentlessly that they won't be 'proper mothers' while at the top of their game (just look at all those stock photos showing babies crying as their suited and booted mums leave for work), or that their work ethic will be destroyed by that ridiculous, anti-medical concept of 'baby brain', decide to not have families, in order to preserve their credibility. They know that if they procreate, the speculation will begin; and if they're 'celebs' in the public eye, so much the worse, because they'll immediately be relegated to the position of 'yummy mummy' on the cover of *heat* or *Reveal*. And the only career progression from *that* position is to MILF.

In 2012, the *Daily Mail* (whose advertising campaign, ironically enough, used to be: 'Behind every successful woman is a *Daily Mail*') went especially insane for newly appointed Yahoo! CEO Marissa Mayer, who famously worked through maternity leave after being hired while she was pregnant. The *Mail* claimed, of course, that female ire had been piqued after she had the audacity to return to work only two weeks after having her son, lauding her nevertheless as proof that certain hard-working women *can* 'have it all'. A guest article in the *Huffington Post*, by a CEO and mother-of-one, quickly followed up the news with the claim that it was possible to 'be a wife' as well as a mum and a businesswoman – and a slew of similar pieces followed. And the same thing will undoubtedly happen when another Marissa Mayer comes along: the endless, tiresome discussion of whether it's possible to be both a wife and a worker, pleasing everyone it's your responsibility to please. Nobody seems to be asking what 'being a wife' entails, and why it has special gender requirements over and above those expected from other human beings, but it definitely comes with a longer job description than 'being a husband' – and it's often subtly implied that it might involve earning less than your male partner, y'know, for the sake of marital harmony. The woman who 'has it all' comes home from her FTSE 50 job and does the homework with her son in between preparing dinner and ironing the school uniforms with a great big smile on her face. In other words, she basically doesn't exist, except in the eyes of the media – but her persistence in those outlets means that real-life women are made to feel inadequate in the workplace every day, stuck in a perpetual panic that they are failing in one of these spheres, when they should probably just be down the pub getting rat-arsed and voguing along to Madonna as they slosh Pinot Grigio from bar to bathroom.

If you're lucky enough not to be a 'yummy mummy' – probs because you're not a sleb – then the moment you touch a keyboard in between breast feeds, you'll be lumped with the term 'mommy blogger' (a charming linguistic import from America that describes women who write online and also have kids) or 'momtrepreneur' (a mother who also sometimes sells stuff). This ensures that, if you're female, the moment you procreate becomes a moment of redefinition. It follows you around like a four-month-old with a malodorous nappy, changing the way you're spoken about, even in the workplace. This, of course, says a lot about our own society and the roles we decide are most appropriate and most natural to females. The 'dadtrepreneur' doesn't exist, not just because it's a shitty word, but because it's assumed that a man's status as father will have little or no effect on his professional life. Meanwhile, Michelle Obama is 'Mom-in-Chief', and Victoria Beckham gets asked at the launch of her Spring/Summer 2014 collection by *Closer* magazine how she 'manages to juggle all her responsibilities' as a 'pretty amazing fashion designer – and . . . a dedicated mum', until Posh Spice shamefacedly admits, 'I do feel guilty.' As long as we're still defined by motherhood and the public perception of women's roles remains so skewed, the question about whether or not women can have it all will seem a little premature.

At the other end of the spectrum, we've been told of readers' and friends' dismay at being made to feel that their decision to stay at home with their newborn baby and take a break is somehow 'beneath them'. Right-wing newspapers jump on this attitude as evidence that their conservative agenda centred on traditional family values is correct, and that high-and-mighty career women need taking down a peg or two.

A sneering article from our favourite right-wing tabloid (the *Mail*, of course) in November 2012 was entitled 'The women who think they're too clever to have babies'. Meanwhile, one in seven women is made redundant after taking maternity leave. It shouldn't be a question of 'us v them', and the arguments just demonstrate how confused we all are. It seems that people are forgetting that feminism – inclusive feminism, anyway – has always been about choice, and who the hell is anyone to pass comment on your decision to work part-time or take a break altogether? Women caught up in the rat race aren't faring much better than stay-at-home mums in terms of media pressure, which is why it's all the more important that we support one another's choices rather than condemning them. Despite its being technically illegal these days, many male bosses seem to think that asking 'Are you planning on having a baby?' in a job interview is acceptable, as is suggesting that your frustration during a particularly challenging project might be because you're on your period.

The gender pay gap in the UK continues to stand at around 16% at the time of writing, with the percentage of women at the top of most careers levelling out at a depressing 22%. Clearly, we're nowhere near 'having it all'; in fact we barely even have a slice of the pie, which we probably baked ourselves while sobbing into the pastry at 4 a.m. One of the reasons that gender inequality in the workplace still exists is the sheer level of the demands made by the current economic system – if you're not clocking in at all hours of the day or night then you're not doing your duty to the company. Despite our increased ability to work from home thanks to new technology, flexible working hours remain as fantastical as the Diet Coke guy in the adverts: an infinitely appealing but untouchable mirage. No wonder so many women are setting up their own patchwork oven glove companies and becoming their own bosses; rather than ask why it is that a full-time job is still so incompatible with having children, the media redefine it as a 'career break'. But if being at home with children is so easy, why aren't more men doing it?

THE MISSING LINKS

This endless reductive pigeonholing of the female public position – the 'yummy mummy out on the town', the 'sassy singleton in the city' with her BlackBerry and her Louboutins, the 'health freak with her high-flying job' (and her requisite even-more-high-flying 'hubby'), or the 'ballsy homemaker mother-of-four, wielding the full force of the PTA' – is just another example of the unfair scrutiny afforded to those in possession of a vagina. While a male politician will always be judged on the work that he does, sadly a 'lady politician' (and what a joyously archaic term that is) can be brought down by a bad haircut. The advice put forward by various outlets reflects this scrutiny of your looks, behaviour and 'business persona'. The *Forbes* article '10 ways body language can help you be more powerful' is a potent example: don't wear too much lipstick, or it will be assumed that your eyes are on your colleague rather than the prize. Don't smile too much – it's a 'sign of weakness'. Don't frown, or you won't seem flexible. Don't peer over your glasses, because 'it makes you look distant and snobby'. Don't expose your wrists (yes, really) because 'an exposed wrist is a sign of submission'. Don't 'act girlish' or 'be overly expressive', because you'll overwhelm your male audience. Similar advice pops up everywhere.

Where genuine career advice is absent, articles about 'job interview conduct' (hair and make-up) abound, including this particularly nauseating example from *Glamour* (September 2013) entitled 'What to wear for a job interview, including hair and make-up tips', written by a Marissa Gold who describes herself thus: 'Lives for love; eats dessert first'. 'Dressing for a job interview can be tough,' it begins. 'You want to appear professional, mature, and serious but still show off a little personal style.' Is that really your principal concern, though? *Teen Vogue* continues the patronising theme by informing its readers that, 'Business professional doesn't have to be boring . . . A sizeable satchel is important . . . though your best accessory is a résumé printed on nice paper – and a smile, of course!' Further up the age range, *Good Housekeeping* tells you the '5 best looks to land the job' – because, as always seems to be the case with these features, the suit is more important than the woman in it. Make sure you get the right type (a skirt suit, because trouser suit says lesbian and everyone *knows* that lesbians are for porn and not the latest business pitch), with the right skirt length (tread the line carefully between 'slutty receptionist' and 'frumpy office mother who brings the boys coffee'), and don't ever, ever be yourself. It may seem that this kind of style spaff is restricted to the media, but sadly it's bleeding into office culture too. In October 2013, law firm Clifford Chance came under fire for emailing a list of 'Presentation tips for women' to the company's female employees which included such gems as 'No one heard Hillary the day she showed cleavage', and 'Talk through your mouth, not your nose.' All sounding a bit like season one of *Mad Men*? That's because it belongs in the 1960s.

Needless to say, there's a lot that could be done by the magazines aimed at women of working age to counteract this madness. Instead of increasing pressure on the gals they often literally claim to love, with constantly reiterated articles on whether 'he' will 'run for the hills' as soon as your pay outstrips his, they could come over from the dark side and get stuck into smashing the glass ceiling, preferably with a sledge-hammer as opposed to a stiletto. Some tentatively progressed in the last couple of years when feminism came back on the agenda (to be fair to them, *Cosmopolitan*'s campaign to tackle the wage gap was a step in the right direction). But the concrete advice that we need is still missing from many a magazine: how to present yourself assertively at a meeting about pay progression, for instance; questions to ask at the end of interviews (thus far *Stylist* is the only mag we've seen tackle this); or where to research different industries and their track records in gender equality. In the conveniently all-female environment of the women's magazine, they could ask questions such as why Virgin Air showed an advert in 2013 in which 'all Virgin Air employees' had magical powers – but in which the male pilots are superheroes, whereas the stewardesses (all of whom bar one are female) have the 'ability' to wear shoes and repel water from passengers. Yep, the guys get superhuman military precision, and the gals get blowjob lips and an enhanced ability to mop up spillages. Is this the advert we want our teenage daughters to watch in between *SpongeBob SquarePants* and the latest music video of bikini-clad girls washing a rapper's car with too many soapsuds? Some would argue that the male-pilot-to-female-steward ratio is merely a reflection of reality – most pilots are, indeed, male. But as many a feminist has said (or indeed yelled) before us, 'You can't be what you can't see.'

If this advice isn't enough, then there's a plethora of books out there just waiting to confuse the general female population with their array of conflicting advice: use your 'flirtatious advantage' to get ahead; be as confident as a man, but not as brash; stay for all of the networking opportunities, but don't stay in the pub past one drink, ever (nobody wants to see a drunk woman); nice girls don't get the corner office; use your inherent feminine loveliness to progress in communications; think 'like a man'. And just when you thought you'd disentangled yourself from that web of inconsistencies and properly settled in your own career, along comes a *Woman's Hour* list of powerful figures that's divided into 'hard power' (finance, war, hereditary positions) and 'soft power' (almost all of the industries where women have a proper foot in the door). Soft power. Suddenly, someone else has decided that your job in legal mediation is the flaccid penis of the business world.

One of the most prominent books of female career advice of late has to be Facebook CEO Sheryl Sandberg's *Lean In*, the international success which urged women not to bow to pressure to remove themselves from the workplace. Acknowledging that society has a problem with successful women, she details how she asked to be removed from a yearbook voting her 'most likely to succeed' at school so that she could get a date to her high school prom. Her advice not to chip away at your career in preparation for a possible family future is solid, and her outspoken dedication to the feminist cause is encouraging. Nevertheless, we are inclined to agree with the *Washington Post* that *Lean In* is 'full of good intentions but rife with contradictions'. Like Louise Mensch or Margaret Thatcher, Sheryl Sandberg pushes individualism and financial power, and assumes the presence of a supportive (male) spouse as well as a good background and an expensive education. She is a woman who 'has it all' – but then, she was born into a world which enabled that.

Meanwhile, books such as *The Essential Difference* (Simon Baron Cohen, 2003) claim women are better suited to nurturing roles such as teaching and nursing – admirable pursuits, but ones that we should never have to muddy with suspect biological determinism. In fact, the *Daily Mail* extrapolated so wildly from *The Essential Difference* during the book's launch that it somehow managed to blame autism on 'the changing role of women in society'. According to the newspaper, in the olden days intelligence wasn't really prized when it came to selecting a woman with whom to procreate. Now that it is, more ladyboffins are having babies with intelligent 'systematising' men, thus producing more autistic children. Because, like, science. So while 'Feminism causes autism' sounds like something that's come out of an online fascist headline generator, it's alarmingly close to a real-life article produced extremely recently.

Thankfully, there are those out there who refused to take such scaremongering articles seriously, and have instead concentrated on founding initiatives for getting more women into science in the twenty-first century. Least successful of these was the $128,000 EU initiative 'Science: It's a Girl Thing', which showed blow-dried, high-heeled lady chemists in little dresses 'doing some science', most of which seemed to involve using massive beakers to mix up nail varnish while gyrating next to a wind machine. As anyone who's ever lit a fag using a Bunsen burner or made their own MDMA knows, that is categorically *not* all we get up to in the science lab. Thankfully a bunch of female neuroscientists from Bristol University were able to provide us with a parody of the whole pathetic campaign by making their own YouTube version where one of them gyrates up against a CAT scan machine to the tune of LMFAO's 'Sexy and I Know It'. The European Commission were laughed out of the building. But it hasn't been the only crap attempt at getting girls interested in science that we've seen in the last year or so. An article in *The Guardian* (no less) told how 'cooking uses both maths and science' and that 'encourag[ing] your daughter to experiment in the kitchen' will increase her interest in science. 'Baking in particular . . . is a scientific activity', the article continued, before suggesting that making 'your domestic scenario more scientific' will help garner her interest, especially as 'shopping is filled with maths problems'. If you're not tearing your face off by now in despair, then perhaps you've fallen victim to the propaganda yourself: the notion that we're only able to do sums when it involves adding up all the wuvely clothes we've bought goes some way to showing why the position of women in the working world still feels so precarious.

It's not just the traditionalists who are irritatingly vocal about women's career choices. The feminist movement was often rather disparaging of 'capitalist feminists' – they wanted a complete social revolution, a new world order where bourgeois gender roles were abandoned, and, presumably, everyone frolicked naked together while the men were all consigned to an island somewhere. When Germaine Greer said, 'I wanted to liberate women from the vacuum cleaner, not put them on the board of Hoover', she expressed the frustration that many feminists were feeling with capitalist power structures. Arguably, both models failed. All you have to do is look around you to realise that capitalist feminism has been a resounding failure. Capitalism has never looked kindly on its underlings, and unfortunately that's what women still are, holding as they do only a tiny percentage of the world's wealth. Our representation in government and public life in the UK and US hovers around that same low percentage mark (17–22%) regardless of the specialism or institution, and we are paid on average £413,000 less over our lifetime than men who follow identical career paths. Meanwhile, the feminist revolution never came. We are in no way a post-feminist society.

ASTRONAUTS, ASPIRATIONS AND AMBITION

When one of our Twitter followers told us that her daughter said she wished she'd been born a man so she could be an astronaut when she grew up, it hit us hard. But who can blame her? The way women in public life are portrayed doesn't exactly foster ambition in the next generation, and it goes all the way back to when you were first given that doll to play with while your brother got a Superman costume, and thus registered (probably unconsciously, because not that many toddlers are that perceptive, even when subjected to hours and hours of Baby Einstein DVDs) notions of what constitute specific 'male' or 'female' behaviours. These are reinforced by adverts such as a 2013 effort from Weetabix showing sibling rivalry between a doll-and-disco-dancing obsessed little girl and her (much cooler) superhero little brother. The idea that in order to achieve career success you have to be aggressive and ruthless – not qualities deemed traditionally desirable for 'little ladies' – demonstrates that there is still a deep mistrust of women who have made it to the top of the career ladder. Girls still shy away from science and maths subjects in school, finding themselves often discouraged from pursuing them by their own teachers and classmates; the fact that it is only in single-sex schools that a significant number of girls choose to take these subjects at

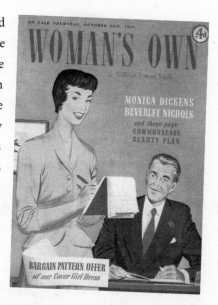

A Level should speak volumes. The few who battle onwards and end up in, say, engineering careers often have to endure entrenched sexism from their male bosses and co-workers from the outset. So begins a lifetime of inappropriate comments, double standards and overlooked promotions that add up to the social equivalent of screaming at a nuclear physicist, 'Why didn't you just shut up and become a nursery school teacher?' It's a cultural environment which slowly and surely erodes our ability to choose.

Yes, sexism in the workplace is alive and well, folks, and allusions to PMT are the tip of the iceberg. There are fusty old dinosaurs wandering around the offices of this country who genuinely believe that women need to get back in the kitchen where they belong, managers who think that rating female colleagues out of ten for attractiveness and then putting the results on the wall is an acceptable workplace practice, and organisations where bum-spanking or pinching is still de rigueur. One of our readers told us that, while working for a male gynaecologist, she and other colleagues were not allowed in the operating room for fear of 'perineal fallout' (aka the charming little completely unscientific notion that because you are a woman and therefore wearing a skirt, germs will literally FALL OUT of your vagina and contaminate the hospital). That we have this to put up with as well as what is, let's face it, an unfair amount of tedious housework just hammers home how important it is that we support one another. In the society we currently inhabit, none of the choices we make can be said to be truly autonomous anyway – having to leave your job because you can't afford the childcare or not being able to leave your job because you can't afford the childcare are not really choices at all. If your friend decides on a different path to yours, try to back her. The support we've received from older women since we started the Vagenda has been incredible, but it has also highlighted how important it is for us to stick together.

As a wise MP once told us, supporting the next generation of women is one of the best things that you can do – or, as Madeleine Albright put it, 'There is a special place in hell for women who don't help other women' (interestingly, quoted by Taylor Swift in very different circumstances in spring 2013). Women are more likely to be underpaid, or more likely not to be paid at all (unsurprisingly, most interns are women) and are most likely to feel like cutting and running when they realise how much of a cock-heavy sausage fest many offices are. And once you start looking into the mechanisms that work against us, you stop seeing 'I only want to get here on my own merit' as a valid argument against quotas and temporary periods of positive discrimination. Because the fact of the matter is that enough racist, sexist, homophobic, privately educated 'boys of the old school' remain in powerful places to keep you from achieving on your own merit if you happen to be a woman, or not white, or not straight, or trans, or working class, or all of the above. Positive discrimination is a clunky solution to a complex problem, but it's a solution that forces these sorts of people to think again when they appoint another employee in their own image, and to have to explain it when they do it one too many times.

Solidarity with your female colleagues is the first step towards a workplace with equal gender representation and hopefully one day the country will be so full of working women that female politicians will no longer be mistaken for secretaries in the lifts of the House of Commons, and the most prominent picture of a woman in a national newspaper won't be a 16-year-old girl with her tits out (hopefully Page Three will have died a death by then), or of a murder victim or a princess, but of a broad taking charge of her own destiny and doing us all proud. In this ideal world, women who feature in news stories will not be defined purely by their marital status – ('wife and mother of three') – unless, of course, we start seeing similar headlines for men: 'Husband and father of three switched his son to a healthier diet and found it had MORE sugar'; 'Slim father-of-four devours 72 oz steak in three minutes'. Female GPs will be merely GPs, and won't be regularly blamed by the right-wing media for the downfall of the NHS. Perhaps most importantly, parenting will be regarded as a jobshare. Until that happens, as far as the division of labour is concerned, it certainly helps to make sure you settle down with someone who'll at least get up in the night with the baby, iron their own shirt and scrub their own shit off the toilet. It'll save you a lot of problems later in life – and it might just end up being the leg-up you need on the way to the top.

9
Let Us Eat Cake

ATTACK OF THE FRIDGE RAIDERS

Take even a fleeting glance at women's magazines and you'll be justified in concluding that the whole lot of them are engaged in a massive conspiracy to ruin your enjoyment of doughnuts for ever. Mags such as *Cosmopolitan*, *Closer* and *Glamour*, with their calorie-obsessed features, are also hell-bent on destroying your penchant for mayonnaise by informing you how much fat per gram it contains and marking it 'Sinful' in huge capital letters, thus condemning you to a lifetime of watery, tasteless condiments or ridiculous food supplements.

Everywhere you turn, some celebrity is inflicting her food diary on you, recording everything that passes her lips save collagen, only for some tedious nutritionist to inform her that there isn't enough curly kale in her diet. Features such as *Closer*'s 'Fridge Raiders' will purport to have the fridge-owning celebrity's best interests at heart, when really it's an excuse for a questionable dietician to experience a little jolt of *schadenfreude* at the discovery that that lass off *Emmerdale* is addicted to Dairylea triangles and, despite her size-8 figure, is actually a covert midnight Pringles-muncher (this is also known as 'food shaming').

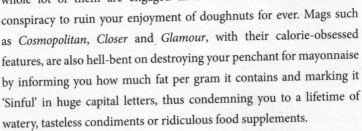

The fact that most celebrities' fridges really only contain a baggie of amphetamines and a Tupperware container full of wheatgrass smoothie is something they choose mostly to ignore, mainly because the headline 'Celeb's diet diaries: what they REALLY eat' sells a lot of copies. Of course it does: we have become a nation obsessed.

Most of these magazines are fairly alert to the fact that they can't be seen to openly tout weight loss to people with healthy BMIs, so their dieting and weight loss features often masquerade as 'healthy eating plans' or 'friendly' advice. Of course, the content itself has always been and will always be centred round being skinny. Women's magazines have a massive vested interest in pushing this message, after all: *Closer* magazine even has its own spin-off weight loss website, Closer Diets.

Weight loss is society's favourite female problem. In the UK, statistics indicate that most women have been on a diet at some point, while a fifth of us are said to be on one most of the time. This amounts to one hell of a lot of women saying, 'No chocolate torte for me, thanks, that spinach salad filled me right up.' And yet, the fact that so many of us persist in our dieting quests can mean only one thing: that most of these diets don't work. At all. Hence the need for newspapers and magazines to continually feature new eating plans and regimes, lest your attention lapse for a moment and you take stock of the fact that your bum is the same size as it ever was. 'LOOK! PALEO DIET!' they scream, drawing you in with clinical trials that have been performed on mice (but my God were those some mad hot, skinny little mice). We are, as we write this, in the midst of an 'obesity epidemic', and yes, that's something we should be worrying about. Yet at the same time, thousands of healthy-sized women are going about their days hungry, buying books such as *Six Weeks to OMG: Get Skinnier Than All Your Friends* (Venice A. Fulton, 2012) which could presumably lead to a national case of competitive starvation if all your friends buy it. If we're to have that 'taut body' and all the 'self-confidence' that comes with it, we shouldn't let ourselves go for one second, let alone throw the baby food out with the bathwater by scoffing something as sinful as broccoli (declared 'carbier than you think' in 2013).

The well-known phrase 'A moment on the lips, a lifetime on the hips' has been the unofficial mantra of the women's magazine for many a year now. For a while, it seemed like men had escaped this twilight zone of strict rationing and routine guilt induction – after all, a man never has to suffer the indignity of a bitchy picture caption describing how he 'poured his enviable curves into this season's tuxedo' – but where once men ate five jacket potatoes of an evening and failed to give it a second thought as their girlfriends wept in the corner with a teacup of carrot soup, now the times are rapidly changing. September 2013 even saw the *Evening Standard* speculate about whether Colin Firth, Jude Law and Harry Enfield were on the 5:2 diet under the headline 'The chaps are going from chunky to chiselled – but why?'

And increasingly we now see similar content in places like *Men's Health* and *Men's Fitness* magazines. Some articles – such as 'Your ultimate smoothie guide' or '12 Foods to remove from your fridge forever' (both found in *Men's Fitness*) – would be welcome on the cover of any of the female counterparts. 'Some refrigerator staples, like pickles, lunch meat, and milk, could explain why your abs are in hiding,' simpers the introduction to the latter article, in that infantilising tone which is almost ubiquitous in its female-oriented counterparts. Meanwhile, *Men's Health* promises 'A year of weight-loss cheats' and holds competitions like the 'Men's Health Fat-Burners' ('How much weight do you think you could lose in one year? . . . One year ago, we asked four *Men's Health* readers to find out. We gave them those 12 months to shed as much fat as possible, armed with nothing but advice from @MensHealthUK Twitter followers.') While men's magazines tend to have much lower circulations than women's magazines (in the first half of 2013, for instance, the UK readership as measured by ABC totalled 400,371 for *Glamour* versus 203,741 for *Men's Health*), it's still a worrying trend that sets a dangerous precedent for both sexes.

However, thanks to centuries of body fascism, women have a pretty hefty head start as far as media scrutiny of their appearance is concerned. Let's not forget that even the buffest of male celebs never really get asked what it is they're consuming and excreting. Until one of them appears in his trunks on the cover of h*eat*, you can consider our sympathy extremely limited. Women have been encouraged to poke around in their own faeces to work out their 'intolerances' for decades. Really want to join us down here, boys? It (literally) stinks.

Celebrity-focused magazines such as *Closer* have made food and body obsessing their central selling points, and word of mouth has it that it can be a pretty lucrative business for those stars who are willing to monetise their yo-yo dieting in the form of pap shots and interviews. Focusing on the diets and fitness regimes of Z-List celebrities and reality TV stars, cover stories have included 'I'm not too thin – Pete loves my size zero body', 'I've gained a dress size but I'll stay curvy for *X Factor*', 'I've dropped a dress size & I'm back in love – sex is amazing' and 'LOVE SPLIT DIETS: it's been a hellish month – I've no appetite' (note the frequent correlations drawn between the quality of your love life and the emptiness of your kitchen cupboards). Inside, where the minutiae of the daily dieting grind are detailed, is even more disturbing. The magazine is full of so many tips on how to be skinny that they often contradict one another – one minute you're being told that Fergie from the Black Eyed Peas is a size 8 thanks to her burrito diet, or that you can 'DROP A DRESS SIZE IN TWO WEEKS' using their slimming plan which includes, as a real-life example, pork kebabs and cream cheese bagels – and the next, you're being told to ditch the junk food and that Kim Kardashian (who, has just been fat-shamed by a rival publication) 'hits the gym five times a day'. It's a minefield of misinformation and manufactured self-loathing.

And then you have the interviews. More common in the higher-end magazines (trash rags will usually just run shamelessly with the diet angle), these features often purport to be interested in the subject's personality, intellect and contribution to society, only to then reveal an obsession with diet to rival the lowbrow offerings. The journalist will be at pains to prove that not only is said celeb refreshingly normal, but she has a normal diet too, and all while maintaining the 'tight little body' (quite probably one of the most unsavoury phrases in the entire English language) required of her as a female in the public eye. 'A model who actually eats?!' the journalist will scribble faux-incredulously, as though the correspondent for (*Fame*) *Hungry Monthly* hasn't been through the whole monotonous routine a million times. 'Oh, I eat all the time,' the celebrity will jovially insist. 'There's nothing I love more than cooking a full Sunday roast for my nearest and dearest on the weekend. In fact, I hate the whole celebrity circus . . . *Her beautiful nose crinkles slightly as she stares into the middle distance, possibly envisaging the tedium of the red-carpet press junket.* 'No, I'd much rather sit at home in Primrose Hill in my pyjamas consuming whatever refined pork product is my current endorsement. I guess I'm just lucky – I'm one of those girls who never puts on weight.' *The silk of her dress flutters over her sample-size frame as she adjusts herself in her seat.*

The pervasiveness of this 'I'm just normal, me' charade was perfectly encapsulated by a headline in *Glamour* that read, 'Heidi Klum is OK With the Occasional Burger' (BREAKING NEWS). This is the sort of editorial that *Glamour* holds particularly close to its cold, dead, sparkly heart. We're talking about the magazine that once featured a full-page picture of spaghetti and meatballs accompanied by 'Some women eat this and stay slim'.

TOFU, CIGARETTES, AND WILD BLUE-GREEN ALGAE

Of course, every now and again a celebrity comes along who makes no bones about the kind of tortuous diet and fitness regime she has to follow (Gwyneth Paltrow, with her 'best green juice' and arugula meatballs is a prime example, though despite saying that she'd 'rather die than let my kid eat Cup-a-Soup' she does, scandalously, allow herself one cigarette per week. 'It's about finding a balance between cigarettes and tofu,' she said. Natch), and when this happens, it's the magazine's official duty to ensure that the minutiae of that celebrity's diet and fitness regime are exhaustively recorded, while *obviously 'not endorsing it' at all*. More often than not, said sleb will be following some awful fad diet or detox regime at the behest of a spaff-peddling expert with a made-up qualification from an uncredited institution. (We have Dr Ben Goldacre's excellent takedown of poo-rummager Gillian McKeith to thank for accurate knowledge of her educational attainments.)

Charlatan nutritionists are always harping on about about this or that superfood (which coincidentally just happens to be the one which last year you were told would give you cancer) and how it removes 'toxins', which usually take the form in this context of non-specific nasties which need 'flushing out' through a punishing liquid diet regime intended to give you the trots for a fortnight. Enter stage-right the 'Saltwater Flush' – an inexplicably popular detox process which involves downing warm, salty water and then spending an agonising half an hour waiting for it to shoot out of your rear end with more kinetic force than an Icelandic geyser.

Or consider 'wild blue-green algae', with which Gillian McKeith was obsessed (so obsessed, in fact, that she wrote an entire book on the subject called *Miracle Superfood: Wild Blue-Green Algae* which is still available for purchase. Form an orderly queue). Unfortunately, as one writer in the *New Scientist* pointed out, wild blue-green algae – also known as cyanobacteria – are toxic. But you know what's really guaranteed to slim you down? Being dead. She could still be on to something.

Alarmingly, this trend for extreme regimes and intense diet scrutiny seems to have extended to the general public. Gone are the days when celebrities were the only ones who had to worry about having their eating habits laid bare; ordinary civilians have to face the nutritionists' food-shaming too. *Red* magazine, for example, ran a feature in June 2012 that saw a variety of perfectly healthy young women berated for their lifestyle choices. Natasha, a lady with a healthy BMI of 21.3, was told to 'swap chocolates and biscuits for a raw bar', while Katie, a gym bunny with an equally healthy BMI and a very healthy diet, was told to ditch the biscuits in exchange for crudités and houmous, because she won't get pregnant unless she loses weight. Pages later, the reader was informed about 'mindful eating' and instructed to 'eat like a calm person'. How the hell can one eat like a calm person when the rules are constantly changing, thus placing you in an endless state of nutritional panic? Poor Katie probably read Mireille Guiliano's bestseller *French Women Don't Get Fat* and thought a little bit of chocolate was OK, but now she's being told by some twat in a national magazine that she's basically a pig in knickers, and a barren one at that. Where do these people get off?

Indeed, it's these fleeting fad diets that really are the most worrying aspects of this hunger-led culture. We've all seen our nearest and dearest make themselves miserable through starvation and deprivation, despite some often unsavoury, and occasionally malodorous, side effects (yes, it's true what they say about the cabbage soup diet).

Back in 2007, *Marie Claire* was singing the praises of what it dubbed 'The Baby Eating Diet', which, despite the name, does not involve the cannibalistic ingestion of infants, but rather 'A-list stars [Jennifer

Aniston, Reese Witherspoon and Marcia Cross] going mushy over the latest diet craze to hit Hollywood – eating jars of baby food'. The article ended with the sentence: 'Sounds like we should all jump on the "choo-choo train" school of eating.' Here, we give you permission to look down at your adult-sized burger and weep for the future of humanity.

Often these diets, the latest being the ubiquitous 'fasting', or 5:2, diet (suggested tagline: 'Making your colleagues even more unpleasant to be around since 2012'), stipulate that you go without the recommended number of calories a day, ensuring that, unless you're a Victorian lady able to spend the working day lolling on a chaise longue, you end up passing out. Not to mention constantly grouchy. Trust us – try one of these fasting diets and you're guaranteed to get to the point where you end up screaming, 'GIVE ME A FUCKING BISCUIT!' in hypoglycemic rage at the supermarket cashier with the wild, yellow-tinged stare of a woman driven mad by malnourishment. But that's cool, right? At least you'll be in 'great shape for a new man', as *Closer* would have it.

It's not just baby food and fasting, either. Take magazine-recommended product Herbalife, which despite sounding like a pretty accurate description of the three years you spent stoned at college is actually the name of a yummy-sounding 'meal replacement programme'. Then you have all the 'beach body plans' which promise to help you drop four dress sizes in four weeks by taking advantage of your anxiety about getting your baps out in a bikini and telling you that the key to shrinking that muffin top lies in something called a 'breadless sandwich.' A *breadless sandwich*. Medical professionals say again and again that the best way to lose weight and keep it off is an oh-so-boring-but-effective combination of healthy eating and regular exercise, yet we're all still hoping for that quick fix.

THE TOP TEN WORST FAD DIETS BY EVERY MAGAZINE EVER

Despite what mendacious, turkey-dinosaur-obliterating tosspot Jamie Oliver would have you believe, a healthy diet combined with frantic Zumba-ing won't be enough to shift your gelatinous arse. Instead, why not try one of these 100% clinically proven diets as invented by an expert near you:

1. **The Tapeworm Diet – early 1900s to 1950s:** If you have a big event coming up and are praying for a spot of slimming norovirus to help you on your way (hot tip: try the oysters), you could do a lot worse than a tapeworm. How exactly you're supposed to go about 'catching' a tapeworm doesn't really bear thinking about (although according to our research on the internet it invariably involves giving a Mexican $1,500 for some parasite-containing pills – a bit dear, considering pig shit costs nothing), but once you've got the bugger in, it can apparently lead to a weight loss of 1–2 lb per week. As recently as August 2013, one woman made the news for buying and ingesting a tapeworm for this very reason. Side effects may or may not include the tapeworm bursting out of your stomach while you lie on a spaceship breakfast table after an artificially induced deep sleep. Once you're skinny enough, sitting in a bath of milk and waiting for it to slide out is apparently one of the few options at your disposal.

2. **The Sleeping Beauty Diet – circa 1966:** This crackpot diet has been peddled for over fifty years on the basis that your body is forced to use up extra reserves of fat while you sleep. Perfect for the ultimate lazy dieter, it involves the bare

minimum of effort and crops up every so often in newspapers and women's magazines. When taken to an extreme conclusion, however, it involves 24/7 sleeping following medically assisted sedation, in order to get your abs fairy-tale firm. Apparently a favourite of Elvis Presley's.

3. **The Lemon Detox, or 'Master Cleanse' Diet – popular since the 1940s:** Starvation is the name of the game, with dieters replacing food with a lemon juice and maple syrup mixture that bungs you up and rots your teeth (Beyoncé is reportedly a fan). Going to a restaurant with anyone on this diet is a miserable experience as they sit there sipping their 'master cleanse lemonade' with barely enough energy to converse.

4. **The Cabbage Soup Diet – circa 1980:** A must-try for the slimming masochist. Everyone knows that cabbage smells like arse, but not only does this diet make you shit molten cabbage-lava, it also makes your house (wherein you have been preparing the devilish concoction) extremely unpalatable to gentleman callers. If you've been craving celibacy as well as IBS, and are prepared to eat unparalleled quantities of the vegetable (perhaps you are a Russian peasant from the 1880s?), then this is the diet for you.

5. **The Hallelujah Diet – popular since 1992 (developed in the 1970s):** The regime of choice for Bible-bashers, this diet is based on something God apparently said in Genesis about how 85% of your food should be raw and plant-based (it's essentially veganism with added sanctimony). It's not the most

balanced of diets, revolving as it does mostly around mung beans, and it flagrantly ignores the fact that cooking kills off some of the bacteria that live in food. God also later reneged on the veggie deal by saying: 'every moving thing that liveth shall be meat for you', which basically means that you can go ahead and eat that tapeworm mentioned earlier.

6. The Dukan Diet – 2000: Offer someone on the Dukan Diet a sausage sandwich and they'll reply, 'No. I'm on phase two of the Dukan Diet and can only eat pork on every second Wednesday providing it's a full moon.' This diet's various phases are harder to grasp than the most complex branches of theoretical physics. Even understanding the Schrödinger's cat thought experiment while drunk (comprehending a cat in a box that is simultaneously both dead and alive is no picnic at the best of times) is liable to become as unchallenging as an episode of *Button Moon* when compared with a Dukan dieter trying to work out whether they're allowed yoghurt on Tuesday. It's based entirely around cottage cheese, which is made from the waste removed during lipo, hence its texture (probably).

7. The *French Women Don't Get Fat* Diet – 2007: *Ooh là là!* Looking a bit portly? Why not take advice from the nation that that eats chocolate bread and cheese for breakfast and loves nothing more than a pig's head fried in butter crowned with baby birds? Apparently, French women are able to enjoy the country's gourmet delicacies, such as baked Camembert, in moderation, while spending every weekend subsisting on leek water that literally makes them poo themselves thin. How the

French have managed to combine faecal incontinence with a reputation for chicness remains one of life's great mysteries.

8. The Air, or Breatharian, Diet – 2010: Perhaps tiring of its daily leek juice, French *Grazia* once featured the Air Diet, an eating plan which involves not eating. Basically, you hold your food up to your mouth – and pretend. It's a regime that sounds even less satisfying than the well-publicised Mastication Diet, in which you chew food before spitting it out. In November 2013, the *Telegraph* reported that Michelle Pfeiffer had become a 'breatharian', believing that she could survive 'on air and sunlight alone'.

9. The Purple Diet – circa 2011: This diet involves the consumption of only purple food (can you tell that we're losing the will to live?).

10. The Liquid Diet – since time immemorial: This is the part where, after exhausting all dieting options, you drink two bottles of Pinot and four tequila shots, while weeping to your best friend about how your life is so miserable and devoid of joy and chocolate mousse that you have become an empty husk of a person. 'Eating is cheating', as the mantra goes, and it's chicer and cheaper just to drown your sorrows in Buckfast than it is to face up to decades of unhealthy eating patterns sanctioned by the mainstream media. In a sense, you have become a human Schrödinger's cat: alive, yet dead, and lying in a box filled with cyanide.

FOOD PORN

Considering the continual cupcakeisation of the media, it's somewhat ironic that they are so keen on preventing us from eating. The way the fash pack have fetishised brightly coloured girlie foods such as macarons, behaving as though these sugary treats are a kind of fashion accessory, begins to look very confusing next to the constant messages we're also sent about hunger and how to manage it. Online magazine *Jezebel* ran a story in 2012 entitled 'A cupcake is never just a cupcake: The psycho-sexuality of a twee treat', pointing out the sudden deluge of teeny tiny iced goods in TV programmes, books and movies, where they apparently often stand in for femininity and even the female orgasm, being as they are a 'private and delicate affair'.

While we may not buy the 'cupcake-as-orgasm' theory, these glorified fairy cakes nonetheless crop up in any number of female narratives. Think about it: Miranda iced cupcakes for Steve's girlfriend Debbie way back when *Sex and the City* was a blazingly honest TV programme rather than a disappointingly consumer-oriented movie franchise for those with hollow eyes and stomachs. Even the brilliant 2011 film *Bridesmaids* featured a love story centred around a cupcake shop, yet this modern obsession with baking is completely at odds with society's current slimming preoccupation, especially in an age when (perfectly healthy-sized) *Great British Bake Off* winner Ruby Tandoh is told by Raymond Blanc that she is 'so thin' it makes him 'doubt her love for great cooking'. (If there was ever a perfect illustration of You Can't Win syndrome for women in the media, this was it.) Then again, when compared to a big fuck-off Victoria sponge, cupcakes aren't really about stuffing your face to satiation – especially the mini ones you get at fashion parties. Likewise, the canapés women are supposed to covet are hardly KFC tower burgers or casserole dishes filled with macaroni cheese. This is girlie food for so-called girlie appetites. And it's probably only a matter of time before someone dreams up the Cupcake Diet.

THINSPIRATION NATION

The continued existence of supposed quick fixes and the enthusiasm they are met with in the media hints at a darker edge to the industry. We've read thinspiration articles in magazines which recommend that you leave the windows open while sleeping because the shivering of your unconscious body will help to burn off calories while you sleep (*Marie Claire*), that you replace food with powder (and not the kind media darlings get on a street corner for £40 a gram, but actual *powdered food*), and tips ranging on the madness scale from taking cold baths every morning to blowing up balloon after balloon to firm up your abs (this from 'Six weeks to OMG'). Celebrity interviews, especially with celebrities who have recently been pregnant, have produced such hyped-up nonsense as the Jessica Alba claim in *Net-a-Porter* magazine (25 April, 2013) that you can 'wear a double corset for three months' after giving birth and, presumably, magically pop back to a size 8. ('It was sweaty, but it was worth it.') *Look* magazine was quick to pick up on this titbit and run it as 'Jessica Alba reveals the secret to her post-baby body: a corset!' The *Mail Online* went with 'Jessica Alba's right – a corset can help you flatten that post-baby bump', and Today.com rather tastelessly ran 'Corsets after pregnancy? It's a thin thing'.

But it's not just celebrities who come under this sort of scrutiny: increasingly, ordinary women are also wheeled out to demonstrate their body flaws and celebrate their dieting techniques. An example of this would be the features which compulsively claim to reveal 'slim women's secrets'. Cue a group of non-celebrities being paraded in front of their readership merely for the supposed virtue of being thin. The slim women in question are always quoted alongside their dress size and weight, for example 'Stephanie (size 6, 8st.)' or 'Chloe (size 6–8, 8st. 7lb)', encouraging you to hold your own weight and dress size up for comparison. Heights are often added too. A feature last year in *Marie Claire* called 'Real women: amazing bodies' informed us Shona is '5ft 8in. tall, weighs 9st 2lb and is a size 8–10', before chronicling her daily diet and exercise regime, just to make all the 5ft 8in. women out there who weigh ten stone and over feel extra, extra shitty. 'I've dropped a dress size and four bra sizes,' continued the article, its photographers lingering over the women's taut muscles. It may be in the health section, and many may describe it as more 'fitspiration' (a mainly internet-based trend that emphasises physical fitness and muscle mass) than thinspiration, but it comes from the same place ('Strong is the new skinny' says *Woman & Home*, as if we were in desperate need of 'the new skinny') and that place is Your Body Isn't Good Enough Central. Which, incidentally, hosts some of the worst nights out of your life.

Magazines which are supposedly aimed at women beyond their twenties and thirties, such as *Women & Home* (a smorgasbord of weight loss advice, recipes, and articles about the perimenopause) and *Good Housekeeping*, don't let up either. Suddenly it's less about 'what's in this season' and more about 'what's in season': food porn mixed in with 'analytical' articles with titles such as 'What's your tummy type?' (Do you have an 'apple tum'? A 'pouty tum'? Or a 'wobbly tum'? If it's the first, then 'Drop all sugar, wheat, processed foods, caffeine, alcohol.' And fun, presumably.) Much like the features listing women's heights and weights, these mags seem to go out of their way to encourage competitive non-eating. As a gender we should all give our thanks to magazines such as *Good Housekeeping*, whose gloating article 'Guess which of us lost the most weight?' last year detailed how weight loss has 'transformed the lives of these four women' while no doubt making its readers want to eat their own faces off in despair (if they weren't so fattening, obvs).

'When I was in my 20s, I was a couple of stone heavier than I wanted to be – at 11 stone I may not have been extremely overweight, but it definitely affected my confidence,' says Jane. 'It was when I started seeing a boyfriend who weighed less than me that I knew something had to change! . . . I signed up for a meal replacement plan – the food tasted completely vile, which probably helped with the weight loss.' Sounds healthy. She continues: 'By ignoring my taste buds I lost two stone over three months, reaching my goal weight of 8 st. 11 lb. Then I married the skinny boyfriend!'

Is this how we now define success: by our ability to deny ourselves pleasure and starve ourselves down to our goal weight? The fact that these magazines aimed at women middle-aged and beyond are still banging the weight loss drum gives us very little hope of ever being at ease around food, but then, it's that insecurity that keeps you coming back for more. A few pages later, in the same magazine, there is an article called 'Beat biscuit o'clock' (why on earth would you *want* to?) which could have been taken pretty much verbatim from a 'pro-ana' message board. It teaches you how to resist cravings by drinking water, 're-training your taste buds' and building a 'mental shield'. 'Try imagining eating chocolate before you eat it . . . you'll end up eating less,' it parrots, before – and this is the killer – telling you to *sniff* the chocolate. Indeed, one of our friends who worked in fashion told us that her colleagues used to sniff birthday cake before throwing it out. When did we stop *celebrating* birthdays and biscuit o'clock, for God's sake, and why are offices up and down the country now filled with women on 'fasting diets' who chew gum rather than having milk in their mid-morning coffee?

It's important to eat for a multitude of reasons, not least because if you don't you eventually die, and, despite what some high-end fashion mags may imply in their photographs, a dead woman never looks good in a dress. The magazines which recommend that women starve themselves are fatally irresponsible: even the ones intended for adult women will make their way into the houses of teenage girls who may already be struggling with low self-esteem and peer pressure at school. Indeed, magazines know that a significant proportion of their readership consists of these young women, although they'd never let slip to advertisers that an economic group with such little spending power makes up their main customer base. But they continue to idolise the hunger deity, and it's not just magazines but newspapers and their columnists too. Back in 2003, prominent journalist Polly Vernon wrote an article for the *Observer Food Monthly* entitled 'Admit it. You hate me because I'm thin'. It detailed her extreme weight loss and how she went from a size 12 to a 6 in a matter of months, concluding that 'contrary to popular belief, being thin has made me happy'. It should go without saying that to equate slimming with happiness so explicitly can be hugely damaging, and when we tweeted about this article, a surprising number of our readers came forward to tell us about the negative effect it had on their eating habits.

Ten years on from Vernon's article, there are magazines which, through their coverage of fasting diets such as 5:2, aim to teach you how not to feel hungry, about how being hungry can be 'addictive', and about the psychological high that you get when you fast. In other words, what used to be the kind of stuff you saw in the darkest depths of the internet is now making its way into our bedrooms, and the impact this could be having on our confidence, our health and our well-being is genuinely terrifying. No matter how we try to combat it, it seems that women are always in the front line for this food-related warfare.

WOMAN FOOD: THE NEW RABBIT FOOD

In a world of 'bitesize' chocolate bars for women and 'man crisps' for men, what we eat remains stubbornly gendered. Years after Susie Orbach's famous treatise on body image, fat is still a feminist issue – and how many lipids you've got to your name can still send the media into a spin. Try looking back at the adverts that launched Cadbury Crispello bar in 2012; most of them had the audacity to suggest that a 'chocolate bar overhaul' had been necessary to cater to women's teensy little feminine hands and their delicate little stomachs which can barely take two bites of pasteurised cocoa butter without recoiling in nauseated horror. In contrast to to a big, imposing rectangular structure stuffed with caramel, raisins and pieces of biscuit, the Crispello was a couple of wispy fingers which was by all accounts more packaging than anything

else. 'A Chocolatey treat for you,' the ads cooed, in that patronising, faux-soothing tone reserved for food that's geared towards gals. 'They'll make your boyfriend's hands looks bigger.' Wait, what? And let's set the record straight here: if you're eating a chocolate bar that's smaller than the size of your finger and you take a couple of bites and then 'save it for later' (as their adverts suggest you'll want to), then *you're doing it wrong*. To eat a Cadbury Crispello in

the way it was apparently intended is basically akin to punching Willy Wonka in the face. In the Chocolate Room. Next to the chocolate fountain. In front of all of his Oompa Loompa friends, you sadist fuck.

Of course, we've experienced this sort of chocolate-based idiocy for years from advertisers: Maltesers commercials where the sweets are so 'light' on your stomach that they float, for instance, or ads where scantily clad models skip around in silk and hide their Galaxy bars in drawers like sex toys, to pull out and consume in masturbatory glory only when they're hidden from the judging eyes of others. It's not difficult to imagine a future wherein Cadbury just charge female customers for buying an empty wrapper to parade in front of their friends and occasionally sniff. As far as turning a profit is concerned, it would be genius.

On the other side of the fence there is the marketing that has long suggested our male counterparts (much like the guy off *Man v. Food*, who unsurprisingly had to retire due to ill health) take big chunks of various forms of junk food and push them into their gigantic, slathering mouths, which are naturally open in perpetual expectation of something nutritionally *masculine*. What the hell is nutritionally masculine? Well, it's preferably meaty (shoving your entire face into a plate of Double Whoppers = manly. Table manners over your tofu curry = icky girlie suspected homosexual). The division even goes as far as your taste buds – beer and whisky are man drinks through and through, while for us lot it's sickly sweet pina colada or Bailey's; 'slag drinks', as they've been dubbed by the *Sunday Times*. If man food absolutely has to be something that was formerly a living, breathing vertebrate, then lady-food consists of a candy treat delivered in pieces that are *far too big* for spindly little girl-fingers to get a proper grip around (which the Crispello would know all about). 'Man food' in marketing speak – and 'man chocolate' and hot dogs, especially – is usually all about handling a big, hard, substantial substitute for a penis, particularly if it used to be alive.

As hilarious and self-parodic as this sort of food PR can become (tattooed truckers chomping away on Yorkie bars under the tagline 'It's not for girls' lent themselves willingly to satire), it's the more subtle targeting of female demographics that gets our backs up. Low-fat spread on a seeded piece of cardboard is supposed to help 'while you're getting into shape for summer' – of course, if you *weren't* 'getting into shape for summer' during the spring months, but were otherwise busy living your life, then this presumption might seem rather insensitive. Probiotic yoghurts such as Activia (known to all as 'that yoghurt that makes you poo') are necessary because your dainty constitution probably can't handle digestion, despite having been honed by millions of years of evolution – including times when we lived in caves, ate speared buffalo rather than leek and potato soup, and snacked on nearby twigs – to do exactly that. Vitamin supplements (at the time of writing it's the pleasingly pink Raspberry Ketone) are a must (see again: 'dainty constitution'). Kale, celery and flax seeds should be the staples of your diet, while the resurgence of the 'no sugar' ideology (up there with fascism as probably one of the most evil ideologies ever posited) means that fruit is plummeting in popularity. No more blueberry porridge for you, babes; this artificial sweetener in a box that looks kind of like a packet of fags should do you fine instead. It's enough to make you want to pick up one of those 'calorie conscious' pizzas with a hole in the middle from Pizza Express and scream through it, 'Let me eat dough!' You'd ruin a polite social occasion, but at least you'd be raging against a society which takes a disturbing interest in what moves through your intestines.

GET OUT OF THE KITCHEN

But, wait: perhaps you actually want to cook your own food, rather than spend hours explaining to the waiter that you want a pizza without a hole in it or a meal deal size *large*, please. (Holly once stood at a counter for fifteen minutes as the man behind it repeatedly asked, 'Are you sure?' to her request for a large falafel wrap, the bastard.) In which case, you'll fit in nicely with the mantra 'Men don't cook, and women are naturally inclined', even if your so-called natural inclinations have only ever resulted in burning the bottom of the pan when you didn't realise that pasta needed to be cooked in water, or, on being asked to put a gigantic Camembert in the oven, making an executive decision to *remove it from the box*, prompting Camembert Armageddon (guilty). And yet, there's still a presumption that vaginas belong in kitchens. (Just check out the internet meme 'make me a sandwich', a taunt regularly made to feminists by sexist a-holes and to which the only possible retort is 'What? So you can try and shag it?') Common mythology has it that whenever people with penises get in the lady-kitchen, they usually mess it up: women are supposed to be all over herbal garnish, of course, while the bumbling, incompetent men envisioned by the advertising output of Tesco, Iceland, Asda, Walmart et al. have to make do with microwavable burgers when their girlfriends aren't around. Oh wait, did you *forget* about microwavable burgers? We know they sound like a piss-take and/ or a vision of society's inevitable slide into *Matrix*-like dystopia, but they're not. They're a food product dreamed up by Rustlers, a company whose advertising imagery compared the easy accessibility and convenience of sticking a pre-packaged piece of meat into an electrical appliance to a scenario in which a man takes a (fully clothed) woman home and, after she agrees to a coffee, presses a button that revolves the sofa once to reveal her in her underwear. Appropriately, the taste it left in our mouths was probably very similar to a Rustlers burger – but, being *women*, we've never tried them. (We've also never tried a Ginsters or McCoy's crisps for that matter.) And if that isn't 'rapey' enough for you, then there's always the infamous Burger King blowjob ad (the 'super seven incher' will 'blow your mind away') or last year's Piri Piri Pot Noodle campaign, entitled 'Peel the top off a hottie' and accompanied by two of the aforementioned Pot Noodles positioned to look like tits (the image in this advert was banned by the ASA in 2013). All these examples demonstrate that, when ad men think 'convenience', the first thing that comes to mind is 'taking a woman's clothes off', whether she's agreed to it or not.

Not only is the idea that men are way too busy and stupid to work an oven and that women have an inborn knowledge of casserole timings and sugar-to-flour ratios pretty equally insulting, but it's also difficult to reconcile with the fact that most famous chefs are men, while Nigella and Delia can only aspire to being a 'cook' or 'domestic goddess'. Granted, most successful *anythings* are men (with the possible exception of burlesque dancers), but the idea that everyday domestic cooking belongs to women, while skilled, career cooking is for men, is especially insulting. It was only in the 1950s that the idea of women's inherent expertise with butter icing and cinnamon came to the fore, yet it's been a persistent assumption since, and a dab of Worcestershire sauce is now seen as the most a man can do with his dinner (cheese on toast), yet the ladies are supposed to magically dispense béchamel from every available orifice. Unless there's payment involved, of course – at which point, the men will step out from behind their veil of incompetence, don a chef's hat, and head up their own TV show and cookware conglomerate.

TAKING CONTROL

The politics of hunger are undoubtedly complex, but one thing's for sure: they're disproportionately skewed towards women. Naomi Wolf, in her hard-hitting book on expectations of womanhood *The Beauty Myth*, referred to women suffering from anorexia as 'political prisoners', and her argument is compelling. She reminds us that, in the same year that women gained the vote, admonitions to 'slim down' cropped up for the first time in the media, after centuries of their celebrating the voluptuous female form as the social ideal. Since then, across all media and in our discussions with each other, this energy-sapping concern with losing 'extra' weight has reached fever pitch. Turning your concerns inward and expressing them via starvation dampens your voice and stamps out your activism. It makes you physically smaller and less threatening. As the potential to gain more power has become more and more real in the outside world, a magazine-driven obsession with diets, slimming and weight has rendered huge swathes of women inactive and ill. Without ignoring the very serious plight of many male sufferers, eating disorders are still much more common amongst women; in fact, they are at almost epidemic proportions (of 6.1 million UK sufferers, it's estimated that 89% are women). And their murky associations with the mass media have begun to seem inherently political.

Where food is concerned, women are expected to tread a difficult line between control and guilt. If we're not worrying about the pastries in the oven, then we're being visually assaulted from all angles by the stock photos of perfectly toned women looking anxiously at the scales in every lifestyle supplement and magazine. Women's bodies are all too often the sites of social discussion, and we're supposed to negotiate the female domains of the cupcake stand and the kinky lingerie rack with exquisite style and no complaints. If an outsider *really* looked into the way we speak to each other – about 'overindulgence', about food that has an abstract morality ('good' foods, 'bad' foods, 'good' and 'bad' days during diets and fasting periods, and cake-eating as 'naughty') – he or she might guess that we remained willingly chained to the oven or the kitchen sink, probably by an extra-strong length of kitchen roll. Being thin is sexy, supposedly, and it's continually implied that being 'naughty' with your food will prevent 'naughtiness' in the bedroom. Rarely will you find your male friend describing his 'man crisps' as a 'guilty pleasure'. But your strawberry cheesecake is exactly that, because it means that you might not fit into your push-up bra and your French knickers without your stomach becoming demonstrably convex, and you won't fit into the role of slimmed-down, anxious, passive sexuality that you're encouraged to conform to, either.

Don't believe us? Then consider that the heartbroken woman, unlucky in love, is nearly always portrayed as having one hand on her weeping brow and the other on a spoon dipped into the nearest tub of double-chocolate ice cream. A woman without a man is a mess of calorific consumption, but a woman who's happily coupled up or celebrating her sexy singlehood on the scene will be chomping the Ryvita at lunch, poising her fork over a cherry tomato and exercising the necessary restraint that comes with being a female adult. The distraught binge-eater is chubby and childish, you see; the powerful, ambitious woman, with her super-green smoothie and her tiny portions, shows self-control through the choices that she makes at the breakfast table. This is a demand not usually made of a man, who can happily slap a steak on the barbecue at a business picnic and be seen to enthusiastically devour it in a matter of spittle-showering bites without any qualms that his professional integrity will be called into question. The same can't be said for his female colleagues – because when 'diet' equals 'control', this bleeds into all variations of life for the workaday woman: she's not only sexually undesirable and probably newly dumped if she's 'pigging out' on such normal fare as spaghetti bolognese, but she's also likely to drop the ball in the boardroom. In other words, if you're not mindful of your food intake, then society will punish you manifold.

An influential study from the *International Journal of Obesity* in April 2012 found that, when being interviewed or in the workplace, 'fat' women experience more prejudice than their similarly rounded male co-workers. Women who are perceived as overweight are judged to be sloppier in carrying out their tasks, lazier in their work ethic, and generally less able to control themselves in business situations. And this has a financial impact: *Business Insider* reported in the same month that research by the American Psychological Association had found 'a fat woman makes $29,419 less per year than a skinny one'. However, this isn't the case with men, where being overweight 'can actually pay'; in other words, can even have a positive effect on their salaries. Little wonder, then, that women who have suffered from eating disorders say again and again how they saw starving themselves or purging themselves of the food that they'd eaten as a way of reasserting lost control. Thinspiration graphics with slogans such as 'Stop stuffing your fat face' and 'Eat. Feel guilty', are a painful reminder of the cycles of self-loathing that can occur. Conflating respect, control, and the restriction of complex carbohydrates results in a toxic social combination. As long as we're being told that we speak primarily through the padding on our elbows and the size of our thighs, we will continue to self-destruct en masse wherever edibles are involved. It might be through a fully fledged eating disorder, or it might be through another hour poring over the seductively titled diet books in the local Waterstones – but either way, it's a waste of talent and a chronic waste of time.

In this climate, where it feels like we drag the chains of social judgement to every leisurely lunch and working breakfast, where the food we eat is supposed to come with a gender attached, where diet plans are part of the average woman's daily casual reading, and where outright hatred of our own constituent parts is normalised and marketed back at us, it's difficult to imagine how to progress. But there is optimism amongst the clamour of the 'chew it then spit it' diets, the starvation inspiration, and the five-year-olds who call themselves fat. The ubiquity of social media means that most of us are now hooked up to a permanent stream of food rhetoric, and using it to promote awareness – and humour – is possible because, contrary to what we're hearing, bread is not the new heroin, and thinspiration can kiss our well-rounded asses. The Twitter account for model Cara Delevingne's thigh gap (@CarasThighGap, if you're interested) has drawn hilarious attention to the idiocy of obsessing over an absence between your legs. And the heart-warming appearance of anonymous handwritten stickers across diet plan adverts in the London Underground in 2011 – stating 'You ARE good enough' or 'You're beautiful the way you are' – not to mention the social media shares of posters proudly proclaiming 'I EAT CARBS' make for a smile on your daily commute. But so much more needs to be done.

We can start by challenging why this overemphasis on food is so tied up with the experience of being a woman. Once you start recognising that your dinner plate is seen as everyone's business and that this is not OK, that the women pushing the message that you are what you eat are often in desperate need of help themselves, then you realise how profoundly unhealthy all this dietary fascism is. And once you realise that the focus on your stomach is bleeding away your ability to act in the real world, you start to call out anyone who tells you that it's a woman's job to focus on controlling her palate rather than her life. We need to arm ourselves with the same sort of scrutiny of the culture that millions of marketers and editors worldwide are affording our muffin tops, until the words that come out of our mouths become more important than the food we put into them.

10
Bad Language

CALAMITY KATE'S SHOEMILIATING BABYMOON

Do men and women speak the same language? If the media are to be believed, the answer is a resounding 'no'. Tabloid newspapers go wild for studies they can feature under headlines such as 'The brain scans which reveal WHY men don't understand women' (*Mail*, April 2013), 'Why your man will NEVER understand how you feel' (*Mail* again, April 2010), and 'Why women are the talkative sex' (*Telegraph*, February 2013), many of which are about as believable as the pseudo-orgasmic screams of an adult movie star pretending to enjoy a spit roast. Either that, or they've been wildly extrapolated from genuinely interesting scientific press releases. There persists a genuine belief that men are from Mars and women are from Venus, along with all the unadulterated toss that comes hand in hand with that proposition. Whether it's the theory that women naggingly persist in forcing men to emote when all they want to do is cower in their cold, detached 'man caves', or some poorly observed stand-up routine regarding our inability to read maps, there are those out there who, if they could, would have us categorised as a different species entirely, or at least as the speakers of a different language. When it comes to women's magazines and the fluffy guff permeating their sentences, it's starting to seem that they are right.

More often than not, the words women's magazines use aren't recognised by any reliable human dictionary. It's not because they're edgy and really into coinage, à la Shakespeare, but because, in their manic quest to recycle popular culture and feed it back to us quickly enough to gain a commercial advantage, they've started believing their own bullshit. Women's magazine journalists appear to envisage their readership as overgrown babies hyped on E-numbers, permanently hooked up to a tweetdrip inserting Justin Bieber soundbites directly into their bloodstream. 'Totes amaze!' an average 'celebrity news' feature will squeal. 'It's #vdayblues for all you singletons on the 14th of Feb, but you're in fab company because F-Tiddy just broke up with her latest squeeze – we've laced next week's issue with her ACTUAL TEARS!' Who is F-Tiddy? She isn't real, but she follows the trend of ridiculous nicknames doled out by the publications in question. (K-Middy, K-Stew, Li-Lo, Jen-An, and now K-Pez: we all know the drill. If you're in a celebrity relationship, it's only a matter of time before you become TomKat, Bennifer, Brangelina or Kimye.) 'Soooo sad and Les Miserables, but we know you'll get through it with the help of your gal pals, Fifi!!!!' the writer continues, with much presumed cackling. Even worse is when the female celebrity in question is given a horrifically patronising and faux-sympathetic nickname, along the lines of 'Tragic Jen' or 'Calamity Kate' (a moniker given to Kate Winslet by the *Telegraph* for being hapless enough to have three children by three different men, the slag). If condescension were flammable, the entire rack of women's lifestyle magazines would be burning in perpetual hellfire next to the fag counter at Morrison's.

Can you imagine the editor at *Zoo* magazine describing their cover-girl as a 'gal pal who dares to bare', with the footnote: 'We here at *Zoo* love you just the way you are. But if you're buying this mag because you totes haven't got a hope of hooking a poster-girl lookalike, then get yourself buff with our #clevergymcheats on page 37'? No? That's because even down in the *Nuts* region, which most definitely counts as the lowest echelon of male reading on offer, they know that a condescending tone isn't going to fly with the dude who's flicking through their sticky pages.

You might think that you haven't internalised this sort of idiocy – but then how come the term 'oh-so-subtle' seems oh-so-familiar, even though it's the most useless phrase ever dredged up by the English language (not counting the portmanteau terms 'cankles', 'manorexia' and 'shoemiliate', that is)? Unless you take heed of the fact that much of what you read is written in oddly patronising baby-talk, it'll only be a matter of time before you start thinking that it's perfectly acceptable to get #YOLO tattooed on your inner thigh, and that doing so doesn't make you, as your friends tell you, an 'incredible tool', but a sexy hot mess with her finger on the pulse of popular culture. (By 'popular culture' we mean whatever it is over-privileged millennials are doing on Instagram this week.)

The strange need to patronise and pigeonhole particularly applies to celebrity coverage, and not just as far as futile nicknames are concerned. The requisite celebrity magazine interview will inevitably advertise itself by saying that Latest Celeb 'opens up' about her childhood/man woes/ hair horror (at one point in 2013, the *Glamour* website included three consecutive reports on celebrities 'opening up' about something, as if it was a description of high-profile women being given their annual smear rather than, y'know, them talking). The endless and totally unnecessary pigeonholing of random and unrelated occurrences is also a well established tactic: *Grazia* once featured Kim Kardashian getting 'pregnancy bangs' (duh. Foetus + hair = fringe) in the same celeb news section that claimed Michelle Obama had 'birthday bangs', and the *Daily Mail* and lifestyle section of *The Sun* are particularly vociferous in claiming that assorted women have 'post-baby curves', 'Christmas curves', 'bikini curves', 'holiday hair', 'hobo style' or a 'new-relationship glow'. Let's also not forget the 'babymoon', a word so unbearably nauseating that it makes us want to mainline six months' supply of birth control immediately. A babymoon is apparently a new kind of twee 'pregnancy escape', which, rather than allowing all those women who have been yelling, 'Get this shitting thing out of me this instant!' for the last fortnight to literally escape their pregnancy, simply means transferring the pregnant lady in question to somewhere glamorous like the Cotswolds, where she will sit, feeling like a heifer, miles from a hospital and her specially hired birthing pool, until the baby comes.

The accolade of the stupidest of all these stupid phrases, however, is reserved for the tabloids' current obsession: the 'sideboob'. Soon to be replaced by the 'underboob', and probably some time after that 'overboob', the 'sideboob' is exactly what it says on the tin, namely – the side of a boob, usually visible poking through the edge of a red-carpet dress. 'Model of the moment shows some SIDEBOOB', the sidebar of shame will holler, apparently unaware that sideboob isn't actually a real thing and that it makes them sound more like an unhinged pervert than usual, which is no mean feat. Ladies – and we use that term with all the gravitas it implies – do we really want to live in a world where 'pregnancy bangs' and 'sideboob' are things? Indeed, we're now proud to announce that 'sidevag' and 'underbum' have been added to the (already long) list of things that are wrong with your body as paraphrased excellently by the comedian Rob Delaney in a 2011 article for *Vice* magazine:

> Saddle bags, upper-arm fat, cottage cheese thighs, midriff-bulge (aka F.U.P.A aka 'gunt'), flat chest, asymmetrical breasts, butt-beard, bacne, pit-cheese, cankles, surprise tampon string cameos, eczema, ham spatula, ashy elbows,

feet of any kind, hairy knuckles, beef knuckles, uncle's knuckles, vaginal halitosis, bald spots, loaf latch, sideburns, flatbottom, creeping jimson weed, dowager's hump, treasure trail, Pepperidge Farm, razor bumps, leakage, phantom dangle, and panty dandruff.

It's as if, by employing this sort of mad phraseology with confidence, magazines expect that we will nod sagely and repeat: 'Yes, post-Halloween pores. I'm sure I remember those from somewhere', before hopefully continuing, 'Now you mention it, I'm pretty sure I've suffered from them for years. Do you have a product advertised that could help me on my way?'

THE ENGLISH CHICKTIONARY

Amazeballs – Something that is so astounding in nature that it warrants comparison to testicles

Babyccino – An espresso cup filled with foamy milk, so that toddlers can play at being grown-up coffee addicts while their mums natter about Botox at Starbucks

Babymoon – A holiday undertaken by the Duchess of Cambridge while pregnant

Bromance – Two men who love one another's company to the point of star-crossed adoration

Buysexual – A sexual compulsion to buy stuff, or the association of the feeling of buying stuff, like shoes, with sexual arousal (see: every episode of *Sex and the City*, ever)

Fauxpology – A pretend apology, often given by a frenemy

Frenemy – A friend you hate, but secretly, who also hates you secretly too, but neither of you have the guts to ever mention it, so you continue to tolerate one another miserably for ever

Hiberdating – This is when you start seeing someone new and temporarily abandon all your friends, only to re-emerge in the springtime two dress sizes larger with a huge stupid grin on your face and a misty-eyed evangelical zeal for the wheelbarrow position

Metrosexual – The 'new man', who uses moisturiser and talks about his feelings (as opposed to the old kind of man, who hunted wildebeest and shaved with a sharpened knife). Alternatively, a niche kind of sexual move that is performed on public transport

Mompetition – Competitive mothers who take their children to baby yoga workshops and Ancient Greek lessons before they reach the age of two

Procrastineating – This is when you eat instead of doing more important things, such as examining your thigh gap or counting your ribs

Sexit – As popularised (but apparently not coined) by the TV show *Girls*, a sexit is when someone makes a sexy exit

Sexorcism – Getting over someone by getting under someone else

Shoemiliate – Being made to wear ugly shoes, most often by your parents, your school headmaster, or the man who works behind the desk at the bowling alley

Tanorexia – This is when, despite spending hours taking your Anglo-Saxon arse down to Tantastic, building up the kind of bronze that screams 'pre-cancer', you still believe yourself to be the colour of ectoplasm and behave accordingly. *NB Not*

> *to be confused with 'Manorexia', an eating disorder that is just*
> *for men*

Tree-book – A book not available on a screen, printed on paper
made from trees and bound together (seriously)

Vagenda – A woman with a hidden agenda

Yestergay – An overnight change of sexuality from homo- to
heterosexual

THE TOTES ADORBS JUICEREXICS WHO DARE TO BARE

The exact reasoning behind magazines' inclination to speak to their readers as if they're missing their frontal lobes is complex and predictably illogical. This problem has persisted for long enough to have been parodied in popular culture: just look at the archetypal public-school girl portrayed by Sally Phillips in slapstick sitcom *Miranda*, who insists on littering her speech with this sort of hyperactive language ('Oh God! This is a Major Disaster and his friend Colonel Cock-up', is a memorable example). You can almost hear an identically grating voice ordering you to 'work your fabulosity' from the glossy pages of *InStyle* – but only if you lose your *flabulosity,* doll (after a Harley Street 'non-invasive treatment', of course). Yes, we can rebrand eyelash extensions as 'spidery confidence boosters' to you – even though you're supposed to 'love your body' with the evangelistic fervour of a Westboro Baptist Church preacher gone freelance – and you'll like it because we're calling you 'babe' and 'loving you just the way you are'. Like, we can't see you but we totes love you. To which we at the Vagenda reply: whatevz, bebz. Lol.

And not only do magazines address you as though they're a cross between your best mate on acid and a machine that perpetually regurgitates social media jargon (a needless hashtag in the middle of a sentence, anyone?), you're also supposed to buy into their equally nonsensical terminology: 'date night' has to be a thing that you do; 'manthropology' is a subject that you're interested in; 'the male menopause' is of genuine concern. You're on a 'healthy eating plan' (diet with a disclaimer) while you 'power walk' to Zumba class, and if you get thrush from your sweaty leggings, then *Cosmo* is there to deconstruct the 'weird little medical terms' it assumes you don't understand your 'vajayjay', 'ladybits' or 'hoo-ha', while the feature editor pats you on the head and mollycoddles your tiny woman brain just a little while longer. Like 'date night', you also need to have a 'baby plan' that tallies with all the fertility anxiety they're waiting to sell you in the pages of the slightly more grown-up rags (hello, *Red*). Oh, and by the way, if you're presently 'coveting' the 'ring bling' of the latest celebrity, look no further than under the rather pornographic sounding banner of 'Finger candy!'

In Girl World, you may have got yourself a 'hunk', while you're rocking 'checkerboard chic' alongside your 'adorbs', 'oh-em-GEE' ponytail, and your 'celeb goss' is so up to date it's from a future parallel universe, but unfortunately your powers of communication are now more akin to the repeated messages that come out of Teen Talk Barbie when you pull a string in her back ('Math class is tough!') Or they would be, if anyone actually spoke like a women's magazine in the real world. Thankfully, they don't. In order to get to the content, you first have to shovel through a steaming pile of gibberish that you'd never bother to apply to your natural environment. They'll feed you all of this with the faux reassurance of a cheap self-help manual designed to be read during interventions: *we're* here to help you; *we* care about your life and where it's going; when we tell you that you'll be better off with a nightly avocado face mask, we're talking un-buh-*lievable* results. Examples from the dreaded magazine archive include 'Here at *Glamour*, we think every body is fantastic and believe that the outfits real women wear 24/7 are just as cool as those found on the red carpet or fashion runways!' (were they snickering behind their hands as they said that, or properly bent over double from laughing?); 'Here at *Glamour*, we love to see women in politics experiment with their fashion' (*why?!*); 'Here at *heat*, we want to make sure you're all taken care of' (creepy); 'We may not be the biggest sci-fi buffs, but here at *heat*, we're are totally obsessed with the three leading hotties'; 'Here at *Marie Claire*, we have a bit of a fetish for stationery' (seriously); 'Here at *Marie Claire*, we go ga-ga for braids!'; and – perhaps most strangely – 'Here at *Tatler*, we are delighted that Camilla Parker-Bowles exists'.

This faceless 'we' (or, even scarier, 'the team') is meant to be taken in the 'support group' way rather than the 'scary Scientologists' way, but one *could* argue that it has the latter effect. And while the bright-eyed, bushy-tailed 'we' get to work on everything from London Fashion Week to the burning pain of cystitis, they're just waiting around the corner to tell you that you get a 'great big thumbs up from the team here' for going it on your own as an entrepreneur, or writing a cathartic letter to your cheating ex and then burning it, or 'daring to bare' (forgoing tights) with a 'super glam' miniskirt. You go, girlfriend. Work it – but not too much. God forbid you stray into slut territory.

KEEPING YOU IN YOUR PLACE

If it were just a touch of 'totes cool beans' and other such linguistic quirks, then we could certainly accuse these mags of being terminally irritating, but little more; unless you melt at the sight of grammar genocide, you can dismiss these linguistic quirks as fairly harmless. But then you're confronted with the terrifying domain of the magazine quiz determined to put you in a box. It all started when you were 13 with 'Which member of the Spice Girls' hairdressing team are you?' and moved swiftly on to the type that you're more familiar with now, such as 'When does *your* skin need you to start wearing night cream?' or, to take a real-life example, 'Classic Mummy or Bling Momma – which fashion mother are you?' (Grazia Daily, January 2013). This sort of banal questioning is an extension of the pigeonhole mentality that convinced you Michelle Obama got 'birthday bangs', and it sucks you into a world where you have to define yourself within the mainstream media's narrow parameters. When you're asked if, in a social situation, you (a) Jump up on the bar to show them your moves! And snog the face off the hot bartender while you're at it; (b) Call up your ex as soon as you've had a G&T, cry, and then storm off to spend the rest of the night harassing strangers and singing sad love songs on the tube train home, or (c) Hang out being a coy wallflower until the perfect man sweeps you up, then pull out the tricks you learnt in this week's pole-dancing class to keep him interested', there's never an option that remotely represents any sane person's reality, such as (d) Unwisely mix your drinks, chat someone up then forget who they are on your way back from the toilets, and do your best fist-pump during a nineties musical resurrection. Reminisce fondly about it all in the morning while eating toast.' The option marked 'normal human behaviour' remains conspicuously absent.

Of course, when someone's breathing down your neck and asking, 'Which pre-surgical treatment is right for you?' you don't get the option of replying, 'None, thanks, and you can piss off before I crush you under the weight of my left thigh's cellulite.' Each time they pull up a couple of questions to 'help' you identify which 'problem area' is leaving your self-confidence in shreds, they're sowing the seeds of self-doubt and negative body image. Like the infamous scene in *Mean Girls*, where each US-bred teenage girl stands in front of the mirror and pontificates upon her flaws as Lindsay Lohan's character, raised outside the Western media sphere, looks on in confusion, every woman has to have something that they hate – and the magazine quiz aims to help you find it.

Women's magazines are also packed with imperatives. Next time you have a free afternoon and nothing to do, try counting how many you can find in any one of them. They're constantly bossing you around, telling you to 'EAT yourself smart' or 'EXPRESS your style' or 'GET your red carpet rocks on' or 'GLOSSIFY your limbs'. And this use of language is a prime example of the way in which advertising speak bleeds into the editorial it's accompanied by: while the latest L'Oréal product wants you to buy it in order to 'reduce fine lines' and 'get rid' of those pesky crow's feet, and the diet practitioners marketing their books will 'make your unwanted muffin top just disappear', the adjacent articles bombard you with the repetitive notion that you need to 'reduce' something, 'fade' something, or 'minimise' various things. '*Reduce* dry skin,' they'll order, '*diminish* cellulite', '*lose* weight', '*vanish* wrinkles'. As a well-known Guerrilla Girls poster points out, it sounds as though someone wants us to disappear.

Every now and then, magazines will run a piece on 'maximising your potential' to throw you off the scent – but don't be fooled. They are making cold, hard cash out of making you feel like you need to become as invisible as humanly possible without slipping down a drain. Once you start counting, you become amazed at the ability of mags to make you feel as if every part of your body is a hideous overgrowth, and your role as the intellectual inhabitant of this endlessly expanding jungle is to desperately keep hacking away at the trees. If *Glamour* were your mate, you'd have no qualms in telling her where to get off as she clung to your bingo wings like a limpet, moaning about how you *existed too much* and directing you towards products with names such as 'Skinny Cow' and 'Zero Noodles' while you tried to go about your weekly shop.

THE FRONT BUM CONUNDRUM: MINKY, VAJAYJAY OR LADYBITS?

All of this is nothing compared to the sheer number of awful euphemisms they've come up with to describe your bits. Men's magazines know better than to refer to their readership's cocks in a weirdly infantilising way. 'Don't worry if after a steamy sesh you get a funny little feeling in your pee-pee or some sensitivity in your A-spot' is not a sentence that's ever likely to appear opposite an otherwise unemployed school-leaver from Nottingham's topless shot. Meanwhile, women's mags use 'vajayjay', 'ladybits' or 'hoo-ha', go apeshit for new genital erogenous zones, whether it's the 'V-spot', the 'C-spot', the 'G-spot', the 'U-spot', or your euphemistically termed 'backdoor', a particular pet hate of ours which conjures up the impression that the writer is one step away from renaming her fanny (a zone which, let's face it, is probably pawed at insistently more than any other) 'my catflap'. Please, just close the backdoor. Close it. Or at least don't call it that. Men's magazines, with their 'Beach and bedroom babes' or 'Best ever Aston Martin?' features, may not be purveyors of deep philosophical nuance either, but at least they don't self-consciously talk down to their audience.

It's as though women's magazines, like an American politician at a Republican conference, are scared that using the word VAGINA will get them ejected from the room. Feminists have long been preoccupied with what to call their vaginas – from an *actual book* called *Cunt: A Declaration of Independence* (Inga Muscio, 1998), to Caitlin Moran's hilarious chapter 'I don't know what to call my breasts!' in *How to Be a Woman*, and despite the fact that feminists almost never agree on anything, we are all pretty united when it comes to referring to it as a 'flower'. Because the worst thing about cutesy vagina monikers is that they prevent women talking about their bodies honestly. You're hardly going to call it a 'muffkin' in the doctor's surgery, or direct a midwife towards your 'front bottom'. And we have it on good authority – from an endless deluge of emails and tweets to the Vagenda blog – that women are fed up with having everyone tiptoeing around their 'ladybits'. Compared to 'minky', even a well-placed 'flange' is preferable – which just goes to show that bad language can sometimes be good.

RECLAIMING THE WORD 'SLUT'

And so we turn from fannies to floozies in order to examine the question 'What makes a slut?' According to our mothers, we're prime examples – although to be fair to them, they were using the old definition of the word, meaning a dirty, slovenly woman (as was *Cosmo* when in 1975 it ran a piece entitled 'Why are women such sluts?' This was somewhat of a disappointment during our period of research). Having your own mother walk into your room and announce that you're the sluttiest person she knows can be something of a shock. Still, it also goes to show that the meaning of words changes over time, and may be part of the reason why every word your grandma has in her vocab to describe a gay person is now wrong (or she might just be a raging homophobe). Perhaps this is something politician Godfrey Bloom should have taken into account before he levied the term at an audience of women last year and caused a media storm.

Back in 2008, a piece in the *Daily Mail* entitled 'So just how many lovers SHOULD a woman have?' denigrated Carla Bruni for her fifteen sexual partners, saying (and we quote) that she was 'starting to demean sex itself'. Meanwhile, in March 2013 a 29-year-old woman wrote to an agony aunt for *The Times* to ask whether or not it's normal to have slept with twenty-five people. The response? 'I don't wish to alarm you but that is more than four times the national average for a woman of your age!' We were suitably alarmed, naturally.

We know that, while guys can pretty much go about their sexual business without anyone poking their nose in too much, gals are still subject to much shaming and scrutiny; Christina Aguilera was singing it in the lyrics to 'Can't Hold Us Down' in the early noughties, and it remains as true as ever. Even if the shaming takes a more subtle tone – as in the case of the young woman seeking advice – the implied criticism about only letting it out of your knickers on very special occasions is still there.

No wonder we're confused – the media tells us that we should be humping the floor in an oily bikini (or 'twerking', as it's now known), but conventional 'wisdom' still insists that just a flirtatious glance and a low-cut top are tantamount to 'putting a leg in bed'. Even magazines which claim to be sexually progressive seem conflicted over whether you should put out on the first date or wank yourself stupid until your wedding night while your boyfriend 'plays the field'. Who the hell cares, and why?

Although we're decades on from the 'sexual revolution', it can still feel as though all a woman has to do is have one shag too many (or, in 'Calamity Kate's' case, one child too many) and suddenly she's labelled a 'slut', a 'skank', a 'tramp' or a demeaner of sex (what a great slogan for a female superhero, though: 'Demeaner of sex, destroyer of WORLDS'). Throw an absent father into the mix and, as far as the right-wing media is concerned, you're basically a massive ho-bag (see myriad articles entitled 'Do absent dads make for promiscuous daughters?'). In this context, it seems that trying to take the word 'slut' and own it will never be anything but a losing battle.

The activists of the past have often focused on the idea of reclaiming things, particularly the night, but let's face it: women never really owned the night in the first place. The same could be said of 'slut'. Although 'cunt' at least refers to something that has, if you'll excuse the crassness, belonged to us, at any rate in a literal sense, have women ever really 'owned' the term 'slut'? It is, after all, a term defined by Urban Dictionary as 'a woman with the morals of a man'.

There's a school of thought that a group claiming a word for itself can minimise the power of that word. SlutWalk, for instance, is a movement of women who call themselves 'sluts' in solidarity with rape victims whose attacks have been 'justified' by the way that they dressed. But as admirable as movements such as SlutWalk are, in saying that being 'sluttish' is not an automatic invitation to every man out there to rape you, we tend to subscribe to what we call the 'Tina Fey in *Mean Girls*' philosophy, which is that 'calling one another sluts and whores just makes it OK for guys to call you sluts and whores'. Right on, sister. Even in jest, you're basically casually employing a word that has been used to shame women for hundreds of years, and from the looks of the 'slut-shaming' rife in the newspapers and on the internet, it's still going on. Gay people and black people have been using 'queer' and 'nigger' respectively for a few decades now, and it hasn't stopped the kinds of people you'd never in a million years want to party with thinking they're big and clever for using those same words abusively. And it hasn't deadened their impact: those words still wound. Calling a woman a 'cow' or a 'slag' may never ever lose its impact, no matter how many 'sup, ho?'s you and your bezzie mate share on the phone. Perhaps it's time to stop using the word 'slut' altogether, because if we want women to make their own sexual choices without fear of society's judgement, then the word shouldn't really exist at all.

You could argue that when women start to adopt terminology such as 'slut', 'bitch' and 'whore' – terminology traditionally used by men to describe women pejoratively – they're internalising a sexist culture that has been against them from the outset. A recent Facebook post by *Cosmopolitan* entitled '13 ways sexy bitches kiss' would be a prime example of this, and there are whole books, such as Ariel Levy's *Female Chauvinist Pigs*, dedicated to it. But, depressingly, those employing bad language often go further than calling a woman a 'whore'.

BEATEN-UP LANGUAGE

You don't have to be part of what the right-wing media like to term 'the politically correct language police' to admit that you feel uncomfortable with certain words, and that those words have the potential, if used, to take a giant dump on someone's day. In the same way that many people recoil from the words 'moist' or 'flaccid', certain turns of phrase are wont to sour the atmosphere during a bout of filthy texting faster than a man can say, 'Did I just say that out loud?' Things like: casually referring to your 'pussy' or 'panties', offering up a 'face-fuck', and actually typing the sentence 'I'd like to smash your backdoors in'.

When compared with that last bit of pre-pillow talk, *Cosmo*'s patronising but benevolent use of the term 'backdoor' seems almost sweet. To those of you less au fait with 'modern culture', in recent years it has become a 'thing' – both in the media and beyond – to use increasingly violent terminology to describe the act of putting a penis in a vagina. So much of a thing, in fact, that you'll get mainstream BBC comedian John Bishop joking on primetime telly that he would 'split Cheryl Cole in half'. While women's magazines we read treat us like little girls, who, being as we are somewhat 'emosh', are in need of endless guidance, orders and advice delivered in a saccharine stream of baby-talk, with sex tips centred around mind-reading male pleasure, their online and offline male counterparts seem intent on perpetuating the myth that sex is something you 'do' to a woman that inevitably 'ruins' or 'despoils' her.

Although things were, obviously, way worse for women in the 1950s, at the same time you didn't get your Don Drapers and your Humphrey

Bogarts pronouncing that they'd 'hit that' when they saw a sexy lady in a bar. Perhaps this is because, since then, the phrase 'rogering', with its Captain Pugwash/posho connotations, has become so passé that not even the most self-confident of toff pirates would use it (and that includes Russell Brand). Or perhaps it's because the internet is saturated with violent pornography and 'Smack My Bitch Up' is really good to dance to. Whichever it is, being told by some internet bottom-feeder/ bar tosser that he wants to 'ruin' you is not only massively disturbing but also a total passion-killer. We're not demanding Shakespeare here, but coming into the office with the opening gambit of 'I was on the hunt last night and I speared one' is hardly going to have the ladies queuing up next to the photocopier.

Apart from its being incredibly unerotic, the use of violent sexual language in media such as lads' mags, internet memes, televised comedy and beyond also hints at something much more disturbing about our society. Violence against women seems to be becoming increasingly accepted, not only as something to 'joke' about but also in actuality – a pertinent case in point being the many, many girls who took to Twitter following pop star Rihanna's domestic violence complaint against Chris Brown to say, 'I'd let him beat me up anytime he wanted.' And that's just the girls. Websites such as the online misogyny bible Uni Lad demonstrate that, in order to joke about women being 'violated', 'fucked senseless' and 'destroyed', you no longer have to be a sick rapist character in a pulp paperback but just your average workaday bloke in a student bar with a couple of Smirnoff Ices in his gut. Of course, most of the boys (for they are mostly boys, and not men) making these remarks would never dream of actually doing any of the things they talk about doing; in all probability they still jizz in their pants from looking at an Actual Live Woman. But the fact remains that the British Crime Survey found in 2011 that teenage girls are the age group most at risk of domestic violence. That so many of their male counterparts seem to find the notion amusing, and are taking to the internet to have a laugh about it together, does not bode well for their future.

Another aspect of this linguistic shift is the lack of agency on the part of the woman in the equation. When a man talks about fucking a woman unconscious or 'ruining' her (and we're not talking financially – we assume all her credit cards are present and correct), where is the woman here? She's certainly not taking an active part in proceedings, which goes to show that the cultural assumption that sex is just something that 'happens' to a woman – while she lies back, all virginal and placid – is never too far away. These stereotypes are enforced again and again by the material we read and watch, and, if a young man displaying a casual attitude to sexual violence might seem to be a big leap from the frothy, childish language of women's magazines, in actual fact they're two sides of a coin. Much like the 'blurred lines' in Robin Thicke's song of the same name, your magazines are telling you you're supposed to be a 'good girl' – interested in lipstick and celebs and spa treatments and *squeeee!* – and not to have too many sexual partners, but his media sources, well, they're teaching him to 'know you want it' and to 'tear your ass in two'.

DID YOU HEAR THE ONE ABOUT THE RAPE?

Which brings us to the topic of rape, and whether or not it's ever OK to joke about it, as many a lads' mag and male comedian has and does. Though admittedly most media sources steer clear of making light of sexual assault, especially following recent controversy, every now and again a new example will rear its ugly head. Indeed, according to Irish comedian Mary Bourke, 'the open-mic [comedy] circuit has basically turned into a rape circle'.

If you're reading this and you're relatively young, you've probably come across increasingly casual uses of the word 'rape', not least on Facebook, where 'fraping' has come to denote someone ruining your social reputation by changing your status to 'Just shat my pants'. The word 'rape' is now employed to describe anything remotely stressful, e.g. 'Work is totally raping me this week', or 'Starbucks was such a butt-rape earlier'. ('They gave me full fat instead of soya.' Apparently, coffee-based anal assault in corporate chains is becoming more common by the minute.) Or even, in the case of the England team's cricketer Graeme Swann, comparing losing a sports game to being 'arse-raped'.

Even if your social circle is relatively benign and mature and no one in it ever uses 'rape' flippantly and instead donates all their money to charity and only eats free-range eggs and reads *The Guardian* every day, you've still probably come across the odd rape joke, because male comedians seem to really enjoy telling them. They are 'taboo-busting' and 'edgy' and anyone who says otherwise is basically the comedy thought police. It's got to such a stage that the making of a rape joke now follows a specific formula: comedian makes rape joke; someone in the audience/Twitter/the newspapers gets angry, prompting a media frenzy; comedian accuses nay-sayers of trying to 'silence' him and stifle his freedom of expression; lots of people sort of agree; we all talk about the Human Rights Act. And repeat. Endlessly.

Recent rape jokes have included Frankie Boyle's 'They say Viagra takes half an hour to work. But by half an hour, I find the woman has been able to wriggle free'; Jimmy Carr's 'What do nine out of ten people enjoy? Gang rape'; Boyle (again) wondering aloud whether glamour model Katie Price's disabled son Harvey might rape her during a tantrum; or Daniel Tosh's 'Wouldn't it be funny if that girl [in the audience, who just told him rape jokes aren't funny] got raped by, like, five guys right now? Like, right now? What if a bunch of guys just raped her . . .' Rape jokers like Tosh will often argue that they're 'equal opportunities offenders', as though being a complete dick to everyone as opposed to some people is actually a point of pride. As American feminist writer Lindy West has pointed out on her online magazine *Jezebel*, such an argument leaves aside the fact that all the people being mocked indiscriminately are likely to be in entirely different positions on the power scale:

> 'It's okay, because Daniel Tosh makes fun of ALL people: women, men, AIDS victims, dead babies, gay guys, blah blah blah' – falls apart when you remember (as so many of us are forced to all the time) that all people *are not in equal positions of power*. 'Oh, don't worry – I punch everyone in the face! People, baby ducks, a lion, this Easter Island statue, the ocean . . .' Okay, well that baby duck is dead now. And you're a duck-murderer. It's really easy to believe that 'nothing is sacred' when the sanctity of your body and your freedom are never legitimately threatened.

Furthermore, the butt of the joke is almost always the woman, and never the rapist. Why exactly is it that, while jokes about attacks on black people or gay men are rarely made in public, violence against women still gets a fair amount of comedy airtime, even on television? Not to mention the fact that women are routinely blamed and shamed in the media for their own rapes, that the clothes they wear, their sexual histories, the drinks they drank, the places they went, or the rules that they didn't follow are routinely held up as examples of how the victim 'asked for it', that advice still focuses on teaching women how to protect themselves ('a can of Elnett doubles up as pepper spray', a magazine once helpfully informed us), and that thousands of rapes go unreported because victims are terrified that they won't be taken seriously. With so many people laughing at these jokes, it's arguably a fair assumption.

That's not to say that all jokes about rape are bad. Horrible things happen in the world all the time, every day, and it's OK to joke about them (if you're British, it's actively encouraged). The ones that are funny, however, are generally crafted by superior comedians who think long and hard about the comedy they're writing, and generally don't use the victim as the punchline. There are plenty of male comedians who can and do make jokes that are close to the bone, and by using comedy to call bullshit on an unpleasant aspect of society they're actually making people question things. In other words, they're doing what intelligent comedy should be doing, rather than following a status quo that sees wheeling out 'surprise sex' as an 'easy laugh'.

The worst part of the current prevalence of sexual assault jokes is that attitude studies have shown that a significant proportion of rapists believe that all men rape. And scarily, every time someone makes or laughs heartily at a rape joke, this helps validate such a world view. No comedian can control how people interpret their comedy, after all – but they have a responsibility to give that interpretation some thought.

Comparing and contrasting the language used by the media sources to which men and women (and particularly young men and women) are exposed shows that it's no wonder so many people are of the belief that the respective genders will never understand one another. Perhaps all those headlines are right, and we'll never speak the same language. The journalists-turned-content-creators delivering information and entertainment to us are certainly in a different world. On one planet it's 'bras', 'babymoons' and 'Brangelina', and on the other it's 'bitches', 'BMWs' and 'banging'. And in between? Nothing more than miles and miles of cold, dead, silent space.

11
Lad Culture

Get yer tits out for the lads

(*or, How men's magazines are ruining your life*)

Nuts magazine, which is now defunct but at the time of writing touted its online presence as 'Britain's number one men's website', isn't exactly the first place you'd expect to go for a spot of feminist reading. But, having dedicated almost an entire book to women's media and the sexist evils it wreaks upon us, it's only fair that we take a brief look at the other, disturbing side of the coin: namely, the media routinely consumed by men, from lads' mags to pornography. Unfortunately, that does mean examining some nuts.

Nuts was a magazine whose introductory tagline on Google is 'Topless Girls, Web Games, Funny Videos, Glamour Models', and whose online brand extensions included one particularly encouraging one called 'Assess My Breasts'. In case its enigmatic name makes you wonder about its content, it did what it said on the tin: women were encouraged to send in pictures of their mammary appendages, and the readers of *Nuts Online* (though *Tits Online* would perhaps be a more appropriate choice of title) would rate them on a scale of 1 to 10. OK, so there's little pretence to intellectual content here – cover girls were asked such probing, Paxman-esque interview questions as, 'What's it like having boobs?' – but it's no wonder that this sort of non-content has aroused its fair share of feminist ire. In comparison to today's porno-inspired offerings, a 1950s issue of *Playboy* with its mix of lifestyle, fiction and photographs of women lounging in bubble baths looks as tame as a modern bush. *Playboy*'s circulation and influence declined from the 1970s onwards, and the rise of the much more explicit lads' mag coincided with the explosion of the porn industry. A rejection of the 'pussyish' pro-feminist 'new man' in favour of hard-drinking, tit-ogling traditional masculinity gave birth to what is now known by some as 'lad culture'. Magazines such as *Maxim, Loaded* (astute tagline: 'For men who should know better') and *Arena* were at the forefront of this boob-heavy counter-revolution.

Lad culture is defined by the National Union of Students (naturally experts on crass behaviour in bars) as 'a group or "pack" mentality expressed in activities such as sport and heavy alcohol consumption, and in "banter" which is "often sexist, misogynist and homophobic"'. It may feel like lad culture has been with us for years, in the same way that thirty seconds of having a drill bored into your skull will feel like it has been happening for ever. But in fact this charming little development had its genesis in the 'post-feminist' nineties, and is described by some as a 'response to feminism', or 'a response to the "girl power' movement". Trying to dress up lad culture as a legitimate answer to the Spice Girls singing 'zig-a-zig-ah' in Union Jack print, however, seems a bit like comparing the aforementioned drill torture with a slow comfortable session of lovemaking. The American equivalent of this British institution is often known as the 'frat boy' mentality, a delicious combo of sport, heavy drinking and dehumanising attitudes to women propagated by close-knit groups of all-male 'homosocial' bell-ends with whom you'd never want to share a tent at a festival. A sociologist researcher described the archetypal 'new lad' as a 'pre-feminist' who contrasts himself with the 'pro-feminist new man'. 'Lads' go 'on tour' and cheat on their 'ball and chain' partners with 'whores' and 'wenches' in strip clubs on their stag nights; meanwhile, everyone repeats the mantra that burlesque shows are different because they involve slightly more people who went to Eton or Roedean and the clothes that the dancers are taking off are a lot more expensive. Make no bones about it: lad culture is not class-specific, and women can espouse it too. If you've got an adolescent mindset and a penchant for militaristic sexism, then welcome to the frathouse. Provided you get your tits out for the lads, of course.

Before you accuse us of being nunnery-inhabiting prudes, we're not saying that there's anything inherently wrong with breasts. They're just mammary tissue, after all. You could easily (and often justifiably) argue that our own attitude to nudity as a society is confused, and that we could do with liberating the breasts and bums and cocks and balls that are presently forced to lurk behind 'XXX' classifications and the post-watershed cutoff. After all, our current film ratings system often looks upon violence or murder as less worthy of censorship than a sex scene between consenting adults, as Evan Rachel Wood drily noted in late 2013 when a cunnilingus scene in her film *Charlie Countryman* was cut: 'The scene where the two main characters make "love" was altered because someone felt that seeing a man give a woman oral sex made people "uncomfortable", she said, 'but the scenes in which people are murdered by having their heads blown off remained intact and unaltered.'

'Why so ashamed of the human body?' a naturist might ask, as you try to focus on looking them in the eye. Why not introduce our children to the full diversity of body types without shame? Well, quite. The problem is that the current range of naked bods on show are hardly 'diverse' – for a start, they're almost always female. Nonetheless, anyone attacking the wall-to-wall representations of naked women in the media is immediately labelled a prude who probably thinks masturbation is dirty and can't even bear to look down in the shower. Journalist Martin Robbins described the No More Page 3 campaign as 'sinister' and indicative of 'a kind of sexual policing', rather than a simple objection by members of the British public who feel that naked breasts don't really constitute 'news'. He even ended his article with the proposition that what we really need is more tits everywhere. This would be all very well were he truly in the game for some proper equal opps nudity. Strangely, though, those who want more nudity always seem to stop short of wanting the whole, full-frontal male shebang and all that that entails, complete with penises unleashed willy-nilly on *This Morning*. We'd hazard a guess that the people of this country would object, though anyone who watched Phillip Schofield and Holly Willoughby awkwardly interview the man with the 'world's largest penis' while his addendum remained safely encased in his trousers may beg to differ. Just whip it out, for Chrissakes.

In reality, erections are probably the most protected species on the planet next to hammerhead sharks. There are more rules and regulations surrounding boners in the media than you could ever imagine: the gigantic fake boobs of Jane from Cornwall might be displayed prominently and at eye level in every local newsagent's, often with a close-up shot of her inner plumbing on the tenth page, but, as the Lose the Lads' Mags campaign has repeatedly pointed out, it's a rare branch of Tesco Extra that markets mags that sexually objectify men on the cover or inside. Don't even think about seeing a turgid willy in a mainstream movie; that shit is not allowed. Meanwhile, the most you'll get from lowbrow women's mags is a torso shot of some ripped dude holding a puppy, which definitely doesn't have the same sexual currency as a pair of GG boobs ('a nipple for a nipple' just doesn't apply here. And isn't even a phrase, but a slightly offensive perversion of a biblical idiom). *Cosmopolitan* once included what they called on the cover 'The naughtiest photo we've ever run of a guy!', which turned out inside to be a topless male model with a hand towel round his shoulders and his boxer shorts on. In the words of unamused online feminist mag *Jezebel*, if this is *Cosmo*'s definition of 'naughty', their next cover better feature 'deranged perverts'.

On top of this, it's worth pointing out that your generic six-pack is achievable with regular gym attendance, whereas we've been told by those working in the industry that certain publications will only print pictures of women whose breast size has been altered by surgery. Where men can work out for the archetypal 'perfect male bod', women are often expected to shell out thousands and undergo major surgery for the female counterpart. And since there are way too many *Telegraph*-reading types who think that seeing a close-up of a bottom will lead to children running wild on crack, we probably need to accept that universal nudity will never happen, and start to address the existing unbalanced representation rather than trying to strip off everybody else's clothes.

Maybe you need some further convincing – after all, we're assuming that if you've got a hold of this book you've spent a least a respectable amount of time in modern society, and perhaps the rows of tatas on 'Assess My Breasts' are no more shocking to you than the average roll of woodchip wallpaper. The media can desensitise you like that. If you had ever delved into the annals (which sounds rude to the average lads' mag reader, but actually isn't) of the *Nuts* website, you might be more offended by the sheer idiocy on show than the misogyny. (Their jokes section included 'Jokes about Women' and 'Jokes about Blondes' – so far, so yawningly sexist – but the total unfunniness of such treats as 'Knock, knock. Who's there? Dozer. Dozer who? Doze are the nicest boobs I've ever seen!' – one that was genuinely trending at the beginning of 2013 –

pretty much swallows up any possible outrage into a sea of anxiety about the rapidly declining IQ of the human race.)

We get that any magazine producing a 'Diamond Boobilee' special edition (that was *Zoo* celebrating the Queen, FYI) is going to come across as more ridiculous than threatening. But it's important to realise that what initially can seem to be 'a bit of a laugh' is acting as a cover for a seriously creepy, dehumanising attitude to women. Even when we avert our eyes from the car crash that is lads' mags for a second and check out where the gentlemen play – that's right, they frolic amidst the pages of that decidedly more discerning institution, *Gentlemen's Quarterly* – things get complicated. Now, *GQ* prides itself on having an audience that is slightly less *Loaded* and slightly more *Vogue Hommes*; its latest feature is more likely to be where to come across the latest brogues than where to *come* across the latest glamour model's boob job (most likely page 37). But, despite its pretensions towards classy behaviour, *Gentlemen's Quarterly* has not been left untouched by lad culture mentality. Don't believe us? Then try googling the latest *GQ* covers, which, if they haven't made a sudden and drastic editorial change, will be mostly men in suits, punctuated by the occasional woman. Invariably, this woman will be wearing one of the following: underwear, a bikini top (most likely with a phallic object in her half-opened mouth), or nothing at all.

In 2013, David Beckham wore a suit and trilby; Leonardo DiCaprio appeared in a fitted coat; Robert Pattinson wore a shirt over a T-shirt; and Joseph Gordon-Levitt sported both a cravat *and* a tie. Meanwhile, Mila Kunis wore a bra; Rihanna appeared naked, with a strategically placed leather jacket to cover her nipples; both top model Ana Sofia Martins and singer Lana Del Rey were naked, contorted into positions that hid their naughtiest parts; and Kate Upton, in a striped bikini top, gave the customary blowjob to a lolly. The message – that men are professionals and women are objects – couldn't have been starker. Just because it's cleverly concealed so-called 'middle-class misogyny' doesn't mean that it's any more civilised.

Despite the moniker 'lad culture', we know that female objectification is not merely the domain of men. Depressingly, it's everywhere, as anyone who was reading the *Evening Standard* (as far as we're aware, a paper for both genders) in September 2012, when they appointed a male 'strip club correspondent', will no doubt be aware. The women on the front of our own magazines are also sexualised and scantily clad – showing that 'laddism' is influencing not just the way men perceive women in general but our own reading material. OK, despite a hefty cleavage, the standard cover girl for a trashy ladymag stops short of nipple exposure, but that doesn't mean women's magazines (and, as we saw, even teen magazines) don't heavily 'laddify' their content. US *Cosmo* ran a trend piece on strip clubs in February 2013 which included the line 'It's not just okay if you get your kicks from stuffing a few ones into a pretty girl's G-string, it's cool', and *Glamour* isn't much better – in early 2012 it not only gave the Playboy Club an overwhelmingly positive review but neatly sidestepped the entire issue of female objectification by stating that 'the bunnies add to the atmosphere of the club', as though they were decorative candlesticks rather than women. *Vogue*, meanwhile, held its fashion week party there.

With newspapers and women's mags waxing lyrical about this Playboy invasion, complaining about it becomes even more difficult, as Vagenda reader Charlotte discovered in her uphill struggle against Playboy in her gym. Charlotte complained to her local Gymbox following the introduction of a 'Bunny Bootcamp', only to receive an email from the manager calling her 'a dick'. The class had received decent PR and had been covered enthusiastically in the *Telegraph* (a newspaper so scarily feminist it has its own 'men' section) in an article explaining the concept of the 'BMI' (that's 'bunny measurement index, folks!'). In the face of such media approval, who cares about one customer's discomfort – or, indeed, the potential discomfort of an entire gender?

YOU GOT A PROBLEM WITH THAT?

Whenever an upset girlfriend writes in to a problem page about how she's upset that her boyfriend went to a strip club, the agony aunt is always suspiciously keen to dismiss it as a harmless embodiment of the saying 'Boys will be boys.' This stance was particularly true of the now-defunct 'ladette' bible *more!* but it has also cropped up on *Cosmo*'s problem pages numerous times. In the August 2012 issue, the magazine 'advised' a young woman who was upset and furious that her boyfriend had attended a live sex show in Amsterdam that 'strip clubs are a stag tradition. I'm sure he meant no harm.' Never mind that the person you thought you might want to settle down with some day paid to have a woman he'd never met wave her fanny in his face last weekend as his erection strained against his sandblasted G-Star jeans; it's all good fun. Don't talk to him about it or anything, because that makes you kinda uptight and totes uncool. This is something for *you* to deal with, not society. Right?

To borrow some lad-speak, we don't want to 'harsh your buzz', but objectifying an entire gender by treating women as things and not as people makes it just that little bit easier to ignore the negative impact that treatment can have. *Esquire* editor (formerly of *GQ*) and professional lady charmer Alex Bilmes summarised it perfectly for us when he stated that his magazine portrays 'ornamental' women 'in the same way that we provide pictures of cool cars' – making it apparently 'more honest' than women's magazines, which do the same thing but deny it (have a gold star for your honesty, Alex): 'I could lie to you if you want and say we are interested in their brains as well. We are not. They are objectified', he said, in March 2013, with characteristic charm. Needless to say, we all swooned.

These sorts of statement just go to show how prevalent dehumanising attitudes towards women have become amongst certain knobhead magazine editors and their readers. To lump us together with cars is typically rude, but at least cars never have to suffer the indignity of knowing that they only exist to be driven. It's *Zoo*, however, that really makes the most of our gender's 'ornamental' potential. Find yourself staring at another page of disembodied arses in *Zoo*'s competition for 'Britain's Best Bum' – or 'Bumblr' – to which women send in pictures of their thong-clad bums stuck out in the 'doggy style' pose beloved of lads' mags, right after you've had a go at 'Crack the Rack' over at *Zoo*'s website ('Guess the cup size and if the boobs are real or fake!'), and you might start to feel a little depressed. That depression might morph into despair when you realise that magazines aimed at teenage girls have been just as guilty of portraying 'women' as nothing more than a series of body parts. Except this isn't even women we're talking about: it's *girls*.

A 2007 Women in Journalism report, for instance, revealed how teenage magazines such as *Mizz* and *Bliss* (in its section called 'How Sexy Am I?') were adopting 'lads' mags' techniques by encouraging young girls to upload pictures of themselves to the internet and post 'ratings' of their own and others' thighs, legs and breasts. This was the same year that *FHM* met with widespread condemnation and a PCC judgment for publishing a topless photo of a 14-year-old girl without her consent.

The (sometimes literal) dissecting of women's bodies doesn't end there. In October 2012, an image on *Zoo*'s Australian Facebook page showed a woman's bikini-clad body that had been chopped in half accompanied by a caption asking followers which half they preferred. 'Right', said one comment, indicating the bottom half, 'because two holes are better than one.' In fact, most of the *Nuts* Australia readers picked right, with one posting: 'Right, 'cause it doesn't have the ability to have its own fucking opinion,' and another: 'Either end there's shit coming out.' It's difficult to not see 'laddish' posts such as this as part of a larger culture that attempts to put women firmly in their place. We're unsure of where a woman's place is exactly, but according to these dickheads, it definitely seems to be under a man, on our back.

One thing is clear: 'lads' such as these don't need the presence of a woman's face in order to get off. The whole 'woman-as-easily-divided-piece-of-meat-thing' has caught on, with skyrocketing media success rates. Perhaps this all started with the zoom-in on the pompom tails of Playboy bunnies, but it's now everywhere. And while Hugh Hefner may have come out publicly against slut-shaming – prompting Yahoo! News to seriously ask if he might be 'the new face of women's rights' – there did seem to be a sneaky bit of self-interest behind his apparently liberal and feminist words. At the end of the day, Hugh, you're still an old man who lives in a Disney porno mansion alongside a collection of dressed-up, pretend, payrolled girlfriends, so forgive us for not hailing you as a feminist icon just yet.

At the end of the long, long day, all of this can be enough to make you feel nostalgic for the annual edition of *FHM*'s Sexiest Women. Sure, it reduces a load of professional female public figures to seedy photographs of submissively posed babydolls in cleavage-enhancing underwear with biros stuck suggestively in their mouths. But hey, at least they have faces.

RAPISTS VERSUS READERS

Attacking the lowest common denominator of men's magazines, we realise, is pretty much like shooting spermatozoa in a Petri dish, i.e. an easy hit. Nobody's expecting *Zoo* to start publishing excerpts from *The*

Female Eunuch any time soon – it wouldn't exactly appeal to the target audience, and if it did appear, we're guessing it would be in the style of *The Sun*'s now-defunct 'News in Briefs', which gave topless models speech bubbles of political rhetoric – the 'hilarious' joke being that silly, decorative women are for getting their boobs out and couldn't possibly entertain highbrow views on the recession or the situation in Syria at the same time. Perhaps we shouldn't expect too much from the titles that reel their readership in with a weekly promise of "The. Naughtiest. Shoot. Ever!' Perhaps we need to pick our battles elsewhere, where a modicum of common sense still exists, before we drive ourselves up the wall with useless indignation. What's the point of even attempting to target the self-proclaimed brainlessness of lads' mags and Page Three? This is a criticism that popular campaigns such as Lose the Lads' Mags and No More Page 3 have faced since their launch.

The problem is, the idea that these rags are nothing more than the print publication equivalent of naughty toddlers with one hand up their nose and another down their pants does everyone a disservice. The men and women working on them know exactly what they are selling, and that increasingly predatory content is becoming more and more mainstream. Perhaps nothing illustrates this more than a 2011 study by researchers at Surrey and Middlesex Universities which revealed that most people couldn't differentiate between quotes from lads' mags and quotes from people who had actually committed serious sexual offences, because both sources displayed the same 'she was asking for it' attitude towards women. Half of the statements (such as 'You do not want to be caught red-handed . . . go and smash her on a park bench. That used to be my trick', or 'Mascara running down the cheeks means they've just been crying, and it was probably your fault . . . but you can cheer up the miserable beauty with a bit of the old in and out') were taken from prominent male magazines *Zoo, Nuts, Loaded* and *FHM*; the other half were taken from a sociology book called *The Rapist File: Interviews with Convicted Rapists* by Les Sussman and Sally Bordwell (2000). Yep, *The Rapist File*. Not one we'll be adding to our Amazon wish lists. When confronted with the anonymous sources, male participants were more likely to agree with the statements taken from testimonies of rapists than to get on board with advice from the bad boys down at *Zoo* and *FHM*. When a quote was attributed to a men's magazine, however, the men who took part in the study were much more likely to identify with it, arguably showing that popular lads' mags normalise misogyny and victim-blaming and make it seem acceptable because of its context. That lads' mags have been found to use the same degrading language as self-justifying convicted rapists says more about these top-shelf publications than a bunch of a fed-up feminists ever could.

And it's not just lads' mags. In 1998, Cynthia Carter looked at over 840 reports of sexual violence and found that many were placed directly beside the topless photograph on Page Three of *The Sun*. Carter's argument is that the reporting of sexual violence is often seen by tabloid editors as part of a 'sexy news package'. One example cited by Rosalind Gill in *Gender and the Media* (2006) was a report on the discovery of a mobile phone and some clothes believed to belong to a 21-year-old woman who was thought to have been raped and murdered (*Mirror*, January 2003), placed next to a story about sex shops illustrated with a photograph of a woman in black lacy lingerie.

So what's a girl to do when confronted with this sort of world; how should she formulate a response to this never-ending strip show of naked, shaven gyrating ladies and the leering geezers who say she's 'asking for it', especially when the standard defence 'It's all banter!' is used to stonewall any sort of dialogue on the subject and make you look like a strait-laced cow? A favourite term of teen and twentysomething misogynists who see the only authentic type of masculinity as involving a predatory attitude to women is that 'banter' can be found anywhere from lads' mags to your local university union. Never mind that 'banter' as a word in serious conversation should have been outlawed and the punishment for its utterance made the only exception to the UN's moratorium on the death penalty. Never mind that categorising your statement as 'banter' immediately after making it is the equivalent of following every sad joke with the instruction: 'THIS IS A FUNNY JOKE. LAUGH NOW.' If it needs signposting, it probably isn't all that funny. Never mind that this irritating phrase is deployed at absolutely any point of wrongdoing for immediate immunity (the 'lads' equivalent of the *Daily Mail*'s 'POLITICAL CORRECTNESS GONE MAD!'). The 'banter' defence has been used to defend statements (amongst others) about 'raping women to death' for speaking in public, and 'smashing [my girlfriend's] head into a wall' to 'knock some sense into her' in a piece by every undersexed predatory troll's online magazine of choice, Uni Lad.

Exactly how far does 'banter' go? Women who star in movies or sing songs or model for fashion labels should expect to pose naked on the covers of magazines, all in the name of good banter. Even in a context that recognises serious professional achievement, that expectation will underlie everything they do: just take a hard look at Seth MacFarlane's 'Boob Song' at the 2013 Oscars. The song called out all of the women actors present whose breasts had been seen onscreen during their careers, in a good old-fashioned sing-song. 'We saw your boobs!' the chorus went. Bantersaurus Rex! It's a bit of a shame that most of those breasts had been seen in emotionally charged scenes about intimacy or serious portrayals of rape – and that all of them featured in movies intended for serious review, rather than for every female actor in them to be reduced to a sexual object – but hey, you can't please 'em all. All is fair in love, war and bantz. And we're pretty sure that makes Seth MacFarlane the Archbishop of Banterbury.

Meanwhile, the 'banter banner' decorates the halls of universities, colleges and schools, where women haven't even had the audacity to begin careers yet. Take the example of Glasgow University Union, which in 2013 hosted a national students' debating competition which ended with the premature departure of two prominent female competitors after their respective breast sizes were commented on repeatedly as they attempted to speak. One was called a 'frigid bitch' as she discussed politics and religion; the other was shouted down with, 'Shame, woman!' every time she tried to continue. The latter reported hearing 'Get that woman out my union' on her arrival, and said that female audience members who had attempted to stop the heckling had been attacked in turn. It goes without saying that this sort of behaviour shouldn't be seen as defensible 'university banter'; that, in fact, it was a very sinister demonstration of how 'lad culture' can literally silence women's voices for no reason other than the nature of the bodies they inhabit.

Neither should this particular example of university sexism be seen as a shameful but isolated incident: during our time at the Vagenda, we've regularly been sent by our readers adverts for student nights that are advertised with 'cheeky' references to rape and pictures of the apparently sprawled, unconscious legs of intoxicated girls in bathroom stalls with their knickers round their ankles. Take the advertisement for a tequila night which was displayed across student halls at Leeds University and sent to us by one of the students; it showed a woman on her knees in front of a faceless man, as white liquid poured out of his genital region, with the headline 'Come and Swallow'. A Freshers' Week event at Cardiff Metropolitan University was advertised with a prominent picture of a T-shirt bearing the slogan 'I was raping a woman last night and she cried'. And in October 2013, nightclub company Tequila UK ran a promotional video for a club night called 'Freshers' Violation', which featured clips of young men talking about 'violating' female students and saying a girl was going to 'get raped'. This kind of misogyny isn't limited to one type of student body or university: a popular chant at the University of Oxford includes the lyrics: 'Fuck a pregnant woman, fuck her on the bed, fuck her really hard until the foetus gives you head'. It was the first thing one of our readers heard on her initial lonely night at college. This from the men who, in all probability, will be running the country one day.

And let us not forget the fraternity at Yale University that stood outside educational buildings to protest against feminist groups discussing sexual consent on campus, holding placards that said 'NO MEANS YES! YES MEANS ANAL!' while yelling the same words in a caveman-like chant. If that's all in the name of 'banter', where are the 'banterous' pictures of dudes collapsed in a toilet with their boxers on show? Where are the advertisements for nights on the town that include a teenage boy with his cheek stuck to a stinking urinal cake? Where are the women actively protesting that if men go to pubs and drink, they should expect to be dragged into fights and assaulted because of their 'naturally aggressive' sex? Where are the men who cannot debate because 'banter' dictates that their entire gender shouldn't be allowed to participate without harassment? Where are the sororities standing outside Yale's campus, chanting intimidating jokes about violent assaults enacted upon their male student counterparts?

The apotheosis of all this university-based skullfuckery here in the UK is, of course, Uni Lad, launched by two male university students in 2010. Uni Lad, or the 'Banter Bible' to associated morons, bridged that gap between interviews with rapists and standard sexist degradation in *Loaded* by actively encouraging its readership to become rapists. The unwise editorial statement that the two students behind Uni Lad came under fire for – '85 per cent of rape cases go unreported. That seems to be fairly good odds' – eventually led to the temporary shutdown of the site, although you'll be pleased to hear that it's now back up and running with a front-page disclaimer about 'not taking it too seriously'. Again, the fault lies at the door of those pesky feminists who got all hot under the collar about various banter-filled articles, including one where a writer detailed how he would forcefully terminate through violence a child that his girlfriend didn't want to abort. Ho ho, what japes!

Uni Lad is a website – or, rather, a phenomenon – that has 588,000 likes on Facebook at the time of writing, and boasts that it has been 'voted number one lads' mag for students'. In other words: it's not a fringe publication, it enjoys frightening popularity, and it's not going away any time soon. In fact, as far as trivialising violence against women goes, it's the tip of the iceberg. There are groups on Facebook entitled 'Sum [sic] sluts need their throat slit', 'It's not "rape" if they're dead and if they're alive its [sic] surprise sex', and, 'Riding your girlfriend softly cause you don't want to wake her up'. In 2012, an image which showed a woman bound and gagged accompanied by the words 'It's not rape. If she really didn't want to, she'd have said something', was widely circulated on the social networking site. And yet, none of these things came under what Facebook refers to as 'hate speech' or 'inciting violence', even when people reported them as such. This inspired feminist campaigners, led by activism powerhouses Laura Bates (of the Everyday Sexism Project) and American feminist Soraya Chemaly, to contact Facebook's advertisers repeatedly and ask them if they knew that their goods and services were being shown next to photographs of women being beaten and raped. Thousands of women and men got involved, including us. Facebook refused to take stock, until a few weeks later when advertisers began to pull out and the business lost significant revenue. Only then did they agree to make gender-based violence unacceptable in the

Facebook terms, just as they had already done for racist slurs and images as 'pornographic' of women breastfeeding their babies. For a long time, they had nevertheless seen banning violence against women as a 'step too far' – something that society implicitly accepted and didn't really mind encountering during a browse on a social network. It's the same kind of implied acceptance that sees T-shirts with slogans such as the disturbing 'I like my women like I like my coffee . . . ground up and in the freezer' and the boringly derivative but no less creepy 'Keep calm and rape a lot' sold by mainstream retailers.

Part of the reason there isn't a bigger outcry from girls and women who come across these websites and publications is because, they tell us, they fear the repercussions if they speak out. Lad culture, which has bled down into the way young men converse and bond with each other, seems so dominant, and so all-encompassing, particularly in schools and univer-sities, that it takes quite some bravery to stand up to it, especially when it's constantly reminding you at every turn of your physical female weakness when faced with the predatory 'wolf pack'. Under this deluge, the casual trivialisation of assault and the routine objectification, the constant raising of the bar of 'harmless banter', the student unions which condone it and the professional institutions which protect it, and the way in which it has suddenly become all-pervasive in the last decade, the room for women to be taken seriously as human beings seems to be getting smaller and smaller as time goes on. In many ways, this is a new and rapidly shifting battleground, where 'lads' mag' media, while not yet bedfellows with sites such as Uni Lad, are becoming disturbingly similar in tone. *FHM*, for instance, revealed exactly how it perceived women's roles when it caused outrage back in December 2012 with the sentence: 'It's never acceptable to wear your girlfriend/mother/victim's socks'. A casual attitude to violence against women is not limited to the internet, but arguably originates in the very magazines the web is now in the process of superseding.

Websites like Uni Lad have undoubtedly changed media perceptions of women for the worse, not least because they're so easy to access and share. Of course, this is far from the only content that your average teenage surfer is going to come across. Porn has been around for ever and a day, but the way its depictions have become fifty shades darker in the last decade has raised concerns about its implications for everyday women. As one Icelandic minister said wryly when the government tabled a motion to ban access to violent sexual imagery in 2013, porn is no longer 'a naked woman in a country field'. Indeed, the playful, bushy frolicking of the 1970s feels like distant archive footage compared with some of the depraved humiliation you can find on the internet.

DO IT LIKE A PORNSTAR

With the wealth of instantaneous filth available at the nation's fingertips online, it's no surprise that lads' mags are facing a crisis in terms of circulation, nor that they are desperately trying to push the bounds of acceptable nudity. By August 2013, sales of *Nuts* magazine were down 25% and in March 2014 its closure was announced. Co-op's decision to withdraw it from sale following IPC Media's refusal to put the magazine in a 'modesty bag' may have played a part in falling circulation numbers, but ultimately the closure probably had more to do with boob-obsessed *Nuts*' inability to compete with the internet in filth stakes. *Zoo*, meanwhile, was down 20% and *Esquire* 14.3%. The slow decline of lads' mags doesn't mean an end to male masturbation fodder, however. As everyone knows, the devil makes work for idle hands, and the internet contains an almost limitless wankbank of hardcore pornography.

Internet porn being a relatively new phenomenon, it's difficult to determine the long-term effects on a child's psyche of regular visual exposure to erect penises aggressively pumping shaved pudenda on squeaky vinyl Argos sofas to tinny musak. Statistics pertaining to the long-term social impact are impossible to compile as the members of 'generation porn' haven't lived much of their adulthood yet, but the anecdotal evidence certainly seems to point towards a shift in where

young people learn and find out about sex. According to one article in the *Sunday Times* by professor of sociology Gail Dines on 19 May 2013, 'on average, the first viewing of porn takes place at the age of 11'. Dines also pointed out that Google Trends data shows 'teen porn' as one of the UK's most searched pornography terms – as well as *the* most searched pornography term in the US and Canada. Searches for the term have jumped 215% in the last eight years, it and continues to be 'the fastest growing genre'. Unfortunately, the most popular forms of pornography are the ones showing a hairless, submissive woman undergoing ritual humiliation. The nature of the acts themselves has also become more extreme: 'choking' during sex, for instance, has, according to our readership, become a fairly mainstream request from their boyfriends and one-night stands. Dines also pointed out that brutal, violent and abusive sex is routinely performed in porn videos by men in the roles of 'predatory fathers, uncles, coaches, teachers, and employers'.

Perhaps the most difficult thing about putting forward feminist criticisms of pornography is that – as with putting forward criticisms of the media's objectification of women – you're immediately assumed to be some kind of frigid, chastity-belt-wearing nun (and not the saucy kind). This seems to have become an accepted party line even in left-wing newspaper opinion pieces. Although we don't believe in being conservative about discussing sex openly, neither do we think that young people's exposure to porn is being exaggerated; after all, 36% of the internet is porn. A 2013 report by the Office of the Children's Commissioner in the UK found that a significant number of children access online pornography and that it influences their attitudes towards relationships and sex, and it also found a correlation between holding violent attitudes and accessing violent media. A study in the *Violence Against Women* journal in 2010 called 'Aggression and Sexual Behaviour in Best-Selling Pornography Videos' found that out of the 50 most watched porn films at the time, 88% depicted physical aggression such as 'open hand slapping', 'gagging', 'hair pulling', 'choking', 'kicking' and 'pinching'.

The claim that porn is influencing real-life relationships is certainly borne out anecdotally. From the teacher in an inner-city state school who claimed she was forced to go on 'blowjob patrol' during lunch breaks, to the 15-year-old girl under pressure to let her boyfriend film her masturbating, only for it to be distributed amongst everyone she knows instantly via BBM, there's a sense that young women, often very young women, are feeling under pressure to behave in the same way as the women they see on the screen. A University of East London study found that 20% of boys 'were dependent on porn to have sex', while University of Cambridge research found that porn addiction leads to the same kind of brain activity as drug dependence or alcoholism. A young man in Beeban Kidron's 2013 documentary about porn, *InRealLife,* speaks of the girls he meets not being able to live up to the women depicted in pornography, saying that 'it's ruined the whole sense of love'. The young women we've met say they sometimes feel that the boys want them to participate in the same acts they've downloaded to their phones, and amongst our own age group there certainly seem to be young men who feel it's appropriate to ask for anal on the first date ('I'm saving it for my honeymoon' is Rhiannon's comeback of choice). *GQ* sex columnist Siobhan Rosen complained about men's expectation of 'pornified sex' in a 2012 article that recounted how men she barely knew seemed to think it was normal to call her a 'dirty slut' in bed or come on her face. We empathise. We've been there.

Of course, if the sexcapades in porn really do get you off, then that's great – your fantasies have come true. It's when there's an expectation that two pumps, a pull out, and some spurting on her breasts is 100% guaranteed to give EVERY woman multiple orgasms, or that we're all secret submissives in search of our very own Christian Grey, complete with vaginal clamps – in other words, when we start seeing highly commercialised pornography as a true reflection of female sexuality – then we're in trouble. Children are confirming in focus groups and interviews again and again that they are getting their sex education from porn. A group of girls interviewed for *The Times* (16 June 2013) said: 'Girls look at porn to see how they should do things. Some think if they don't do it like in porn, then boys won't like them.'

Of course, there are arguments to be made in favour of a more liberated society when it comes to sex – in some cases, especially with regard to prostitution, liberalisation can result in a much safer environment for women, and if, as a nation, we had a more open attitude to sex education, young people wouldn't be looking to porn partly because they're in need of guidance. Seeing all pornography as essentially exploitative to women is, especially in light of all the feminist porn directors who have been springing up in recent years, patronising, to say the least. Pornography has traditionally been made by men for male gratification, but recognising that women too can be visually stimulated by erotic images is an important step towards a culture that sees women's sexual desires as valid and important. We've always found the argument that men are genetically hard-wired to visually objectify women, while women are hard-wired to just, like, imagine stuff, to be more than a bit shit. There's this assumption that, while men are frantically tugging themselves off in XXX theatres, women can get off simply by lighting a few candles, running a bath, and grabbing the latest bodice-ripping bonkbuster featuring a stable hand rummaging around in the lady of the manor's bloomers. ('Your undercarriage awaits, my lady.') *Psychology Today* even went so far as suggesting that women get off on something they nauseatingly called 'the awakening of love'. Please.

But you can't necessarily lump a woman's discomfort with commercialised sexuality and its impact on young people and children together with a 'prudish' agenda. Indeed, by doing that, you're essentially playing into the porn barons' hands. 'It's just a bit of fun, love,' you can imagine them saying, probably while drooling all over their £500 Cuban cigars. 'Nothing to get uptight about. Now drop your knickers and bend over.' Make no mistake: porn is an industry, and those who run the lucrative show have a vested interest in making you accept – and buy into – the status quo.

That's the difficult thing about 'raunch culture': it dominates. As MakeLoveNotPorn founder Cindy Gallop has pointed out, 'The issue isn't porn. The issue is the complete absence of counterpoint to porn.' As a teenager coming of age in these dick-dominated days, the pressure to be 'hot' or 'sexy' can seem overwhelming – we know, because we've donned the schoolgirl outfits and read the sex tips too, in our time. But if you voice the fact that you're uncomfortable with being made to feel as though your body is nothing more than an attractively arranged set of humps and orifices, a spaff receptacle existing solely for the benefit of male pleasure, you're a killjoy. In light of this, it really is no wonder the world is teeming with female chauvinist pigs such as those featured in Ariel Levy's book. These 'girls gone wild' with their Playboy Bunny tracksuit bottoms and their insistent appreciation of hardcore pornography have bought into raunch culture so enthusiastically/completely that they're often condescendingly sexist towards members of their own gender who refuse to participate.

Take the way anal sex has been normalised in the last twenty years. Once upon a time, the blowjob was the height of depravity. Now it's so run-of-the mill that it's almost surprising that it's not on the national curriculum (and with our sex ed advocacy hats on we would argue that, actually, it should be). As oral sex became less taboo, pornography turned its attention to the anal variety – to the point where many young men now expect it as standard. And, despite some women protesting that 'it feels like doing a poo backwards', many of our readers and acquaintances told us that they just give in to the pressure to do it, rather than have to explain to their partner that it's not their thing. The same goes with being ejaculated on: young women are reporting that it's now being expected of them, rather than something that can be discussed and then consented to if it feels right. If their partners knew, most likely they would feel terrible, but raunch culture can alienate women from the men that they're having sex with because under the crushing weight of pornographic expectations, some women don't even feel their own preferences count for anything in the bedroom any more. There's this feeling that, unless you're hogtied or brandishing a vibrating two-way cock ring like everyone else, your sex must be hopelessly sad and vanilla.

The popularity of hardcore porn, rough sex and BDSM has definitely seen certain sexual behaviours hit the mainstream – as the huge popularity of E. L. James's spank-and-chain-fest *Fifty Shades of Grey* demonstrates. BDSM in itself is not oppressive of women, of course, and many women find it intensely erotic, just as they might anal sex or bukkake. But it's worrying when the pressure to perform certain sexual acts becomes so great that some women, especially young women, feel pushed into a corner. As a society, we're exposed to increasingly violent forms of sex, and yet there seems to be no proper education system to help explain to young people what this means. If you're being sold the message that this is what women are, and that this is what they enjoy, is it so strange that young men are surprised when their sexual partners don't want to act out what they have seen on screen? An interviewer for *The Times* article mentioned above asked groups of young people whether they believed it was true or false that 'women fantasise about being raped', and only a small handful said 'false'.

As a commercial enterprise still mainly owned and dominated by men and their sexual urges, the porn industry is unlikely ever to be wholly un-exploitative of women. Does that mean that we should boycott it? Not necessarily. But it does mean that, as *Guardian* writer Tanya Gold once suggested, we should question its provenance. 'Why not treat it as some of us do meat, and ask where it came from and how was it made?' she asks. It's a fitting analogy, considering many performers are treated as little more. Take Linda Lovelace, the actress from *Deep Throat*. To some, the 1972 retro filthfest about a woman with a clitoris somewhere around her tonsils may just be a bit of harmless kitsch, but according to Lovelace, 'Virtually every time someone watches that movie, they're watching me being raped.'

Consent is a problem not just in porn, but outside it too. Sexual health workers have told us that teenage boys have expressed confusion as to whether or not a girl crying, shouting and begging 'no' counts as standard foreplay. Much like the lads' mags that sound like rapists, pornography rarely exhibits a firm grasp on the meaning of consent, and, with the depictions of sex in the media doing little to counteract this, and in the absence of mandatory sex education in the UK, there is a real possibility that this might bleed over into real life.

It's possible to object to how women's bodies are objectified, debased and commercialised for entertainment purposes, and also to love sex more than anything else in the world ever. It's possible to understand that sex workers need unionising, and legislation to protect them, without saying that you agree with the way many women are having to turn to sex work or porn to pay the bills partly because in these industries women are valued so much more for their bodies than their minds. You can see the decision to enter the sex industry as both a personal choice and one that reflects the male-dominated society we inhabit. You can buy a dildo from Ann Summers, have someone spank your arse with a paddle in a room full of strangers in gimp masks, and invest in anti-gagging BJ spray ('squirt to eliminate the taste of spurt'), and still be a feminist, provided you still fundamentally believe that you are in control of your own vagina. In other words, IT'S POSSIBLE TO HOLD MANY DIFFERENT IDEAS IN YOUR HEAD AT THE SAME TIME, such as loving sex and believing in the fundamental equality of men and women. It's when you stop believing that the trouble starts.

Yes, you can be a feminist and watch porn – videotaping two people getting down to it is neither inherently feminist nor anti-feminist. But it's crucial to realise that while sexual freedom is essential to the ultimate liberation of women, sexual freedom does not necessarily involve submitting to gagging on a massive cock on camera in order to pay the rent. Freedom of choice is definitely not born out of limited options and opportunity. Not all porn is violence against women, and to say so wrongly paints all women in the sex industry as victims. But the male boner still dominates, to the extent that questions of morality and ethics often don't stand a chance when pitted against some random dude's wank. The man who wilfully ignores female concerns about the current state of the porn industry is essentially saying: 'But . . . MY PENIS!' which is the same old justification that has been wheeled out for the existence of Page Three and nudie mags since time immemorial. In 2014, an age when most porn consists of a submissive woman being penetrated by multiple cocks and we're simultaneously seeing a resurgence of the misogynistic, violent attitudes to women that belong in the Stone Age, that excuse just isn't good enough any more.

RAPE CULTURE

The sexist, demeaning treatment of women in our society can range from street harassment (and some sleazy guy thinking it's his prerogative to walk up to you in broad daylight and describe exactly what he'd like to do to you), to sexual harassment (and having to rely on a protective dance circle of girlie mates every time you visit a club to avoid being dry-humped by a guy in a diamanté T-shirt), to violent language, sexual assault, and ultimately rape. The degrading attitude towards and treatment of women ultimately originates in the belief that as a sex we are lesser creatures, universally weaker in both physical and mental terms, and it is still pervasive. Every time a guy makes a rape joke he is, whether consciously or not, essentially reminding you of your apparently inferior position as a woman in the world. He is reminding you where the power lies – in his hands, or in his pants, and in the hands and pants of his gender. The joke is putting you in your place. When a group of men holler at you across the street as you walk home in the dark, alone, they are putting you in your place. (No, they don't seriously imagine that you will run towards them with open arms, crying out, 'Finally, Prince Charming is here! Take me home for a good hard shag!') Similarly, when a male colleague or a guy at a bar pinches your arse or tweaks your nipples and when you complain tells you that 'it's just a bit of harmless fun', he is putting you in your place.

This is what people mean when they talk about 'rape culture'. Rape culture simply means a culture in which sexual violence and rape are not only common but normalised. In other words, it's a culture in which rape is tolerated to various extents, when it should be condemned. The now infamous Steubenville rape case is a prime example of these mechanisms at work. When, in August 2012, a 16-year-old girl claimed that members of the local football team had taken her, drunk, from party to party and raped her, the small community in Ohio closed ranks and a culture of silence sprang up. Rather than believing the victim, onlookers claimed that condemning the men to prison was unfair, considering they were talented sportsmen whose minor slip-up shouldn't ruin lives with so much promise. They also claimed that the girl's drunkenness, her attire and her sexual behaviour meant that she was complicit in what happened to her. This was despite physical evidence suggesting otherwise: a widely circulated Instagram photo, showing two of the young men holding a clearly unconscious teenage girl by her arms and legs, as though she was an animal, surfaced shortly after the allegations were made. Status updates and tweets referring to her as 'dead' and a 'sloppy drunk bitch', as well as a video in which a classmate joked about the assault, also appeared. 'She wasn't moving,' a male voice laughs in the footage – 'She's dead!' he repeats, over and over. 'She's so raped her pussy is as dry as the sun right now.' Against the tirades of laughter we hear a lone voice pipe up: 'That's rape. It's not funny. They raped her. What if this was your daughter?' More heartbreaking still are the text messages sent by the victim, one of which, to a friend, reads: 'I wasn't being a slut. They were taking advantage of me,' as though her being a 'slut' would have excused what happened to her. Another photograph emerged of her naked, unconscious body. There was semen on her chest.

The victim-blaming that went on during the Steubenville trial is in no way unique. In 2009, the feminist blog Shakesville ran a powerful post entitled 'Rape culture 101', citing some then-recent examples of rape culture as a way of explaining the phenomenon. Since then, there have been many more examples. Rape culture, for instance, is a judge during a UK-based trial in December 2012 telling a rape victim who was drunk during the assault that 'she let herself down badly'; or the Israeli judge who said in June 2013 to a 13-year-old girl who had been sexually assaulted by a gang of teenage boys that 'some women enjoy rape'. It's another British judge, in August 2013, calling a 13-year-old female abuse victim a 'sexual predator', after she has been accused in court of 'egging her abuser on'. It's Jimmy Savile getting away with it for decades and decades. It's the footballer Ched Evans being found guilty of rape in 2012 and his victim being referred to on Twitter as a 'money-grabbing slut'. It's the threat of rape and sexual violence being used to silence women, just as it was used against feminist campaigner Caroline Criado-Perez in the summer of 2013 for having the audacity to campaign for the UK to have a woman's face on a banknote, and against Member of Parliament Stella Creasy for having the audacity to support her. It's police officers failing to investigate rape claims properly, or a police officer telling his then-colleague Brian Paddick that the victim of a sexual assault 'was asking for it'.

Rape culture is articles appearing in national newspapers which claim that by wearing a short skirt, or being drunk, or even being out at night alone, you are bringing it on yourself. Rape culture is the *Mail Online*'s Liz Jones claiming that pop star Rihanna's clothes 'invite rape'. Rape culture is Robin Thicke singing 'I know you want it', as though sexual consent is a blurred line, and that being a 'good girl' and the 'hottest bitch in this place' is reason enough to 'tear your ass in two'. Rape culture is all those Facebook groups and posts and pictures, all those stand-up routines, and all those implied threats of violence. It's one in four women in the UK being victims of sexual violence, and, out of nearly 100,000 rapes, only 1,000 rapists being sentenced. It's the National Survey of Sexual Attitudes and Lifestyles revealing that one in ten women in the UK reported that they had experience of 'non-volitional sex' (sex against their will), and that of those women only 42.2% had told anyone about it, with 12.9% going to the police. It's the idea of 'legitimate rape' and 'not rape-rape'. Rape culture is elected US politician Congressman Todd Akin claiming that true rape victims can never be pregnant because 'women's bodies have ways to try to shut that whole thing down', presumably because our vaginas are full of magical elves that can gobble up the semen of the 'wrong men'. It's Justice Secretary Kenneth Clarke suggesting that some rapes are more 'serious' than others. It's George Galloway reducing a man having sex with a woman without her permission to 'bad sexual etiquette'. It's Tony Benn saying that 'a non-consensual relationship' is 'very different from rape', when actually, if some guy decides he's your boyfriend without your agreement, and then goes on to screw you without your consent, then that is, actually, very straightforwardly, rape.

Rape culture is old white men in positions of political power trivialising sexual assault, implying that there's some kind of scale, a rape spectrum or rainbow, with 'proper rape' at one end (in a dark alley, by a stranger) and 'not so serious' rape at the other. Rape culture is predominantly white men in positions of political power legislating for women's bodies, wanting to subject those who want abortions to transvaginal ultrasounds against their will – rape as a medical procedure. It is the fact that, up until 1994, it was legal for a man to rape his wife in the UK (it's worth bearing in mind that in huge swathes of the world, particularly in Africa and Asia, rape within marriage is yet to be outlawed). It's the knowledge that most rapists are someone the victim knows and that they occur at home, where you're supposed to be safe, and yet the same old arguments revolving around stranger rape – against wearing skimpy clothing, or drinking too much, or avoiding taking the short cut – are wheeled out again and again. Rape culture is comparing the violation of your body to a burgled house; it's telling you that going out alone with your female body is tantamount to leaving your house with the door unlocked.

Rape culture can be seen in the idea that a woman's sexuality may be dangerous, and that if it becomes too potent then it must be controlled. The tweets and photographs distributed in Steubenville as a way of 'slut-shaming' the victim are not a million miles from some of the things we are starting to see regularly on the internet. Making a woman feel guilt and humiliation for engaging in sexual practices is as old as the hills, but the way these ideas are being disseminated through mobiles and the internet is relatively new. Memes featuring teenage girls smirkingly saying, 'Hey girl, you spread Nutella, not your legs' are only the beginning of a massive turd of sexist nastiness. Groups of students speak of 'slut-dropping', where they'll pick up a vulnerable drunk 'slut' from a nightclub and drop her off, alone and scared, in the middle of nowhere. Teenage girls are being coerced into giving their classmates head or jacking them off on camera, and that footage is then pinged around schools and used as a tool to shame and humiliate them. We know that young women have committed suicide over the existence of these videos, and yet some still seem to feel that shaming the 'promiscuous' is socially beneficial.

Rape culture is Uni Lad. Rape culture is *FHM* joking about stealing a victim's socks. Rape culture is certain porn-addled teenage boys hearing 'no' and not understanding what it means, because the internet is teeming with seemingly non-consensual sex, and telling girls to wear a longer skirt and stay home with a movie at the weekend.

Your teenage years are some of the most confusing and isolating that you will ever experience, and with the prevalence of hardcore porn and social media things are getting even more stressful for teenage girls. Everywhere you look there's an objectified female body, and yet living up to those images will only get you shamed. How can you be both a porno princess and a dirty slut? How do you tread that delicate tightrope between 'frigid' and 'tight' and 'loose' and 'whorish'? First and foremost, we need to be teaching young people the difference between sexual exploration and exploitation. We need to be teaching both sexes the meaning of consent, and that sex isn't shameful or dirty and that female sexuality, particularly, is to be celebrated rather than concealed, feared, forced or repressed. We need to overhaul our frankly bollocks attitude to sex education, our legal system and the way we treat rape victims, and we need to start making porn where the woman not only looks like she's participating in the act but also looks as though she's enjoying herself, doing things that other women might enjoy too (maybe even in a room that actually looks like a real lounge). Maybe she'll even have a proper orgasm, or a couple. We need to realise that patriarchy (yep, we waited until the end to drop that in there) – in other words, the status quo where men run the world and women run their households – is bad for men too, because it limits who they can be as people and as sexual beings. But most of all, we need to confront those people who still claim that we don't live in a man's world, that we don't need feminism any more, and we need to laugh them right out of the fucking park.

Conclusion

The ideal magazine

When we started the Vagenda blog back in the heady days of 2012, we never thought we'd be sitting here two years later at the conclusion of this book, waiting for our lukewarm takeaway fish and chips to arrive. Then again, we never in a million years imagined that we would be commissioned to write 'a call to arms for young women' – or that you could actually get fish and chips *delivered*. Obviously, we hope that our dazzling rhetoric has left you with no choice but to pick up the nearest pitchfork and make for *Cosmopolitan*'s head office, but we'd be satisfied with your just being proud to call yourself a feminist. We're flexible like that. Though we may not have harped on about it, this is a feminist book.

Feminism gets one hell of a bad press for a mixture of reasons, not least because of the assumption that one woman, in the media, talking, should somehow represent everyone on the planet with a vulva. Until there are more women in the media generally, we can't avoid a certain amount of all being tarred with the same brush, which is something women have been dealing with since the dawn of humanity. Despite what popular shows like *Sex and the City* might tell you, we don't all start rolling around and speaking in tongues when confronted with an Hermès Birkin bag. On the contrary, some of us would yell, 'CHRIST ALIVE, THAT £12,000 WOULD BUY ME ENOUGH MDMA TO SEE ME TO THE OTHER SIDE OF CHRISTMAS,' thus embarrassing everyone at the family buffet. Being a feminist is exactly like that. OK, not exactly, but the point is that we don't all act the same just because we have two X chromosomes.

Some would have it that you can't be a feminist and . . . vajazzle. Wear make-up. Apply fake tan. Enjoy dressing up. Shave your legs. Be sexy. Make your own pies out of hemp and feed them to your fourteen naturist children. The list is endless, but they all boil down to essentially the same thing. Namely, 'You can't be a feminist and make choices which are different to mine.' Although during the course of this book we've looked at why women are treated and represented in a certain way, we hope that we've stopped short of telling you what to do with your life. We can give you the facts about the media, and how we feel about them, but only you can make your own decisions. It's what the feminists of the past fought for. And if that choice involves getting up on a podium with hundreds of tiny specks of diamanté attached to your hairless flange with eyelash glue, and shaking it like a Polaroid picture, then by God, we defend your right to do that.

The idea that feminism is obsolete is one of the most dangerous myths being bandied around at the moment. Many women 'find' feminism because they are fed up with all the sexism and misogyny that is happening to them and their nearest and dearest. Whether it's because they are getting a lower pay cheque, suffering from workplace sexual harassment, being told that choosing to have an abortion is 'selfish individualism', or are simply fed up with bleaching their moustache, these gals have realised that our society can be a pretty shit place to be a woman. This is why someone going, 'Oh, we don't need feminism any more,' as they grind along to 'Bitches Ain't Shit' by Dr. Dre is so annoying. Once you notice that some sexism has happened to you, you suddenly start to see it in all kinds of places, especially ones where you may never have looked before – just witness the success of projects like Everyday Sexism, a prime example of women in their hordes suddenly opening their eyes to (and their mouths about) the misogyny that still exists all around them. Before you know it, you're wondering what you ever saw in that ex-boyfriend who answered most of your political opinions with 'Yes, dear' before telling you that a blowjob was a 'fitting apology' for having a period, and you're wishing that you'd told him to make his own fucking sandwich.

As any reader of this book may have guessed, the belief in gender equality has informed our view of the way the media speak to women, how they continue to fall back on tired old stereotypes and try to make you feel bad enough about yourself to buy more products. But this doesn't mean that we don't enjoy reading magazines – we've read a scary number in our short lives, and have even, occasionally, learnt from them. We just wish, in our heart of hearts, that they were better. And, in light of falling circulation rates, we presume that lots of other women wish that too.

In our version of a perfect magazine, all the models would have their own limbs. Nary a tacked-on, photoshopped leg nor slimmed-down waist would mar the pages. The diversity of the models' ethnicities and body types would directly reflect those of the population. Being a size 14 would no longer be treated as an urgent health condition, and fashion spreads would cease to look like a brochure for a summer camp for Aryan teenagers. There would be no cosmetic surgery advertorial, and the women on the cover would be women who have done incredible, inspiring things. There would be no picking over their diet and exercise regimes, no PR puff, and instead of asking them formulaic questions about their beauty routines, journalists would think outside the box, asking such questions as: 'If you could live inside a painting like the little girl in Roald Dahl's *The Witches*, which painting would it be?'

Since many of us do have a legitimate interest in why Kanye called his baby North West, the celebrity section would remain, but there would be no covert paparazzi shots from snappers hiding in bushes, and no body snark. There would be no circle of shame, and wheeling out the same old Topshop jeans to illustrate 'What to wear' would be replaced with something a little more inspiring, such as what women the world over are wearing. Rather than the same old fashionista friends of the editor, we'd really like to see Anna from Norway's amazing hangover grocery-shopping outfit, and how she has successfully merged the steampunk aesthetic with silky pyjama bottoms and a beanie. Also: no fascinators. Oh, and stop telling us 'this dress will change your life'. It won't.

There would be artistic fashion photography and an encouragement to experiment with style. If you like those embroidered knee warmers, then you should go ahead and wear them without judgement.

There would be a ban on the phrases 'OMG', 'totes' and 'amazeballs', and a shift towards the use of plain English. Hashtags would remain the preserve of Twitter, and portmanteau phrases such as 'babymoon', 'momtrepreneur' and 'yestergay' would be consigned to the dustbin. The female columnists would write hilarious, clever pieces on a wide range of issues. We've got to the point now where there's nothing more to be said about multi-dating, and referring to your partner as 'the boy' when you're in your mid-thirties and peppering your copy with 'lolz' just begins to look as though you're desperately trying to be down with the kids. Can we get some new blood, please? Preferably someone with an interesting life. Books, too. We read them.

Please, stop reminding us about our ovaries having a sell-by date. Believe us, we know. At present, magazines are failing to cover the full spectrum of things that can go wrong with your vagina. They have the twin pillars of cystitis and thrush pretty much down, but we're talking rarer conditions, like vestibulitis and syphilis. On the Vagenda blog, we've been running a series called 'TMI' for the last year, where women write in anonymously to discuss the realities of living with their various health issues. The response has been extremely positive. It's good to share, and it's good to be aware.

In our perfect magazine, the sex tips would immediately become more female-focused: no more 'Slap on a PVC G-string and gyrate around a £200 pole until your boyfriend feels up for it', and no more pretending that getting your boyfriend to test spaghetti sauce by licking it off your breasts is conducive to good sex or good cooking. The 'U-spot', 'T-spot', 'VV-spot', and all the other imaginary 'spots' that have been made up by desperate editors will be replaced by a more sensible and fruitful focus on the clitoris. Oh, and no more orgasm-shaming. Reading another feature called 'The 45 orgasms you must totally have NOW (otherwise you're a loser)' is only going to be detrimental to our mental well-being.

And editors: if you could mention a woman in print without putting her height and weight next to her name in brackets, then that would be awesome, ta.

Of course, feminism doesn't stop at laughing at and laying into women's magazines. Nevertheless, we intended this book to act as something of a shield against the torrent of projectile bullshit they tend to throw your way on a daily basis – and maybe that will free you up to embark on your own personal feminist revolution. For starters, a new generation of alternative women's magazines is now cropping up online, most notably teenage-oriented *Rookie*, as well as websites such as *Jezebel*, *The Hairpin*, and *XOJane*.

There are a million awesome feminists out there campaigning on a range of different issues – go forth and find them! Kat Banyard's UK

Feminista is at the forefront of the Lose the Lads' Mags campaign, while Lucy Holmes's No More Page 3 campaign against *The Sun* has been going from strength to strength. The Women's Institute as well as the Girl Guides are defining themselves as feminist organisations and reaching out to the community to spread the message. Groups such as Hollaback!, Reclaim the Night and SlutWalk have marched in defence of our right to walk the streets free from harassment and assault. And, of course, charities such as Refuge and Women for Refugee Women continue to do tireless work for the most vulnerable women in our society. One of the best parts of this new wave of feminism is that so many different women are coming out in force to campaign on so many diverse fronts: from Photoshop and airbrushing in the media, to eating disorders, to violent porn. They can do all of this without feeling that they have to sign up to the Acceptable Feminist Behaviour Checklist. This time around, the only membership criterion is a steadfast belief in equality – other than that, the more the merrier.

But hey, before you go galloping off into the night to join your nearest branch of the WI (ours is called the Dalston Darlings), here are a few helpful mantras for you to take away with you like a battered saveloy from your local finest fish bar. Feel free to repeat them in front of the mirror, self-help style, at will.

There's no such thing as the 'perfect body' (or the 'perfect female face'), and I don't have 'problem areas', 'fat armpits', or 'cankles'.

The sex I have is normal and nobody else's business unless I willingly involve them (yeah, even *that* thing). I am not a 'slut' or a 'prude' – I am simply in control of my own sex life.

There are no 'relationship rules'.

When I walk down the street, I don't have to take wolf-whistling as a 'compliment', and if I'm wearing a short skirt or I'm drunk, I don't 'deserve' to be raped.

The only things that define my career are my achievements, my experience and my choices – not my lipstick, my husband or my heels.

Any arse-chafing, pain-giving pants are just not worth it.

My clothes are an expression of my personal taste, not that of a fashion editor.7

I will have my cake and eat it.

I am not a 'slag', or an 'office bitch', or a 'prude', or a 'fat cow', or a 'princess', or a 'tramp', or a 'ball and chain', or a 'cracking pair of tits', or a 'fashionista', or a 'momtre-preneur', or a 'wench', or a 'womb-in-waiting', or a 'whore in the bedroom and an angel in the kitchen'. I am a composite human being, and nothing about my gender changes that.

No matter how many magazines imply that I should, I refuse to disappear.

Notes

p. 5   Stice, E.; Shaw, H. E. (1994). 'Adverse Effects of the Media Portrayed Thin-Ideal on Women and Linkages to Bulimic Symptomatology'. *Journal of Social and Clinical Psychology*, quoted by The Body Project study by the Women's Studies Program of Bradley University, (2012).

'Predictors of Media Effects on Body Dissatisfaction in European American Women', University of Missouri–Columbia, (2007).

p. 8   Anne O'Hagan, quoted in 'Out on Assignment: Newspaper Women and the Making of Modern Public Space', University of North Carolina Press, (2011).

p. 11   Katharine Whitehorn, BBC News Magazine, (August 2008).

p. 12   Naomi Wolf, *The Beauty Myth*, William Morrow and Company, (1991).

p. 33   Hayes S. and Tantleff-Dunn S. (2010) 'Am I too fat to be a princess? Examining the effects of popular children's media on young girls' body image.' Study published in *British Journal of Developmental Psychology*, (2009).

p. 44   NHS statistics on labiaplasty quoted by Liao, Lih Mei, and Creighton in 'Requests for Cosmetic Genitoplasty: How Should Healthcare Providers Respond?' in the *British Medical Journal*, (26 May 2007).

Data from survey conducted by WhatClinic search engine, (2013).

Data from research conducted by the Cosmetic Surgery Guide, (2013).

p. 65   'Sex differences in the structural connectome of the human brain', published in the Proceedings of the National Academy of Sciences of the United States of America and conducted by the University of Pennsylvania, (December 2013).

p. 67   'Does red lipstick really attract men?', *International Journal of Psychology*, (June 2012).

Research carried out by Nicolas Guéguen and Céline Jacob at Université de Bretagne-Sud, France, published in *Journal of Hospitality and Tourism Research*, (2012).

p. 72   Research carried out by Cosmetic Executive Women UK, (February 2012).

p. 78   'Girls' Attitudes: What Girls Think About . . .' www.girlguiding.org.uk/girlsattitudes Girlguiding UK, (2012).

p. 86   Christopher Ryan and Cacilda Jethá, *Sex at Dawn: How We Mate, Why We Stray, and What It Means For Modern Relationships*, Harper Perennial, (2010).

p. 113   Germaine Greer, *The Female Eunuch*, MacGibbon & Kee, (1970).

Prof. Jean-Denis Rouillon, University of Besançon, quoted on *France Info*, (April 2013).

p. 133   Data from 'Media Values Survey', IPC Magazines, conducted by Research Services Ltd, (1992).

p. 134   Guy Consterdine, 'How Magazine Advertising Works', PPA, (August 2005).

p. 185   'Sex and Power', survey by the Equality and Human Rights Commission, (2011).

p. 233   'Obesity discrimination: the role of physical appearance, personal ideology, and anti-fat prejudice,' by the University of Manchester and Monash University, Melbourne, published in the *International Journal of Obesity*, (April 2012).

p. 267   Horvath, M.A.H., Hegarty, P., Tyler, S. & Mansfield, S., 'Lights on at the end of the party: Are lads' mags mainstreaming dangerous sexism?', study by Surrey and Middlesex Universities, published in the *British Journal of Psychology*, (2011).

p. 268   C. Carter, G.A. Branston and S. Allan (eds), *News, Gender and Power*, Routledge, (1998).

Rosalind Gill, *Gender and the Media*, Polity Press, (2006).

p. 276   'Basically . . . porn is everywhere: A Rapid Evidence Assessment on the Effects that Access and Exposure to Pornography has on Children and Young People', Office of the Children's Commissioner [UK], (May 2013).

Bridges A.J., Wosnitzer R., Scharrer E., Sun C., Liberman R., 'Aggression and sexual behaviour in best-selling pornography videos', *Violence Against Women*, Sage Journals, (2010).

Online Sexual Imagery Study, conducted by Dr A. Roberts, Psychology department of the University of East London (2013).

Research conducted by Dr Valerie Voon, Department of Psychiatry, Cambridge University, featured on Channel 4, 'Porn on the Brain', (September 2013).

p. 285   Data from 'The National Survey of Sexual Attitudes and Lifestyles', published in *The Lancet* (2013).

Acknowledgements

We'd like to thank a few (read: lots) of people without whom this book would not have been possible. Firstly, our hilarious agent Diana Beaumont, who saw potential in us when others didn't, and who always provides us with glasses of cold white wine. Rosemary Davidson, our excellent editor, who's been there every step of the way with support and witty observations, and refused to allow us to rush things. The book is better for it. Ellah Allfrey and Sara Holloway, for their razor-sharp edits, some of which almost made us cry (it needed to be done). Beth Humphries for her incisive copy-edit and our proofreader Alice Brett for her eagle eye on the text. Thank you! Humungous thanks to everyone at Square Peg and Vintage Books: Kate Bland, Faye Brewster, Alice Palmer-Brown, Rich Carr, Julia Connolly, Tom Drake-Lee, Lada Kris, Penny Liechti, Crystal Mahey-Morgan, Malissa Mistry, Victoria Murray-Browne, Susannah Otter, Simon Rhodes, Rowena Skelton-Wallace, Christina Usher, Ruth Warburton, Natalie Wall and Vicki Watson.

We'd also like to thank Helen Lewis at the *New Statesman*, who gave us our big break in the world of journalism, and has remained hugely supportive (and amazingly chipper) in the face of so much bullshit ever since. Also Caroline Crampton, who tirelessly edits our columns every week, and leaves all the swearing in.

To all our editors on the comment desk at the *Guardian*: Becky Gardiner, Natalie Hanman, Maya Wolfe-Robinson, Katherine Butler, Libby Brooks, Joseph Harker, David Shariatmadari and Sarah Phillips, a million thank-yous. Thanks to all the Vagenda contributors including Rosie Cowling of ohdearism.com.

To Rosamund Urwin, who put us in the *Evening Standard* when we were just a baby blog, and to everyone at *Elle*, who, despite being a women's magazine, were chilled enough to still want to work with us on a brilliant feminist campaign, and everyone at Wieden+Kennedy and Mother, who made it happen. It meant a lot.

We'd also like to thank our friends, both online and offline, who, lucky for us, are too many to name here, and our supporters – both inside and outside the media, who have encouraged us and mentored us, and gently told us when we've got it wrong.

And our bemused families, of course. The support and friendship of Victoria Armstrong, in particular, have been so much appreciated. Rhiannon would particularly like to thank Tim, who once stood on a chair and said he was more of a feminist than she was. He isn't, of course, but his love and support has meant the world to her.

Lastly, thank you to our readers, who are side-splittingly funny and outraged in equal measure. Without you, none of it would matter at all.